SAFETY AND RISK IN SOCIETY

OCCUPATIONAL STRESS

RISK FACTORS, PREVENTION AND MANAGEMENT STRATEGIES

SAFETY AND RISK IN SOCIETY

Additional books and e-books in this series can be found on Nova's website under the Series tab.

SAFETY AND RISK IN SOCIETY

OCCUPATIONAL STRESS

RISK FACTORS, PREVENTION AND MANAGEMENT STRATEGIES

NICOLA MUCCI
GABRIELE GIORGI
FRANCESCO SDERCI
AND
GIULIO ARCANGELI
EDITORS

nova
science publishers
New York

Library of Congress Cataloging-in-Publication Data

Names: Mucci, Nicola, editor. | Giorgi, Gabriele, editor. | Sderci, Francesco, editor.
Title: Occupational stress : risk factors, prevention and management strategies / editors, Nicola Mucci, MD, PhD (Junior Researcher in Occupational Medicine, Department Experimental and Clinical Medicine, University of Florence, Italy), Gabriele Giorgi (Organizational Psychology, Department of Human Science, Universitaÿ Europea di Roma, Italy), Francesco Sderci, MD (University of Florence, Italy).
Description: Hauppauge, New York : Nova Science Publishers, Inc., [2019] | Series: Safety and risk in society | Includes index.
Identifiers: LCCN 2019017075 (print) | LCCN 2019019187 (ebook) | ISBN 9781536154054 | ISBN 9781536154047 (hardcover)
Subjects: LCSH: Job stress. | Medicine, Industrial.
Classification: LCC RC963.48 (ebook) | LCC RC963.48 .O235 2019 (print) | DDC 158.7/2--dc23
LC record available at https://lccn.loc.gov/2019017075

Published by Nova Science Publishers, Inc. † New York

Contents

PREFACE

Stress related work, although always present, is considered one of the new risks for occupational medicine. This is largely due to a general change in the organization of work, inevitable in a constantly evolving market. It is also due to the presence of objective and subjective indicators that allow a satisfactory, though very complex, risk assessment.

Related work stress generates repercussions on the company at every level, with a reduction in productivity, a reduction in the corporate image, a reduction in the quality of service, an increase in absenteeism and the dissatisfaction of workers. Some of these aspects are often submerged and difficult to identify.

Related work stress also generate significant costs, both direct and indirect, for companies. A budgeted economic investment will be useful for forward-looking companies, especially for large companies. This book, written by authors from all over the world, will analyze some aspects of this increasingly relevant subject.

Chapter 1 - Human adaptation to stress involves the understanding of contextual and personal variables, and also the specific stress event. This complexity is a challenging topic not only for researchers interested in the topic of stress but also for delivering public policies dedicated to control the negative effects of stressful work conditions to individuals, families, and organizations. In this chapter, the authors will debate occupational stress in a dual perspective. First, the authors propose the Interactive Model of Human Adaptation to Stress that gives particular relevance to processes of cognitive appraisal on the relation between the stressful event and the individual responses to stress. Second, the authors will analyze implications of the interactive model for intervention, emphasizing techniques that can be useful to prevent the negative effects of stress and that can indeed promote positive adaptation to work demands.

Chapter 2 - This abstract offers summary results from three recent applied work analysis projects. The first set of data are associated with an academic medical unit, the second data set is associated with an academic strategic marketing and communications unit and the third data set is connected to an academic international program. In all projects; a seven-point; Likert-type scale was utilized to collect work analysis data by way of interviews with 7 representing the most important or intense factor. With regard to Project 1; mean values and standard deviations for each work analysis factor are depicted in the following chart.

Chapter 3 - The term burnout was first introduced in the 70s. Since then scientific publications on this topic have proliferated. Human services professions have been identified as a group vulnerable to developing burnout due to significant degree of interpersonal contact with troubled client population. Burnout has significant impact on the delivery of service, the quality of service, the emotional and physical health of the person experiencing it and their interpersonal/social functioning. There is also some evidence to suggest burnout may have protective effects on the psyche of the person experiencing it. Burnout serves as an emotional brake by slowing down the working and thus scope of further strain on the person. Distancing oneself from demanding work situations may also be protective against emotional drain and depletion of empathy. Key lessons from opinions and research studies on the prevention and management of burnout are reviewed in this chapter. Active screening of burnout, helping employees develop resilience and positive coping and developing a strong organizational culture of tackling burnout early are methods which can help prevent this global problem from developing further. A combination of intensive individual or group therapy sessions based on cognitive behavioral principles along with booster sessions appears to be most effective in managing burnout once it has developed. Treatment interventions for reducing scores on the three dimensions of burnout have also been identified.

Chapter 4 - This chapter focuses on adrenal fatigue and hormonal imbalance induced by work related stress. Occupational stress can be described as work associated stress, which brings about drastic variations in the physical, emotional and mental responses of an individual when exposed to excessive work and pressures that challenges their abilities. During a stressful event, the hypothalamus sends signals to the adrenal glands to dispense, epinephrine and nor epinephrine into the bloodstream, in order to exert the fight or flight response effectively. With further increase in time, the adrenal glands begin to release excessive cortisol into the circulation which in turn escalates the blood glucose levels and eventually leads to adrenal fatigue or adrenal exhaustion. Stress has been found to be a critical factor in several health conditions ranging from cardiovascular damage to digestive impairment as well as immune suppression. Elevated production of stress hormones (adrenaline and cortisol) has been found to have a predominant contribution in several medical complications. Adrenal fatigue indicates a substantial decline in the optimal cortisol levels, due to sub optimal functioning of the adrenal glands under stress. In this chapter, the authors discussed about the stress induced adrenal fatigue and hormonal imbalance, and the use of bio-identical hormones to prevent and replenish the activity of the adrenal glands. This overview of stress induced adrenal fatigue and hormonal imbalance and its associated treatment using bio-identical hormone therapy, when properly formulated, tested as for stability and optimal sublingual absorption, will give us a better knowledge about the dysfunction and its concomitant therapeutic and preventive measures.

Chapter 5 - Metals are commonly prevalent in the body along with various other fundamental molecules. However, an alteration in their concentration may damage vital physiological functioning. Several toxic metals may be predominant contributing factors in the occurrence of several chronic diseases which often produce only subtle clinical signs leading to misdiagnosis or being left undetected. The terminology “heavy metal” is referred to a toxic metal which does not normally belong to our biological system and is harmful when accumulated in the body. The accumulation of these heavy metals is more prominent in industrial workers. The toxic effects of heavy metals which have entered our body can be effectively counteracted by utilizing natural substances such as “Zeolites” which assist our organs to gradually cleanse and discard the toxic metals. Although natural zeolites were discovered over 250 years ago, people have begun to realize the true potential and capabilities of zeolite only in recent times. Zeolites, due to their specific internal structure, are able to trap heavy metals, mainly by their ability to exchange inherent cations for other cations on the basis of ion selectivity mechanisms. Novel studies have indicated that not all zeolites possess the same “trapping ability.” In this chapter, specific studies have been highlighted that exhibit a new class of zeolites that are far more effective than the ones that are currently available. Metabolic syndrome and various other associated cardiovascular and neurological complications, affects various social classes, mainly the workers under stressful conditions, invariably tend to be forced towards more detrimental dietary and lifestyle attitudes (pre-cooked food in company cafeteria, junk food, night shifts, lack of exercise, limited inclination to healthy food choices, eating while commuting etc. to mention some). This opens the way to a creeping, silent fatty liver infiltration (NAFLD) which is far more than a simple excess fat accumulation, but it does represent the first step leading to a much worse cascade of events. NAFLD at the moment has a prevalence of 23-34% in USA, China (with reports up to 46%) and alarmingly rising in Middle-East too. Patients with T2DM and NAFLD have a 2-3 fold higher incidence of acute myocardial infarction than those without NAFLD. In this regards,, late in 2004, some research studies had been done on a promising mixed herbal compound made in China (YHK) with a number of positive experimental and scanty clinical reports, following some empirical observational data. Further studies making pure extracts of the main ingredients together with inner enrichment of specific bioactive fraction (FOLHK) proved through very stringent, either in vitro or in vivo animal studies and clinical trials its effectiveness. This was shown to be significantly better over the common silymarin-based liver protectors as well surpassing the benefit of the initial prototype formulas while confirming its safety. While better working environment, healthy food and attitudes maintain their fundamental role as main pillars of health and disease prevention, the above non-chemical interventions may represent a convenient aid to support health protection.

Chapter 6 - Occupational exposure to different hazards is thought to be one of the greatest health challenge in the contemporary era. Although many studies are performed with animal models and *in vitro* evaluating the toxicity of single compounds, the real exposure occurs through the use of mixtures of different chemicals, establishing a complex scenario in occupational risk assessment. The use of biomarkers of early effects is a major tool in approaching the occupational exposure to complex mixtures, helping to increase risk prediction. The most significant use of biomarkers in occupational health have been in biological monitoring of workers from different areas: industry, primary production, agriculture, and urban workers, as some examples. This review will discuss the three major biomarkers of early effect used in the last few years by the authors' research group: (1) Comet assay, which evaluates genotoxicity, being a versatile and sensitive method for measuring single- and double-strand DNA breaks; (2) Micronucleus assay, which can be applied to both lymphocytes and buccal cells; it is a mutagenic test that evaluates different chromosomal aberrations and cell death and can provide information of cytostasis; and (3) telomere length (TL) quantification, a relatively new method applying for identification of chromosomal instability linked to accelerated cellular senescence, several age-related diseases and neoplasia. The use of those three biomarkers has been proven useful in the assessment of occupational risk of individuals exposed to pesticides, coal, polycyclic aromatic hydrocarbon, lead, solvents, traffic air pollution, among other xenobiotics. Those tests may characterize the exposed from non-exposed individuals. Data from literature has shown that demographic characteristics, such as age, gender, and period and time of exposure may alter individual's response to chemicals. Additionally, lifestyle habits, as alcohol consumption, hours of sleep, smoking habits and dietary intake may also play a significant role in occupational risk evaluations. As human inter-individual variability is a major source of uncertainty in risk assessment, this review will also address those factors. Finally, in order to understand how biological systems and processes interact, System Biology tools are being used to integrate biological data. This approach is based on consideration of common biological processes and how chemicals may disrupt them, allowing to observe the interaction between the xenobiotic agent and the mechanisms of damage. This review will investigate the use of System Biology for connection of biomarkers of early effect to adverse outcomes as regard occupational risk concern. Biomarkers of effect indicates the biochemical or functional alterations including a wide range of biological responses; they are mainly used as group indicators, being sensitive but not specific, and aiming to decrease the inter-individual differences. As those biomarkers are recognized to have an association with several diseases, including cancer, they may help in early detection and prevention of such pathologies. Given this, studies in occupational exposure area are discussed in this chapter, approaching the use and the importance of such biomarkers as key strategies to help in management decisions.

In: Occupational Stress
Editors: N. Mucci, G. Giorgi et al.
ISBN: 978-1-53615-404-7

Chapter 1

THE INTERACTIVE PROCESS OF ADAPTATION TO STRESS AND IMPLICATIONS FOR INTERVENTION

Clara Simões*[1,2,*]*, PhD and A. Rui Gomes*[3,†]*, PhD
[1]School of Nursing, University of Minho, Braga, Portugal
[2]Institute of Health Sciences, Portuguese Catholic University, Porto, Portugal
[3]School of Psychology, University of Minho, Braga, Portugal

ABSTRACT

Human adaptation to stress involves the understanding of contextual and personal variables, and also the specific stress event. This complexity is a challenging topic not only for researchers interested in the topic of stress but also for delivering public policies dedicated to control the negative effects of stressful work conditions to individuals, families, and organizations. In this chapter, we will debate occupational stress in a dual perspective. First, we propose the Interactive Model of Human Adaptation

* Corresponding Author's E-mail: csimaes@ese.uminho.pt.
† Corresponding Author's E-mail: rgomes@psi.uminho.pt.

to Stress (Gomes, 2014) that gives particular relevance to processes of cognitive appraisal on the relation between the stressful event and the individual responses to stress. Second, we will analyze implications of the interactive model for intervention, emphasizing techniques that can be useful to prevent the negative effects of stress and that can indeed promote positive adaptation to work demands.

INTRODUCTION

Worldwide in every-day living contexts, specifically those related to work performance are becoming further more demanding and stressful. Work related sources of stress are also becoming wider, incessant and intense, pushing the individuals to be constantly more efficient in their ways of coping, in order to achieve a positive adaptation to work. Although that, the relationship between stress and human adaptation is far from being linear, and requires to take into consideration the contextual and personal factors involved in the ways individuals perceive and respond to their work context. Therefore, to promote human adaptation to work stress is both necessary to understand the conceptual models that can help to recognize the complexity of the adaptation process to stress, and analyze the implications of those models for the intervention. Specifically, how individuals can achieve their best performance in their work contexts and how they can use those same contexts to be fulfill as human beings.

Stress is a word widely used in day-to-day living (e.g., common sense talks, media and scientific world), being object of several theoretical conceptualizations, conditioned by the continuous and obsessive nature of men, in the task of discovering and explaining the mechanisms that regulate human reactions and behaviors of adaptation to their performance contexts (Tavares, Soares-Fortunato, & Leite-Moreira, 2000; Vaz Serra, 2007). The stress has been subject of several research domains, in the last few years, constituting a particular area of interest in the field of health psychology, allowing to establish the border between the normal and the pathological, emphasizing the influence that psychosocial factors have on the health-illness process (Aldwin & Gilmer, 2004; McIntyre, 1994). The field of research in the health domain is large, embracing different points of view that vary from ethology, human and social sciences, physiology, physiopathology, up to the causal factors for physical and mental morbidity (Vaz Serra, 2007).

Stress related to work has been considered the "plague of the century" (McIntyre et al., 2007, p. 5), and theme of the debate in the contemporary scientific field of research, due its impact on several domains of the person´s life (e.g., family, marital and societal domains) (Ashforth, Kreiner, & Fugate, 2000; Carter & McGoldrick, 1995; Coupland & Júdice, 2002; Davila, Karney, Hall, & Bradbury, 2003; McIntyre, 1994; Rodell & Judge, 2009; Rosenstock, 1997; Vaz Serra, 2007). The relevance of occupational stress raises from the increasing interest on the conditions that determine the person's productivity, satisfaction and well-being in the work place, for its negative effects on health quality of life and work performance (e.g., Burke & Greenglass, 1999; Hasselhorn, Müller, & Tackenberg, 2005; Simon, Kummerling, & Hasselhorn, 2004; Simon et al., 2008). A great number of studies emerge from fundamental questions and perennial doubts that stress researchers have talk over. That is, will be individuals who are more vulnerable to stress than others are? Are there professions inherently more stressful than others are? What are the causes of stress related to day-to-day work? In addition, what is the relationship between work-related stress and the person's health? How and when should we intervene? (Barling, Kelloway, & Frone, 2005; Kopp, Skrabski, Szekely, Stauder, & Williams, 2007; Rosenstock, 1997; Vaz Serra, 2007).

Occupational health constitutes a primordial and pioneer area for the investigation of these problematics. Moreover, the *National Institute for Occupational Safety and Health* (NIOSH), identified psychological disorders as one of the ten main categories of pathological conditions related to work, specifically to occupational stress (Quick, 1999; Rosenstock, 1997). Occupational stress has been identified worldwide, as being associated to cardiovascular and musculoskeletal diseases (Johnson, 1996; Kopp et al., 2007; Quick, 1999; Schneiderman, Ironson, & Siegel, 2005) (Huang, Feuerstein, & Sauter, 2002; Simon et al., 2008); physical and psychological distress (Blustein, 2008; Klainin, 2009; Rosenstock, 1997);

absenteeism, *turnover* and *burnout* (Gomes, Cruz, & Cabanelas, 2009). Affecting, interpersonal relationships and performance at work (McIntyre et al., 2007; Queirós, 2005), as well as, general satisfaction with life (Netemeyer, Boles, & McMurrian, 1996; Rodell & Judge, 2009; Simon et al., 2004; Yildirim & Aycan, 2008).

In this domain, aid professions (e.g., psychologists, teachers, health professionals) had been identified as being in particular risk of experience the negative effects of occupational stress, demanding the implementation of primary prevention policies, by organizations (McIntyre et al., 2007). However, most of studies have a general character in his nature, showing some gaps with respect to the process of adaptation to stress, demanding intervention guidelines (McIntyre et al., 2007).

The aim of this chapter is to discuss the factors that are involved in human adaptation to stress and its implications for the intervention, being proposed specific strategies to prevent occupational stress negative effects and to promote a positive adjustment to work demands. The chapter moves from the theoretical analysis of the interactive process of stress, proposed by the Interactive Model of Human Adaptation to Stress (Gomes, 2014), to discuss intervention possibilities to promote a positive adaptation to stress, according the main dimensions included in the model (e.g., characteristics of the stressful events, personal antecedent factors, cognitive appraisal, responses, and event outcomes). There will be proposed approaches in order to turn the stress situation a positive context for excellence, the individual adaptable to stress conditions, and human resources adequate to multiple stress conditions.

STRESS AS AN INTERACTIVE PROCESS

The Interactive Model of Human Adaptation to Stress, proposed by Gomes (2014), relies mainly on the cognitive-motivational-relational theory of stress and emotions of Lazarus (1991, 1999) and the succeeding adaptations proposed by Fletcher, Hanton, and Mellalieu (2006) and Folkman (2008). Furthermore, the model counts with the contributions of concepts related to the sources of stress (Occupational Stress Model; Cooper & Marshall, 1976), the fit between the person and the environment (Person–Environment Fit; Edwards, Caplan, & Van Harrison, 1998), and the importance of personal control over work (Job Demands-Control model; Karasek, 1979; Karasek & Theorell, 1990).

For a better understanding of the Interactive Model of Human Adaptation to Stress (Gomes, 2014) according to the author, some assumptions should be taken into consideration. Human adaptation to stress is best understood and accomplished through a process-oriented approach, which adopts the dynamic nature of the relationship between the individual and the environment. The apprehension of this dynamic process implies the analysis of the temporal sequence of the demands, the antecedent factors at the situational and personal levels, the cognitive appraisal at the first and second levels, the responses, and the event outcomes of human adaptation. The most influent model that theorizes stress as a process is the transactional (or relational) model, proposed by Lazarus (1991), which assumes that stress is not a property of the individual nor of the environment, as separate entities, but resides in the transaction between the two. Numerous aspects can characterize both the individual and the environment, but the dynamic experience of stress can only be achieved when both factors are analyzed in conjunction.

The model is interactive, since it considers that human adaptation is an ongoing process, with advances and setbacks in the coping process with stress, assuming interactive influences between the first level of cognitive appraisal, the responses, and the second level of cognitive appraisal in a bidirectional way, as such: first level of cognitive appraisal ↔ responses ↔ second level of cognitive appraisal. Stress is an ongoing transaction between environmental demands and personal vulnerabilities and resources. Strain (*negative human functioning*) is a consequence of an imbalance between these demands and resources (Cox, 1985; Lazarus, 1999; McGrath, 1970) and well-being (*positive human functioning*) is a consequence of a balance between these demands and resources.

For the interactive model, the process of adaptation involves the processes of cognitive appraisal, the responses (at the emotional, cognitive and behavioral levels), and the adjustment to the appraised conditions. Cognitive appraisal is a central component to understand human responses during stressful events. Cognitive appraisal is involved in the onset of psychological, physiological, and behavioral responses, and in how these responses will be interpreted and managed. The process of human adaptation does not need to go through all the steps proposed in the model, it can end when the individual does not give importance to the stressful event or when he has achieved an event outcome of positive or negative human functioning. There is no reason to believe that human adaptation to stress finishes after primary and secondary cognitive appraisals, and that, tertiary and quaternary cognitive appraisal are only mobilized if a positive adjustment is not achieved. Further, even if a positive adjustment to stressful events is achieved, after primary and secondary cognitive appraisals, additional efforts can be developed to improve personal adjustment to the situation.

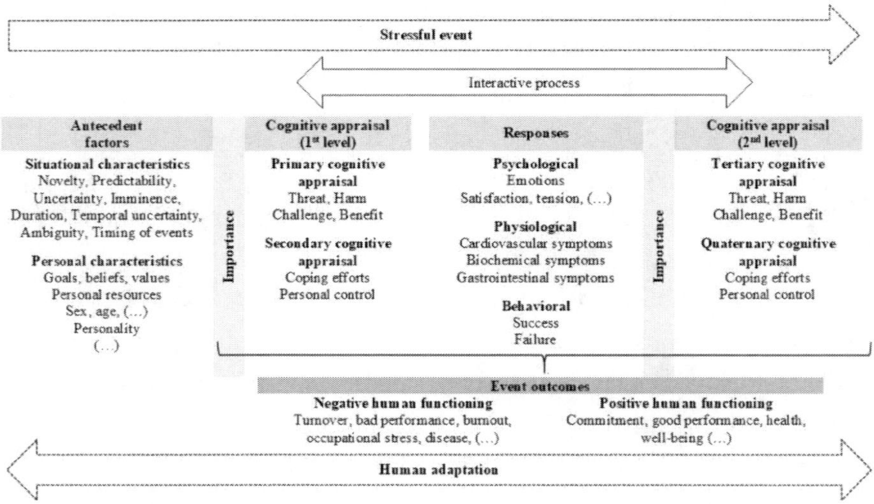

Figure 1. Interactive model of human adaptation to stress (Gomes, 2014).

The model takes into consideration that the relationship between stressful events and the events outcomes, can be mediated by cognitive appraisal and moderated by antecedent factors. Stressful events can be a source of influence along the all process of human adaptation, and not only at the beginning, strengthening the dynamic nature of the person-environment relationship.

After these core considerations, we will explore in more detail the theoretical dimensions that define the Interactive Model of Human Adaptation to Stress (Gomes, 2014), which is presented in Figure 1.

Stressful Event

Research on stress has been developed essentially along three axes, which define three conceptual perspectives: the biological, environmental and the psychological (Mason, 1975; Paúl & Fonseca, 2001; Soares & Pereira, 2006; Vaz Serra, 2007). The biological perspective focuses on the study of the mechanisms by which specific physiological systems are activated, and on their modulation by certain physical and psychological conditions. The environmental perspective is interested in the study of specific environmental factors, and to what extent its assessment by the individual determines feeling the environment as a stressing agent, affecting health and well-being. Finally, the psychological perspective, highlighting the cognitive evaluation factors, is centered on the subjective interpretation of the meaning around environment events, or specific experiences, and on the subjective evaluation of the available resources, so that the individual can deal with the demands perceived (Aldwin & Gilmer, 2004; Paúl & Fonseca, 2001; Soares & Pereira, 2006).

Accordingly, stress has been analyzed in one of three ways: as a stimulus (factors that can induce distress), as a response of the individual to stressful events (psychological, physiological, and behavioral), and as an interaction between the person and the stressful situation (for a review, see Cooper & Dewe, 2004). The Interactive Model of Human Adaptation to Stress reflects more the last approach to stress (as an interaction), without underestimate the other two (as a stimulus and as a response). The conception of the stress as a stimulus and as a response, have the merit of highlighting the factors that can disrupt human functioning in performance contexts (e.g., work) and the consequences that stressors can have on human functioning. Actually, it is fundamental to comprehend if the nature of stressors is changing across time, leading to "new" or "more intense" responses to stress, in order to promote an appropriate intervention. The interactive model proposes that stressful events play a major role in human adaptation to stress. This means that stressful events are not a static entity prior to processes of cognitive appraisal or coping efforts that are assumed by the individual in order to deal with stress. In contrast, it assumes an interactive and dynamic nature established between the individual and the situation. This means that the stressful event plays a major role during all processes of human adaptation to stress; changing its nature according to the continuous efforts made by the person to cope with stress along this adaptation process, (this is why there is a dashed line to signalize the stressful event in Figure 1).

Considering research on stress related to work, Lazarus (1995) proposed that sources of stress at work are, to somewhat, an individual phenomenon, as well as the ways people cope with stress. In addition to describing the sources of stress that can promote negative human functioning, it is important to perceive the way the individual appraises and manages the stress situation. Yet, the author recognizes the importance of describing the conditions of work, since some types of stressors (e.g., time pressures, work overload, lack of decisional control) can be stressful enough for a great number of workers. The interactive model considers Lazarus's perspective, giving relevance to the individual process of human adaptation to stress, but also recognizing the importance of the effects of some occupational stressors. The interactive model assumes that a deep understanding of the process of human adaptation to stress will be achieved if the nature of the stressful situations and the following process of human adaptation are considered (appraisal and coping). This interactive perspective of stress gives attention to the ongoing process that is involved in the relationship between the environment and the individual, considering the dynamics between these two factors and the subjective meaning the individual builds when facing a stressful event. Stress is conceived as a transaction between the set of demands associated to each stress event and the individual personal resources. Therefore, strain arises from an imbalance between these two aspects (Cox, 1985; Lazarus, 1991; McGrath, 1970). This dynamic perspective can be best understood by analyzing the relational meaning that the individual attributes to the stress situation; that is, the meaning a person gives to the relationship he or she has with the environment (Lazarus, 1991).

Antecedent Factors

Stressful events include two of the most important factors involved in human adaptation to stress; that is, situational characteristics (e.g., type of organization, culture) and personal characteristics (e.g., personality traits). Both represent antecedent factors that can influence the process of human adaptation to stress events and for that, they are consider in the Interactive Model of Human Adaptation to Stress (see Figure 1).

Regarding situational characteristics, the transactional perspective of Lazarus (1991; Lazarus & Folkman, 1984) considers that, besides describing the stressful event, it is important to identify the reasons why an individual appraises events as stressful. So, situational characteristics in the model, involve not only aspects related to the organizational culture and the type of work to perform, but also the underlying properties that can turn the situation into a stressful event, as proposed by Lazarus and Folkman (1984). Those properties are: (a) the novelty of the situation for the individual; (b) the predictability of the situation for the individual; (c) the uncertainty of the event's occurrence; (d) the imminence of the event in terms of time available to anticipate before its occurrence; (e) the duration of the event; (f) the temporal uncertainty of the event, which is related to the individual ability to know the precise time when the stressful situation will occur; (g) the ambiguity of the information needed for the appraisal of the event; and, (h) the timing of the event occurrence, in relation to the life cycle, which analyzes whether more events are happening in the person's life when the stressful situation occurred. There are scarce studies on this topic, but some existing findings do support the importance of these properties to the stress response (Dugdale, Eklund, & Gordon, 2002; Kirschbaum, 1999; Marchant, Andersen, & Morris, 1997; Perrez & Reicherts, 1992; Thatcher & Day, 2008).

Concerning the personal characteristics, Lazarus (1999) describes the importance of analyzing goal commitment, values, beliefs about the self and the environment, and situational intentions. Goal commitment is considered a central factor because "it implies that a person will strive hard to attain the goal" and that "if there is no goal commitment, there is nothing of adaptational importance at stake in an encounter to arouse a stress reaction'' (Lazarus, 1999, p. 76). These aspects are included in the interactive model as antecedent factors that can determine the ongoing process of stress confrontation (see Figure 1). The advantage is to split the personal meaning of the event (included in the concept of importance for the interactive model) from the factors involved in human adaptation to stress (e.g., appraisal, coping, and event outcomes). For example, if the stressful event affects valuable personal goals (antecedent factor), the chance of being attributed importance to the event increases, giving start to the process of adaptation to the stressful event. For the interactive model if no personal significance is given to the situation, then it cannot be appraised as stressful because it has no importance.

The interactive model considers other aspects related to personal resources (e.g., educational level, economic resources, social skills, life experiences, social support, health status, physical abilities) that can influence what an individual will be able or unable to do (Lazarus, 1999; Lundberg & Cooper, 2011; Payne, 1988). Personality factors are also included as antecedent factors in the interactive model. Certain types of persons (e.g., rigid personalities, addicted to drugs, neurotic, depressive tendencies) are likely to react with stress more often or more intensely than others (Lazarus, 1995). Research has partially confirmed this idea, namely, the tendency to be more vulnerable to stress and to perceive job situations as more stressful in individuals who are high in negative affectivity (Cassar & Tattersall, 1998; Spector & O'Connell, 1994), who have an external locus of control (Newton & Keenan, 1990; Ress & Cooper, 1992), and who have a Type A behavior pattern (Newton & Keenan, 1990; Payne, 1988). Other dispositional variables have been suggested to buffer the impact of stressors on an individual's experience of strain, for example, hardiness, self-esteem and self-efficacy, and optimism (for a review, see Cooper, Dewe, &

O`Driscoll, 2001). Finally, demographic variables (e.g., sex, age) also constitute personal antecedent variables in the interactive model, because they can affect vulnerability to stress, as demonstrated by research (e.g., Jenkins, 1991; Nelson & Quick, 1985; Shirom, Gilboa, Fried, & Cooper, 2008).

It is important to note that situational and personal characteristics should be conceived together (Lazarus, 2000a), meaning that personal factors make sense when they are analyzed in the context of the situation, and the situation makes sense in the scenario faced by each individual. The situation can be meaningful to the individual, but it will not be appraised as stressful if it does not assume one or more of the described underlying properties; further, the situation can assume at least one underlying property, but it will not be appraised as stressful if no personal significance is given by the individual (Thatcher & Day, 2008).

Considering these aspects, the Interactive Model of Human Adaptation to Stress suggests the concept of "importance" as the *gate* that opens the process of human adaptation to stress, resulting from the conjunction of situational and personal characteristics (see Figure 1). This personal meaning attributed to the stressful event will determine if the situation will be faced by the individual; if no importance is attributed to the stressful event, then this event can become, for example, a frustrating or sad situation, but it does not represent an event that requires efforts of human adaptation to stress. The concept of "importance" or personal meaning of the Interactive Model of Human Adaptation to Stress also results from the relation between a particular individual and a specific situation, indicating if the process of human adaptation to stress will begin or end at this first moment of confrontation with the stress event.

Cognitive Appraisal: 1st Level Processes

Appraisals are evaluations that affect people's beliefs, values and/or goals (Arnold, 1960; Lazarus & Folkman, 1984), having an adaptive function because they indicate whether an event may be good or bad for the individual, generating subsequent action tendencies (Arnold, 1960). Therefore, cognitive appraisal represents reactions to stressful situations that vary according to the way the individual perceive the stressful events. This turns cognitive appraisal a central concept for human adaptation to stressful events.

The Interactive Model of Human Adaptation to Stress defines two processes of cognitive appraisal that arise directly from the transactional proposal of Lazarus (1991): primary and secondary cognitive appraisals (see Figure 1). Primary cognitive appraisal refers to whether what is happening is personally relevant to one's values, goal commitments, and beliefs about the self and the world, and situational intentions, thereby meaning if there is any personal stake in the stressful encounter. Secondary cognitive appraisal refers to coping options and prospects, evaluating if there are available personal resources for dealing with harm, threat, or challenge appraisals.

Specifically, regarding the Interactive Model of Human Adaptation to Stress, it is worth remembering that the concept of "importance" already analyzed whether the stress event is *personally relevant*. In this way, when primary cognitive appraisal happens, the event already has a significant personal meaning that requires to be coped by the individual. In this way, for the interactive model, primary cognitive appraisal refers to the first impact of the stressful event in the individual. The results from the primary cognitive appraisal, for the interactive model, are described as by Lazarus (1991, 2000b, 2001) (see Figure 1): (a) threat perception (i.e., harm or potential loss that has not yet happened); (b) harm perception (i.e., damage that has already occurred); (c) challenge perception (i.e., difficult-to-attain, yet anticipated gain); and, (d) benefit perception (i.e., gain that already occurred). The result of the interaction between the individual and the stressful encounter generates a *relational meaning* (Lazarus, 2000b) that can be organized according to a loss or a gain attributed to anticipated results (i.e., threat and challenge) or to results that are already occurring (i.e., harm and benefit). Additionally, it can coexist in the same situation the threat and challenge perceptions because the same stressful encounter may exhibit aspects that implicate a potential loss while others implicate a potential gain; however, as assumed by Lazarus (1999), one or the other usually dominates.

Secondary cognitive appraisal includes coping efforts made by the individual to deal with the situation and personal control over the situation (see Figure 1). As discussed by Lazarus and Folkman (1984), coping involves cognitive and behavioral efforts that an individual makes to manage demands that exceed the personal resources. These efforts can be organized into problem-focused coping, when the person tries to alter the actual relationship between the person and the environment for the better (and if the efforts are successful, then the threat and harm can be reduced or even eliminated); it can also be organized into emotion-focused coping, when the individual tries to regulate emotional distress caused by threat or harm by using, for example, avoidance of thinking about the sources of stress. Some authors also include a third type of coping related to meaning-focused coping that is used to manage the meaning of a situation (Folkman & Moskowitz, 2004). Regardless of the dimensions that can characterize the concept of coping, this factor is central to explain the stress process and its adaptational outcomes. In fact, psychological stress only occurs if the person evaluates the internal or external demands as taxing or exceeding the individual's resources (Lazarus, 1999). In addition to coping efforts, the interactive model includes personal control in the secondary cognitive appraisal. Personal control can make a difference in the selection of coping strategies used by the individual to deal with the stress situation (see Figure 1). If the person feels that the stressful encounter can be subject to control by his or her actions, then problem-focused strategies predominate; in contrast, if the person feels that nothing can be done to change the situation, then emotion-focused strategies predominate (Lazarus, 1991). The model assumes that more important than the set of job demands that can exert pressure to the individual and create strain, it is crucial to consider if he or she has some control over the set of demands to be deal. This assumes an interactive effect between the demands and the control on stress levels, meaning that control will buffer (moderate) the impact of demands (pressures) on strain (Dewe, O'Driscoll, & Cooper, 2013). Thus, primary and secondary cognitive appraisals represent central dimensions for the interactive model.

Cognitive Appraisal: 2nd Level Processes

The interactive model proposes a second level of cognitive appraisal that comprehends tertiary and quaternary cognitive appraisals. Tertiary and quaternary cognitive appraisals are targeted to deal with the entire set of responses at the psychological, physiological, and behavioral levels (as will be described in the next section). This level is particularly important, if after the first level of cognitive appraisal the situation is not resolved, although, the interactive model considers that favorable (or not so good) situations can also trigger the need for the second level of cognitive appraisal. For example, quaternary cognitive appraisal maintains its relevance when the individual feels that he can achieve an even better situation, or when he feels that, despite the positive effects, there are personal or situational aspects that can be improved.

More specifically, for the interactive model, tertiary cognitive appraisal reflects the personal significance of the *same* stressful event that can result in threat/harm or challenge/benefit appraisals. Tertiary appraisal assumes that the situation maintains the significant personal meaning that requires coping by the individual (importance). Quaternary appraisal includes the *new* coping strategies and personal control, which are involved in the efforts to manage the impact of the responses to the stressful events (see Figure 1). The final goal of using the second level of cognitive appraisal is achieving a better personal situation, compared to the one that resulted from the first level of cognitive appraisal. Thus, all subsequent evaluations and efforts of resolution after the first level of cognitive appraisal should be included in the second level of cognitive appraisal. This is important to say, because long and complex processes of human adaptation to stress can trigger more than one process of the second level of cognitive appraisal. That is the case when one has to deal with sources of stress that change their nature along the process. For example, health professionals have to deal with chronic or fatal diseases, and the process of being ill can start with a problem that was benign and only after a period it becomes malignant and terminal. Therefore, the second level of cognitive appraisal can assume different forms and results along the process of human adaptation to stress.

Psychological, Physiological, and Behavioral Responses

For the interactive model, the main aspect related to the three levels of responses to a stressful situation (e.g., psychological, physiological, and behavioral) is cognitive appraisal. Cognitive appraisal not only explains the type of responses obtained in a stressful event (e.g., anxiety, threat, increased heart rate, decrease of motivation toward the task) but also explains how the individual interprets the responses and the way he will respond. The cognitive appraisal at the first level will determine the responses to the stressful event, whereas the cognitive appraisal at the second level will determine how these responses will be interpreted (e.g., positive or negative; facilitative or debilitative). After this interpretation, adaptation to stress can terminate (turning to event outcomes) or can be assumed the need of additional efforts in order to deal with the situation (e.g., quaternary cognitive appraisal).

Considering the set of responses that follows the first level of cognitive appraisal, the interactive model proposes responses at the psychological, physiological, and behavioral levels (see Figure 1). Nevertheless, the model makes a distinction between *immediate and proximal* outcomes that occur *during* the process of human adaptation, and *stable and prolonged* outcomes that occur *after* the same process of human adaptation. For example, it is accepted that the individual can feel fatigue and lack of energy due to a very demanding situation (outcomes). Yet, it is not likely that same person experiences immediately the process of burnout (event outcomes), because this process results from a prolonged exposure to chronic stress (Maslach, Schaufeli, & Leiter, 2001). This distinction, assumed in the interactive model, can reflect better the ongoing process between the first level of cognitive appraisal, the responses, and the second level of cognitive appraisal. This will result in an interactive relationship between the first level of cognitive appraisal ↔ the responses ↔ the second level of cognitive appraisal (that correspond to immediate and proximal outcomes) and the final process of human adaptation reflected in the event outcomes (that correspond to stable and prolonged outcomes).

Regarding the psychological level, the interactive model highlights the emotional responses involved in human adaptation to stress. As emotions are triggered by cognitive appraisal, they play a central role in the comprehension of adaptation to stress. This means that stress and distress are not independent of the environmental conditions or of the individual characteristics, but instead are the "functional juxtaposition of both" (Lazarus & Cohen-Charash, 2001, p. 46). Furthermore, it is assumed that processes of cognitive appraisal related to threat and harm tend to be associated with negative emotions (but not always) and that processes of cognitive appraisal related to challenge and benefit tend to be associated with positive emotions (but not always). Regarding the physiological responses, the model considers the three main types of physiological symptoms focused in general research (Fried, Rowland, & Ferris, 1984; Jex & Beehr, 1991): cardiovascular (e.g., blood pressure, cardiac activity, and cholesterol), biochemical (e.g., catecholamines, cortisol, and uric acid), and gastrointestinal (e.g., peptic ulcers). Regarding the behavioral responses, the interactive model proposes the analysis of the success or failure obtained by the individual by using his coping efforts in order to deal with the stressful event. These behavioral responses correspond to immediate and proximal results achieved by the individual when trying to resolve or mitigate the effects of the stressful event. From this point of view, they are somewhat different from the results achieved in the event outcomes as these effects tend to be more prolonged in time and often occur after a long exposure to the stress situation.

For the interactive model, using the example of occupational stress, all three types of responses (psychological, physiological, and behavioral) deserve equal importance, and they should be integrated in the understanding of human adaptation to stress, where cognitive appraisal plays a major role. This need is based on research that supports the influence of cognitive appraisal in psychological, physiological, and behavioral responses to stress (Blascovich, Mendes, Hunter, Lickel, & Kowai-Bell, 2001; Tomaka, Blascovich, Kibler, & Ernst, 1997).

The Interactive Process

The interactive model proposes a sequence of steps that occur since the stressful event activates cognitive appraisal, the three types of responses, and the occurrence of event outcomes in human adaptation. Although that, it also considers the process is quite complex.

First, human adaptation to stress adaptation can be completed after the first level of cognitive appraisal or even before when the individual evaluates the personal meaning – importance – of the situation to his well-being. The process will be finished when the individual assumes that: (a) the stress situation is not so important to challenge/threat his well-being or to mobilize coping efforts, in order to deal with the source of stress; (b) coping efforts (both at first and second levels) succeeded in dealing with the situation (e.g., positive human functioning); (c) coping efforts (both at first and second levels) did not succeed in dealing with the situation, and the individual feels harm in the event outcomes (e.g., negative human functioning); and, (d) coping efforts (both at first and second levels) did not succeed in dealing with the situation, and the individual feels that there is nothing that can be done to solve the problem, thereby accepting the situation. The split between situations (c) (where there is negative human functioning) and (d) (where there is not necessarily negative human functioning) is important, because the way the individual copes with the failure of dealing with the stressful event can determine the event outcomes of human adaptation to stress. In fact, there is evidence that avoidant emotional coping (e.g., denial or self-distraction to avoid the source of distress) leads to mental health problems when compared to other forms of emotional coping (Coyne & Racioppo, 2000).

Second, the relation between first and second levels of cognitive appraisals is interactive, meaning that they can influence each other along the process of human adaptation to stress (and both can produce psychological, physiological, and behavior responses). For example, the harm resulting from having a bad job performance (second level of cognitive appraisal), resulting from a threat perception of having too much work to do (first level of cognitive appraisal), can be followed by negative emotions, physical disturbances, and a tendency to avoid the situation. That scenario can become even more difficult (e.g., threatening) for the individual, not only to face the same situation in the future (e.g., too much work to do) but also similar situations that can happen to the individual (e.g., having a difficult task to do). Thus, the interactive model assumes that processes of cognitive appraisal can interact in such a way that can cause negative cycles of human functioning (resulting in the incapacity to deal with stressful events), or can promote positive cycles of human functioning (resulting in the capacity to deal with stressful events). Along the interactive process between the first and second levels of cognitive appraisals, people can feel advances and setbacks, and progress and regress, through a point where the individual positively or negatively adjusts to the situation.

Third, the need to not consider coping and emotion as separate entities (Lazarus, 1999) is accepted because separating the elements involved in the adaptation to stress can only provide a partial vision of the phenomenon. For the interactive model, cognitive appraisal (which includes the evaluation of the effects of the stressful event and the coping efforts) and the event outcomes (including psychological, physiological and behavior outcomes) interact in a continuous way, influencing each other until event outcomes of human adaptation to stress are reached.

Event Outcomes: Human Adaptation

The interactive process means that human adaptation results from the combination of a certain individual and a specific situation, that interact with each other along the occurrence of the stressful event, being highlighted the dynamic characteristics of this process (because of that there is a dashed line to describe the process of human adaptation to stress; see Figure 1). The dynamics of this process can turn difficult to study human adaption to stress, not only because the person or the situation can change along this process, but also because it can change the relation between the individual and the situation.

The model proposes two main effects of adaptation to stress, positive human functioning and negative human functioning. From an historical point of view, there has been a great interest in studying the maladaptive reactions to stress (e.g., decreases in productivity, turnover, burnout, depression, anxiety), but more recently, psychological science has paid more attention to the adaptive reactions to stress (e.g., increases in productivity, will to stay in the organization, commitment, happiness, satisfaction) (for a review of these topics, see Beehr, 1995; Cooper et al., 2001; Folkman, 2011; Payne & Cooper, 2004). In effect, if cognitive appraisal can result not only in threatening and harmful appraisals but also in challenging and beneficial appraisals, then not only can negative reactions occur in stressful situations, but positive reactions can also be observed when studying human adaptation to stress.

For the interactive model, cognitive appraisal will mediate the relationship between stressful events and event outcomes, meaning that it can change or alter the relationship between both sets of variables. It is assumed that positive human functioning will derive from an ability of the individual to use effective coping strategies, in order to deal with the existing demands. Therefore, when a correspondence between existing demands and individual resources has been achieved, the conditions for positive human functioning are increased. For the interactive model, the role of cognitive appraisal is crucial to explain the final result of human adaptation to stress.

PROMOTING POSITIVE ADAPTATION TO STRESS: SOME POSSIBILITIES

The Interactive Model of Human Adaptation to Stress besides contributing for the theoretical understanding of the stress process, it allows to propose some possibilities for the intervention. Then, considering the ongoing process of human adaptation to stress, and the dynamic nature of the relationship between the individual and the environment, we propose two focus for the intervention: antecedent factors and cognitive appraisal. With respect to antecedent factors, the model highlights the role of the situational and the personal characteristics, in the process of human adaptation to stress. Therefore, our proposal for the intervention aims to turn the situation a positive context for excellence, and to turn the individual adaptable to stress conditions. With respect to cognitive appraisal, the model emphasizes the role of threat perception and challenge perception (primary and tertiary cognitive appraisal), and the role of coping potential and control perception (secondary and quaternary cognitive appraisal) on the process of human adaptation to stress. Consequently, concerning cognitive appraisal processes, our aim for the intervention is to turn human resources adequate to multiple stress conditions.

Research on occupational stress interventions are unanimous in considering the primary and secondary health prevention levels, as the most desirable and efficient in reducing the adverse effects of stress related to work. Centering the intervention either on the sources of occupational stress, reducing job stressors by eliminating their causal factors, and by capacitating the individuals with appropriate skills to deal with the inevitable stress conditions, thus altering the way the individual respond to them (Campos et al., 2010; Grant & Langan-Fox, 2007; Lamontagne, Keegel, Louie, Ostry, & Landsbergis, 2007; Quick & Quick, 2004). Additionally, interventions can address three different entities: (1) the organization, by changing work situation through organizational-based interventions; (2) the individual-organization interface, by increasing the individual resistance to specifics sources of stress; and, (3) the individual, by turning the individual more capable of coping with stress, thus preventing stress negative effects (Le Blanc, de Jonge, & Schaufeli, 2008). Joining all those perspectives, we analyze the implications of the interactive model for the intervention, considering both the antecedent factors and cognitive appraisal.

Antecedent Factors: Turning the Situation a Positive Context for Excellence

Turning the situation a positive context, implies an organization of the job context, in such a way that it can be able to promote a well-being of excellence to the employee. To do so, we must consider in the intervention plan the situational characteristics (antecedent factors) proposed by the interactive model. Specifically, it is important to implement strategies to reduce the novelty and the uncertainty of the situation for the individual, as well as, to increase its predictability and imminence, in terms of the time available to anticipate its occurrence and duration. It is also necessary to implement strategies to decrease the ambiguity of the information needed for the appraisal of the event, and to recognize the timing of the event occurrence in relation to the life cycle. To turn the situation a positive context for excellence, we consider that the main target of intervention will be the organization.

With respect to organizational-based interventions, strategies should be focused in implementing a positive organizational climate and a collaborative organizational culture, in order to reduce job sources of stress and to promote a better organizational functioning. As proposed by Le Blanc, de Jonge, and Schaufeli (2000; Le Blanc et al., 2008) in an overview of job stress interventions, first it is important to identify the stressful working conditions, that is, to analyze the situational characteristics that turn the job context into a source of stress. This implies a diagnosis of the employees' working conditions, which can be achieved through a stress audit. The next step for the intervention, aims to remove or reduce the diagnosed job stressors and/or turn the inevitable stress events more predictable for the individual. This task can be accomplished by improving workload, job content and work environment (e.g., work enlargement, job enrichment and job rotation); better time scheduling and role clarification, improving communication among different hierarchies, decision making and conflict management; optimize the use of equipment and technologies; improve healthier and safer physical work conditions; implement corporate wellness programs and improve organizational development. Additionally, it becomes necessary to change the ways employees respond to job stress by improving the fit between the individual and the organization. This can be enhanced by improving career management and career development plans, anticipatory socialization, and management development. Furthermore, when occupational stress is identified and the consequences are significant, it becomes fundamental to improve the institutionalization of occupational health and safety services, and employees' assistance programs.

Antecedent Factors: Turning the Individual Adaptable to Stress Conditions

Turning the individual adaptable to stress, implies to consider the personal characteristics (antecedent factors) proposed in the interactive model, as contributing for the ongoing process of human adaptation to stress. It is not our intention to explore in detail personal characteristics, since most of the individual level of interventions are well established in clinical and health psychology. However, some aspects should be addressed, when we talk about implications for intervention. As proposed by Le Blanc, de Jonge, and Schaufeli (2000; Le Blanc et al., 2008) individual-based interventions in occupational stress should address the following purposes: i) increase the individual's consciousness (e.g., self-monitoring and didactic stress management); and/or, ii) reduce negative arousal (e.g., implementing healthy life styles, cognitive-behavioral techniques, biofeedback and relaxation, physical fitness programs). To do so, we must consider the way individuals see their work environment, and what personal goals they expect to achieve professionally and in their job. We must consider among several characteristics, personal values, believes, personality traits, personal resources, age, gender, and to what extent they feel and believe that their work environment allows them to accomplish their personal goals. Therefore, intervention can focus on dysfunctional believes or in redefining realistic personal goals, and increase personal emotional and instrumental resources to turn the indivual more prone to deal with inevitable job stressors.

Considering the dynamic and interactive nature of human adaptation to stress, we can not conceptualize intervention without acknowledge the role of cognitive appraisal in this process.

Cognitive Appraisal: Turning Human Resources Adequate to Multiple Stress Conditions

Turning human resources adequate to several work stress conditions, implies the implementation of strategies that can address primary cognitive appraisal processes (i.e., that can reduce threat perception and increase challenge perception), and secondary cognitive appraisal processes (i.e., improving control perception and coping potential).

With respect to primary cognitive appraisal, challenge perception constitutes, a priori, the stress-inducing interpretation that is less harmful for the individual. Although of being a demanding or complex situation, it is perceived as capable of being overcome, and as resulting in personal benefits, a sense of gain, control perception and self-efficacy, being associated with a sense of mastery and positive emotions (Rodell & Judge, 2009; Schwarzer, 2001). On the contrary, the perception of threat, damage or loss, imply less positive consequences for the individual. Specifically, the perception of damage or loss, implies the conclusion that some form of damage or harm has already occurred (e.g., low self-esteem, salary reduction) in a given situation (e.g., a negative evaluation at work). However, an event can also be evaluated as a threat, when the subject anticipates that it may result in damage or loss, in the short or medium term future, being associated to more negative emotions (e.g., anxiety, pressure, anger, sadness) (Folkman & Greer, 2000; Lazarus, 1993; Rodell & Judge, 2009; Straub, 2005).

Therefore, if the individual was not indifferent to the situation, having appraised it as a threat, damage or challenge to his personal goals and well-being, a process of secondary cognitive appraisal begins. The purpose of the secondary cognitive appraisal is to evaluate the adequacy of the personal and social resources available for the individual, to confront the demands placed to him, to solve the problem and to eliminate the negative emotions experienced, which usually are covered with high intensity. That is, the secondary evaluation concerns the evaluation of individual *coping* resources (Lazarus, 1993; Lazarus & Folkman, 1987; Straub, 2005). Specifically, in this level of cognitive appraisal the individual makes judgments regarding the abilities and resources that he owns, the options he can have and the limitations of each option. Those judgments are influenced by several factors, such as the novelty, the predictability, controllability, clarity or ambiguity of the occurrence, but also by the state of mind, physical and mental health, and the expectations of personal self-efficacy (Rodell & Judge, 2009; Schwarzer, 2001; Vaz Serra, 2007).

The expectancies of self-efficacy, as proposed by the social learning theory, concern personal beliefs about the individual abilities to take the necessary attitude in order to achieve the desired result. Those beliefs are related to the individual’s personal confidence, sense of coherence, locus of control, sense of personal competency and mastery, influencing his response or action, including the direction of the individual's interpretation of the situation and emotional reactions (Folkman & Greer, 2000; Folkman & Moskowitz, 2004; Lazarus & Folkman, 1987). Consequently, there will be a higher probability for the individual to appraise the situation as a challenge, and not so much as a threat, if he has positive expectations of self-efficacy and personal sense of competency, allowing the individual to feel more confident about himself, and more able to respond to the demands (Folkman & Moskowitz, 2004; Lazarus, 2006).

Together primary and secondary cognitive appraisal determines to what extent the situation is assessed as damage or loss, threat or challenge, or a combination of all, as well as the intensity and types of emotional, neurophysiological, autonomic, endocrine, cognitive and behavioral responses, which are associated to these appraisals (Folkman & Greer, 2000; Folkman & Moskowitz, 2004; Ganzel, Morris, & Wethington, 2010; Lovallo, 1997). Thus, if the available coping resources are perceived as weak and/or ineffective, in such a way, that the imposed demands exceed the individual’s ability to cope, generating negative emotions, then there is a high probability of initiating and maintaining a stress process, especially by perceived lack of control (Straub, 2005). As a result, we consider that a threat perception to stressful work conditions can be reduced and turned into a more challenging situation, if the individual appraises some personal control over the situation, and the availability of some personal coping resources to mobilize and face the demands.

Lazarus and Folkman (1984) conceptualized *coping* "*as constantly changing cognitive and behavioral efforts to manage specific external /or internal demands that are appraised as taxing or exceeding the resources of the person*" (p. 141). This concept, besides considering coping response as a process, it underestimates coping behaviors and coping thoughts, which seam apparently disconnected from the personal situational meaning. This meaning is fundamental, because it gives vitality to all individuals' lives, embracing the personal goals, believes and situational intentions (Lazarus, 2006). Therefore, we consider a more detailed definition of coping, as proposed by Folkman and Greer (2000), conceptualizing *coping* as *"thoughts and behaviors a person uses to regulate distress (emotion-focused coping), manage the problem causing distress (problem-focused coping), and maintain positive well-being (meaning-based coping),* (p. 12). In this perspective, we highlight the usual dichotomous distinction between two forms of coping: (a) problem-focused coping, characterized by the mobilization of cognitive and behavioral strategies to change the situational characteristics or the problem that is causing distress (e.g., construction of an action plan, concentration at work, seek for social support and for information); and, (b) emotion-focused coping, when the individual mobilizes strategies in order to improve the experienced negative emotions that are associated with the problem (e.g., involvement in distractive activities, smoking, consumption of alcohol or other substances, denial, detachment, avoidance, emotional expression). However, although these forms of coping constitute the most used nomenclature in the literature and research, a third type, the meaning-focused coping, is also highlighted. The latter is characterized by the mobilization of cognitive strategies in order to change or assign a meaning to the situation that the subject is experiencing (e.g., give a new meaning to the fact of having lost a job promotion) (Folkman & Moskowitz, 2004).

Despite the distinction, both types of coping are provided with adaptive and maladaptive strategies and, what may be adaptive in one relational context may not be for the same person in a different context or moment (Schwarzer, 2001). Because of this, the coping process is complex, highly contextual and dynamic over time, influencing the outcome of the situation and the cognitive evaluation that the individual does of the same (Folkman & Greer, 2000). At the same time, both different types of coping should be interpreted theoretically as coping functions, since they are often mobilized in a joint and complementary way, influencing the situations and the attributions that the individuals construct from them (e.g., in a chronic illness situation). A process that should not be dissected when it comes to the arduous task of understanding the individual's behavior. That is, just as a tree only makes sense in a landscape context, the coping process must also be contextualized and meaningful (Lazarus, 2006). Yet, the coping strategies adopted are largely determined by the intensity of the individual's emotional response and the ability to regulate these responses, along with the situational opportunities to solve the problem, the changes and characteristics of the established relational substrate between a given individual and a particular situation (Folkman & Greer, 2000). A series of classical stress studies developed by Lazarus and colleagues, emphasize the relevance of cognitive appraisal as a cognitive filter in the conceptualization and subjective experience of stress (e.g., Folkman & Lazarus, 1985; Folkman, Lazarus, Dunkel-Schetter, DeLongis, & Gruen, 1986), constituting as a fundamental legacy in the study and understanding of this phenomenon.

Therefore, to increase coping human resources, the intervention must go further the organization and the individual, and take place at the individual/organization interface level. According to Le Blanc, de Jonge, and Schaufeli (2008), the intervention at the individual/organization interface must pursue the following purposes: (a) improve consciousness (e.g., personal screening); (b) increase personal coping skills (e.g., time management, interpersonal skills training, improve a realistic image of the job, balancing work and family life; (c) provide emotional and instrumental support at work (e.g., peer-support groups, co-worker support, supervisor support, coaching and consultation, and career planning); (d) cure target complains by intensive treatment (e.g., specialized counselling and psychotherapy); and, (e) rehabilitate employees (e.g., individual guidance and assistance).

Let us consider the example of occupational stress in health professionals. One of the first areas of intervention should be at the basic training level of health professionals (Gillespie & McFetridge, 2006; McIntyre et al., 2007; Vaz Serra, 2007). In particular, there are studies that reveal a relevant incidence of stress in students from health professions (e.g., Khademian & Vizeshfar, 2008; Loureiro, 2006; Loureiro, McIntyre, Mota-Cardoso, & Ferreira, 2008). Consequently, the teaching of appropriate communication strategies, as the active listening, assertiveness and the understanding of clients' reactions to illness, permits to capacitate the upcoming health professionals in strategies that will enable them to deal and solve conflicts and problems in the future, in an assertive way, reducing the levels of experienced stress. In this context, we highlight the importance of learning in laboratorial context, with resort to simulated practice and Role Play (Arnold & Boggs, 2003; Grilo & Pedro, 2005; Phaneuf, 2004; Riley, 2000), as well as the workshops of professional continuous training, promoted by the organizations so that employees can have the chance of developing and updating their competences (Akerboom & Maes, 2006).

In addition, it is important to educate health professionals about the reality of their work and the roles they have to play. That is, provide knowledge about what the organizations expect from employees and about what they can obtain, in order to avoid creating high expectations, which subsequently can be translated into a "sea of frustrations," leading to a bad performance, illness, and the abandonment of the profession (Arnold & Boggs, 2003; Glazer, 2005; Khademian & Vizeshfar, 2008; Phaneuf, 2004; Vaz Serra, 2007). Likewise, being able to get help when needed, knowing how to plan and stablish priorities about both professional and private life, constitute fundamental skills health professionals should develop, especially those that experience high levels of stress (McIntyre, McIntyre, Araújo-Soares, Figueiredo, & Johnston, 2000; Seixas & Pereira, 2005; Vaz Serra, 2007).

In order to reduce emotional tension, in result of occupational stress, there have been suggested the practices of relaxation according the cognitive-behavioral model (McIntyre et al., 2000). Besides, a meta-analysis conducted by Richardson and Rothstein (2008) reveals that cognitive-behavioral programs are the most efficient in terms of intervention. In this field, it is also important to know how to laugh and how to have a sense of humor, as essential competences health professionals should develop, because they have a direct action on health and well-being, by improving the function of the immune system (José, 2002; Vaz Serra, 2007).

However, dealing with stress goes far beyond a simple relaxation strategy, or a good laugh. As valuable as they are, the process is much more complex, while based on the development of a realistic conception of the situations and the assumption that each individual acts in the most competent way that he can, according to its theoretical-practical knowledge, personal resources, context and moment. That is, "dealing with stress is knowing how to deal with time ... it is having your own way of gathering information, solving problems, planning enjoyable activities, taking advantage of people and their environment, as well as generating ideas, thoughts and emotions. Caring for patients should also include caring for oneself" (Vaz Serra, 2007, p. 606).

Globally, review studies indicate that occupational stress interventions with an organizational focus and a systemic approach, involving a high number of professional groups, in comparison to the individual interventions, constitute the ones with higher impact on both the individual and the organization, in terms of job stress reduction (Lamontagne et al., 2007). In this area, it is highlighted the role of chiefs and supervisors, and the leadership style adopted by them, as a determining factor of the organizational climate (Stone et al., 2007). So, an intervention on those hierarchical groups, considering an transformational leadership style, focused on the competencies, virtues, abilities and personal integrity of employees, has shown to be effective in reducing the occupational stress levels experienced by the team, resulting in a more positive and productive environment (Jennings, 2008; Quick & Quick, 2004; Stone et al., 2007; Stordeur & D'Hoore, 2007).

Recent studies showed that the perception of discriminatory work environments have a negative impact on employees' health, which can be buffered by high levels of job satisfaction (Donatella Di et al., 2016). So, intervention with human resources managers, in order to recognize and reduce work discrimination and, turn work environments more inclusive and equitable, are suggested. Additionally, managers should focus on the promotion of employees' job satisfaction (e.g., by allowing the participation of employees in decision-making processes) (for further detail see, Donatella Di et al., 2016).

Workplace bullying is also a topic that deserve our consideration, since it constitutes a relevant source of occupational stress, with significant impact on physical and psychological health (Giorgi et al., 2016). Being considered a form of dysfunctional and toxic relationship, workplace bullying influences the employee's emotional intelligence and the ability to self-management. This relationship is mediated by psychological distress (for further detail see, Giorgi et al., 2016). Thus, intervention with human resources managers should focus on the promotion of positive and inclusive work relationships, reducing the levels of psychological distress, and the improvement of self-management ability. In addition, an individual intervention with managers might be important. To this respect, Li and colleagues (2017) showed the effectiveness of a psychotherapeutic stress management intervention at work based on the ERI model, observed over a 9-year period (for further detail see, Li et al., 2017).

More, Campos and colleagues (2010) proposed that to achieve an efficient management of the occupational stress experience, we must consider group-oriented interventions, which should embrace the following elements: encouraging group cohesion; stimulation of assertive communication within the multidisciplinary team; promoting the training of stress management skills, such as communicational skills in the face of difficult patients or in the transmission of bad news, through simulation and role play; encouraging active listening and interprofessional decision-making, by creating critical reflection groups and a constructive supervision. Underlying this strategy is Winnicot's concept of "holding," characterized by affectionate, empathic and caring relationships, which promote bonding, support and cohesion among group members (Campos et al., 2010). In this field, is inscribed the concept of "group field," as a promoter of a "lap" that gives support to the organization and the standardization of procedures, through stimulating interpersonal relationships and experiences, by facilitating brainstorming and ideological disclosure, fundamental to problem solving, critical spirit, initiative and innovation, especially in moments of crisis and vulnerability (Campos et al., 2010). Additionally, the regular practice of physical exercise, has been shown a significant strategy to reduce the negative effects of the occupational stress experience (Coury, Moreira, & Dias, 2009), namely in health professionals, resulting in increased levels of professional satisfaction and mastery (Ribeiro, Gomes, & Silva, 2010).

CONCLUSION

Along this chapter, we analyzed the Interactive Model of Human Adaptation to Stress, conceptually and its implications for the intervention in order to promote a positive human functioning. Considering the discussion so far, some topics deserve a final comment.

Regardless of considering the process of human adaptation to stress in its individual nature, intervention to promote a positive human functioning related to workplace must above all, provide "friendly places to employee's performance." Therefore, designing predictable and fair workplaces can be a way of turning the situation a positive context for excellence, constituting a preventive strategy to reduce the stress experience, and probably more effective than the individual training to prepare employees to face "unfriendly workplaces." However, since some personal characteristics are hard to change (e.g., personal traits), there are advantages in helping individuals to be aware of their personal strengths and weaknesses, so they can make changes in order to become more adaptable to face stress conditions. Additionally, the importance given to a certain situation is many times considered a sign of commitment and motivation toward the job or task, but excess importance can turn the situation much more significant than it really is. Therefore, we believe there are advantages in educate individuals to include all different sides of their lives in a meaningful living perspective, consequently being more likely to appraise job stressful events as "just" one part of their everyday life.

The definition of specific and realistic personal goals by individuals, along with an appraisal of their job performance in terms of personal standards, instead of external indicators, constitute an effective strategy in order to promote a challenge perception. The majority of workplaces are sensitive to programs of goal setting, in the view to promote the individuals' feelings of mastery. Having individuals that are more confident about their abilities to face stress and focused in their own job performance, reduce the probability of making threat and harm evaluations. In addition, more relevant than the number of coping abilities the individuals have, it is important to train them to use their coping skills in an effective way. This training should include strategies that individuals ought to use when something can be done to change the situation (problem-focused), as well as, when nothing can be done to change the situation, but adapt in the individual best way (emotion-focused). To this respect, is important to allude that human adaptation to stressful situations is a process highly dependent of personal control. Therefore, individuals must have at least some control over their work and roles in the job performance situation. Supervisors should give control to individuals, including some degree of participation in decision-making and autonomy, in order to do their work. Some control is better than no control.

Responses to stressful events are spontaneous. Nevertheless, individuals can be trained to change their responses or, to control their reactions to those situations. The majority of individuals are not even aware of the relationship between a stressful event and a specific personal reaction, so when they do that association, they start to gain control over the situation. Training this kind of awareness in advance, increase individuals' probability of controlling stress negative effects. More, coping with stressful events is an ongoing and often unfinished process. This implies that individuals should be educated regarding the cycles of stress and most important, people should be trained in how to use their coping skills in their lives.

Lastly, society and all human beings should expect no less than a positive human functioning, besides the recognition that a negative human functioning is a part of becoming a better person. However, what seems intolerable is having individuals in performance situations where what they can expect is to not make the situation worse than it is. Human beings should expect to be happy most of the time, even when they are in very demanding work performance situations.

REFERENCES

Akerboom, S. and Maes, S. (2006). Beyond demand and control: the contribution of organizational risk factors in assessing the psychological well-being of health care employees. *Work & Stress,* 20 (I): 21-36.

Aldwin, C. M. and Gilmer, D. F. (2004). *Health, Illness, and Optimal Aging: Biological and Psychosocial Perspectives.* London: SAGE Publications, Inc.

Arnold, E. and Boggs, K. U. (2003). *Interpersonal Relationships: Professional Communication Skills for Nurses* (4th ed.). USA: SAUDERS, Elsevier Science.

Arnold, M. B. (1960). *Emotion and Personality* (Vol. 1: Psychological aspects). New York: Columbia University Press.

Ashforth, B. E., Kreiner, G. E. and Fugate, M. (2000). All in a day's work: boundaries and micro role transactions. *Academy of Management Review,* 25 (III): 472-491.

Barling, J., Kelloway, E. K. and Frone, M. R. (2005). *Handbook of Work Stress.* Thousand Oaks, CA: SAGE.

Beehr, T. A. (1995). *Psychological Stress in the Workplace.* London: Routledge.

Blascovich, J., Mendes, W. B., Hunter, S. B., Lickel, B. and Kowai-Bell, N. (2001). Perceiver threat in social interactions with stigmatized others. *Journal of Personality and Social Psychology,* 80 (I): 253-267.

Blustein, D. L. (2008). The role of work in psychological health and well-being: a conceptual, historical, and public policy perspective. *American Psychologist,* 63 (IV): 228-240.

Burke, R. J. and Greenglass, E. R. (1999). Work-family conflict, spouse support, and nursing staff well-being during organizational restructuring. *Journal of Occupational Health Psychology,* 4 (IV): 327-336.

Campos, E., Chaves, A., Pereira, C., Fontaine, J., Santos, L., Cardoso, L., . . . Silva, V. (2010). Equipes do programa saúde da família: estresse profissional e dinamica de trabalho. *Revista APS, Juiz de Fora,* 13 (I): 46-54. [Family health program teams: professional stress and work dynamic. *Journal of Primary Health Attention,* 13 (I): 46-54].

Carter, B. and McGoldrick, M. (1995). Changes in the family life cycle: a framework for family therapy. In B. Carter and M. McGoldrick (Eds.), *Changes in the Family Life Cycle - A Framework for Family Therapy* (pp. 7-29). Porto Alegre: Medical Arts.

Cassar, V. and Tattersall, A. (1998). Occupational stress and negative affectivity in Maltese nurses: Testing moderating influences. *Work & Stress,* 12 (I): 85-94.

Cooper, C. L. and Dewe, P. J. (2004). *Stress: A Brief History*. Oxford: Blackwell.

Cooper, C. L., Dewe, P. J. and O`Driscoll, M. O. (2001). *Organizational Stress: A Review and Critique of Theory, Research, and Applications.* London: Sage.

Cooper, C. L. and Marshall, J. (1976). Occupational sources of stress: a review of the literature relating to coronary heart disease and mental ill health. *Journal of Occupational Psychology,* 49 (I): 11-28.

Coupland, D. and Júdice, M. A. (2002). *Todas as famílias são psicóticas* [*All families are psychotic*]. Lisboa: Teorema.

Coury, H. J., Moreira, R. F. and Dias, N. B. (2009). Evaluation of the effectiveness of workplace exercise in controlling neck, shoulder and low back pain: a systematic review. *Brazilian Journal of Physiotherapy,* 13 (VI): 461-479.

Cox, T. (1985). *Stress* (2nd ed.). New York: Macmillan.

Coyne, J. C. and Racioppo, M. W. (2000). Never the twain shall meet? Closing the gap between coping research and clinical intervention research. *American Psychologist,* 55 (I): 655-664.

Davila, J., Karney, B. R., Hall, T. W. and Bradbury, T. N. (2003). Depressive symptoms and marital satisfaction: within-subject associations and the moderating effects of gender and neuroticism. *Journal of Family Psychology,* 17 (IV): 557-570.

Dewe, P. J., O'Driscoll, M. P. and Cooper, C. L. (2013). Theories of psychological stress at work. In R. J. Gatchel and I. J. Schultz (Eds.), *Handbook of Occupational Health and Wellness* (pp. 23-38). New York: Springer.

Donatella Di, M., Rocío, L. C., Alicia, A., Gabriele, G., Giulio, A. and Nicola, M. (2016). Approaching the discriminatory work environment as stressor: the protective role of job satisfaction on health. *Frontiers in Psychology,* 7: 1313. doi:10.3389/fpsyg.2016.01313/full.

Dugdale, J. R., Eklund, R. C. and Gordon, S. (2002). Expected and unexpected stressors in major international competition: Appraisal, coping, and performance. *The Sport Psychologist,* 16: 20-33.

Edwards, J. R., Caplan, R. D. and Van Harrison, R. (1998). Person-Environment fit theory: conceptual foundations, empirical evidence, and directions for future research. In C. L. Cooper (Ed.), *Theories of Organizational Stress* (pp. 28-68). New York: Oxford University Press.

Fletcher, D., Hanton, S. and Mellalieu, S. D. (2006). An organizational stress review: conceptual and theoretical issues in competitive sport. In I. S. Hanton and S. D. Mellalieu (Eds.), *Literature Reviews in Sport Psychology* (pp. 321-374). Hauppauge NY: Nova Science.

Folkman, S. (2008). The case for positive emotions in the stress process. *Anxiety, Stress, & Coping,* 21 (I): 3-14.

Folkman, S. (2011). Stress, health, and coping: synthesis, commentary, and future directions. In S. Folkman (Ed.), *The Oxford handbook of stress, health, and coping* (pp. 453-462). Oxford: Oxford University Press.

Folkman, S. and Greer, S. (2000). Promoting psychological well-being in the face of serious illness: when theory, research and practice inform each other. *Psycho-Oncology,* 9 (I): 11-19.

Folkman, S. and Lazarus, R. S. (1985). If it changes it must be a process: study of emotion and coping during three stages of a college examination. *Journal of Personality and Social Psychology,* 48 (I): 150-170.

Folkman, S., Lazarus, R. S., Dunkel-Schetter, C., DeLongis, A. and Gruen, R. J. (1986). Dynamics of a stressful encounter: cognitive appraisal, coping, and encounter outcomes. *Journal of Personality and Social Psychology,* 50 (V): 992-1003.

Folkman, S. and Moskowitz, J. T. (2004). Coping: pitfalls and promise. *Annual Review of Psychology,* 55: 745-774.

Fried, Y., Rowland, K. M. and Ferris, G. R. (1984). The physiological measurement of work stress: a critique. *Personnel Psychology,* 37: 583-615.

Ganzel, B. L., Morris, P. A. and Wethington, E. (2010). Allostasis and the human brain: integrating models of stress from the social and life sciences. *Psychological Review,* 117 (I): 134-174.

Gillespie, M. and McFetridge, B. (2006). Nurse education - the role of the nurse teacher. *Journal of Clinical Nursing,* 15 (V): 639-644.

Giorgi, G., Perminienė, M., Montani, F., Fiz-Perez, J., Mucci, N. and Arcangeli, G. (2016). Detrimental effects of workplace bullying: impediment of self-management competence via psychological distress. *Frontiers In Psychology,* 7: 60-60. doi:10.3389/fpsyg.2016.00060.

Glazer, S. (2005). Six of one, half a dozen of the other: problems with working fixed and rotating shifts. *International Journal of Stress Management,* 12 (II): 142-163.

Gomes, A. R. (2014). Positive human functioning in stress situations: an interactive proposal. In A. R. Gomes, R. Resende and A. Albuquerque (Eds.), *Positive Human Functioning from a Multidimensional Perspective: Promoting Stress Adaptation* (Vol. 1, pp. 165-194). New York, NY: Nova Science.

Gomes, A. R., Cruz, J. F. and Cabanelas, S. (2009). Estresse ocupacional em profissionais de saúde: um estudo com enfermeiros Portugueses [Occupational stress in health professionals: a study with Portuguese nurses]. *Psicologia: Teoria e Pesquisa,* 25 (III): 307-318.

Grant, S. and Langan-Fox, J. (2007). Personality and the occupational stressor-strain relationship: the role of the big five. *Journal of Occupational Health Psychology,* 12 (I): 20-33.

Grilo, A. and Pedro, H. (2005). Contributos da psicologia para as profissões da saúde [Contributions from Psychology for the Healthcare Professions]. *Psicologia, Saúde & Doenças,* 6 (I): 69-89.

Hasselhorn, H., Müller, B. and Tackenberg, P. (Eds.). (2005). *NEXT Scientific Report*. Wuppertal: University of Wuppertal, NEXT-Study Coordination.

Huang, G. D., Feuerstein, M. and Sauter, S. L. (2002). Occupational stress and work-related upper extremity disorders: concepts and models. *American Journal of Industrial Medicine,* 41 (V): 298-314.

Jenkins, R. (1991). Demographic aspects of stress. In C. L. Cooper and R. Payne (Eds.), *Personality and Stress: Individual Differences in the Stress Process* (pp. 107-132). New York: Wiley.

Jennings, B. (2008). Work stress and burnout among nurses: role of the work environment and working conditions. In R. G. Hughes (Ed.), *Patient Safety and Quality: An Evidence-Based Handbook for Nurses* (pp. 1-12; Chapter 26). Rockville, MD: Agency for Healthcare Research and Quality.

Jex, S. M. and Beehr, T. A. (1991). Emerging theoretical and methodological issues in the study of workrelated stress. *Research in Personnel and Human Resources Management,* 9: 311-365.

Johnson, J. V. (1996). Conceptual and methodological developments in occupational stress research: an introduction to state-of-the-art reviews I. *Journal of Occupational Health Psychology,* 1 (I): 6-8.

José, H. (2002). *Humor nos cuidados de enfermagem: vivências de doentes e enfermeiros* (1th ed.) [*Humor in nursing care: experiences of patients and nurses* (1st ed.)]. Loures: Lusociência.

Karasek, R. A. (1979). Job demands, job decision latitude, and mental strain: implications for job redesign. *Administrative Science Quarterly,* 24 (II): 285-308.

Karasek, R. A. and Theorell, T. (1990). *Healthy Work: Stress, Productivity, and the Reconstruction of Working Life*. New York: Basic Books.

Khademian, Z. and Vizeshfar, F. (2008). Nursing students' perceptions of the importance of caring behaviors. *Journal of Advanced Nursing,* 61(IV): 456-462.

Kirschbaum, C. (1999). Mental stress follows mental rules. *Journal of Clinical Endocrinology and Metabolism,* 84 (XI): 4292.

Klainin, P. (2009). Stress and health outcomes: the mediating role of negative affectivity in female health care workers. *International Journal of Stress Management,* 16 (I): 45-64.

Kopp, M. S., Skrabski, A., Szekely, A., Stauder, A. and Williams, R. (2007). Chronic stress and social changes: socioeconomic determination of chronic stress. *Annals of the New York Academy of Sciences,* 1113: 325-338.

Lamontagne, A. D., Keegel, T., Louie, A. M., Ostry, A. and Landsbergis, P. A. (2007). A systematic review of the job-stress intervention evaluation literature, 1990-2005. *International Journal of Occupational and Environmental Health,* 13 (III): 268-280.

Lazarus, R. S. (1991). *Emotion and Adaptation*. New York: Oxford University Press.

Lazarus, R. S. (1993). From psychological stress to the emotions: a history of changing outlooks. *Annual Review of Psychology,* 44: 1-21.

Lazarus, R. S. (1995). Psychological stress in the workplace. In R. Crandall and P. L. Perrewé (Eds.), *Occupational Stress: A Handbook* (pp. 3-14). Washington, DC: Taylor & Francis.

Lazarus, R. S. (1999). *Stress and Emotion: A New Synthesis*. London: Springer.

Lazarus, R. S. (2000a). Toward better research on stress and coping. *American Psychologist,* 55 (VI): 665-673.

Lazarus, R. S. (2000b). How emotions influence performance in competitive sports. *The Sport Psychologist,* 14 (III): 229-252.

Lazarus, R. S. (2001). Relational meaning and discrete emotions. In K. R. Scherer, A. Schorr and T. Johnstone (Eds.), *Appraisal Processes in Emotion* (pp. 37-67). Oxford: Oxford University Press.

Lazarus, R. S. (2006). Emotions and interpersonal relationships: toward a person-centered conceptualization of emotions and coping. *Journal of Personality,* 74 (I): 9-46.

Lazarus, R. S. and Cohen-Charash, Y. (2001). Discrete emotions in organizational life. In R. L. Payne and C. L. Cooper (Eds.), *Emotions at*

Work: Theory, Research and Applications for Management (pp. 45-81). Chichester: John Wiley & Sons, Ltd.

Lazarus, R. S. and Folkman, S. (1984). *Stress, Appraisal, and Coping*. New York: Springer.

Lazarus, R. S. and Folkman, S. (1987). Transactional theory and research on emotions and coping. *European Journal of Personality,* 1 (III): 141-169.

Le Blanc, P. M., de Jonge, J. and Schaufeli, W. B. (2000). Job stress and health. In N. Chmiel (Ed.), *An Introduction to Work and Organizational Psychology: A European Perspective* (pp. 148-177). Oxford: Blackwell.

Le Blanc, P. M., de Jonge, J. and Schaufeli, W. B. (2008). Job stress and occupational health. In N. Chmiel (Ed.), *An Introduction to Work and Organizational Psychology: A European Perspective* (2nd ed., pp. 148-177). Oxford: Wiley-Blackwell.

Li, J., Riedel, N., Barrech, A., Herr, R. M., Aust, B., Mörtl, K., . . . Angerer, P. (2017). Long-term effectiveness of a stress management intervention at work: a 9-year follow-up study based on a randomized wait-list controlled trial in male managers. *BioMed Research International*, 1-11. doi:10.1155/2017/2853813.

Loureiro, E. (2006). *Study of the relationship between stress and lifestyles in medical students.* (MasterThesis), University of Minho, Braga.

Loureiro, E., McIntyre, T., Mota-Cardoso, R. and Ferreira, M. (2008). A Relação entre o stress e os estilos de vida nos estudantes de medicina da faculdade de medicina do Porto [The relationship between stress and life-style of students at the Faculty of Medicine of Oporto]. *Acta Médica Portuguesa,* 21 (III): 209-214.

Lovallo, W. R. (1997). *Stress and Health: Biological and Psychological Interactions*. USA: Sage Publications.

Lundberg, U. and Cooper, C. L. (2011). *The Science of Occupational Health: Stress, Psychobiology, and the New World of Work*. Chichester Wiley.

Marchant, D. B., Andersen, M. B. and Morris, T. (1997). Perceived uncertainty of outcome as a contributing factor in competitive state anxiety. *Australian Journal of Science and Medicine in Sport,* 29: 41-46.

Maslach, C., Schaufeli, W. B. and Leiter, M. P. (2001). Job burnout. *Annual Review of Psychology,* 52: 397-422.

Mason, J. W. (1975). A historical view of the stress field. *Journal of Human Stress,* 1 (I): 6-12.

McGrath, J. E. (1970). *Social and Psychological Factors in Stress.* New York: Holt, Rinchart and Winston.

McIntyre, S., McIntyre, T., Salgado, J., Pereira, P., Dantas, J., Johnston, D. and Jones, M. (2007). *Serving Two Masters: Job Characteristics as Predictors of Psychosocial and Psychophysiological Responses to Stress in Physicians and Nurses in Managerial Positions.* Maia: Bial Foundation.

McIntyre, T. (1994). Stress e os profissionais de saúde: os que tratam também sofrem [Stress in health professionals: those who care also suffer]. *Análise Psicológica,* 12 (II-III): 193-200.

McIntyre, T., McIntyre, S., Araújo-Soares, V., Figueiredo, M. and Johnston, D. (2000). Psychophysiological and psychosocial indicators of efficacy of a stress management program for health professionals: phase 1. In T. Cox, P. Dewe, K. Nielsen and R. Cox (Eds.), *Occupational Health Psychology: Europe 2000* (pp. 112-116). Nottingham: European Academy of Occupational Health Psychology Conference Proceedings Series.

Nelson, D. L. and Quick, J. C. (1985). Professional women: are distress and disease inevitable? *Academy of Management Review,* 10: 206-213.

Netemeyer, R. G., Boles, J. S. and McMurrian, R. (1996). Development and validation of work-family conflict and family-work conflict scales. *Journal of Applied Psychology,* 81 (IV): 400-410.

Newton, T. J. and Keenan, A. (1990). The moderating effect of the Type A behavior pattern and locus of control upon the relationship between change in job demands and change in psychological strain. *Human Relations,* 43: 1229-1255.

Paúl, C. and Fonseca, A. M. (2001). *Psicossociologia da saúde* (1ª ed.) [*Psychosociology of health* (1st ed.)]. Lisboa: Climepsi Editores.

Payne, R. L. (1988). Individual differences in the study of occupational stress. In C. L. Cooper and R. L. Payne (Eds.), *Causes, Coping and Consequences of Stress at Work* (pp. 209-232). New York: John Wiley.

Payne, R. L. and Cooper, C. L. (2004). *Emotions at Work: Theory, Research and Applications for Management*. Chichester, UK: Wiley.

Perrez, M. and Reicherts, M. (1992). *Stress, Coping and Health. A Situation-Behavior Approach Theory, Methods, Applications.* Seattle: Hogrefe & Huber.

Phaneuf, M. (2004). *Comunicação, entrevista, relação de ajuda e validação* [*Communication, interview, helping relationship and validation*]. Loures: Lusociencia.

Queirós, P. J. (2005). *Burnout no trabalho e conjugal em enfermeiros Portugueses* [*Burnout in work and conjugal in Portuguese nurses*]. Coimbra: Edições Sinais Vitais.

Quick, J. C. (1999). Occupational health psychology: historical roots and future directions. *Health Psychology,* 18 (I): 82-88.

Quick, J. C. and Quick, J. D. (2004). Healthy, happy, productive work: a leadership challenge. *Organizational Dynamics,* 33 (IV): 329-337.

Ress, D. W. and Cooper, C. L. (1992). The occupational stress indicator locus of control scale: should this be regarded as a state rather than trait measure? *Work & Stress,* 6 (I): 45-48.

Ribeiro, L., Gomes, A. R. and Silva, M. (2010). Occupational stress in health professionals: a comparative study between physicians and nurses working in hospital context. In C. Nogueira [et al.] (Ed.), *Proceedings of the VII National Symposium on Psychology Research* (pp. 1494-1508). Lisbon: Portuguese Association of Psychology.

Richardson, K. M. and Rothstein, H. R. (2008). Effects of occupational stress management intervention programs: a meta-analysis. *Journal of Occupational Health Psychology,* 13 (I): 69-93.

Riley, J. B. (2000). *Comunicação em enfermagem* [*Communication in Nursing*]. Loures: Lusociência.

Rodell, J. B. and Judge, T. A. (2009). Can "good" stressors spark "bad" behaviors? The mediating role of emotions in links of challenge and hindrance stressors with citizenship and counterproductive behaviors. *The Journal of Applied Psychology,* 94 (VI): 1438-1451.

Rosenstock, L. (1997). Work organization research at the National Institute for occupational safety and health. *Journal of Occupational Health Psychology,* 2 (I): 7-10.

Schneiderman, N., Ironson, G. and Siegel, S. D. (2005). Stress and health: psychological, behavioral, and biological determinants. *Annual Review of Clinical Psychology,* 1: 607-628.

Schwarzer, R. (2001). Stress, resources, and proactive coping. *Applied Psychology: An International Review,* 50 (III): 400-407.

Seixas, P. C. and Pereira, P. (2005). *Relações e situações criticas na enfermagem* [*Critical relations and situations in nursing*]. Porto: Universidade Fernando Pessoa.

Shirom, A., Gilboa, S., Fried, Y. and Cooper, C. L. (2008). Gender, age and tenure as moderators of work-related stressors' relationships with job performance: A meta-analysis. *Human Relations* 61 (X): 1371-1398.

Simon, M., Kummerling, A. and Hasselhorn, H. M. (2004). Work-home conflict in the European nursing profession. *International Journal of Occupational and Environmental Health,* 10 (IV): 384-391.

Simon, M., Tackenberg, P., Nienhaus, A., Estryn-Behar, M., Maurice Conway, P. and Hasselhorn, H. M. (2008). Back or neck-pain-related disability of nursing staff in hospitals, nursing homes and home care in seven countries: results from the European NEXT-Study. *International Journal of Nursing Studies,* 45 (I): 24-34.

Soares, A. J. and Pereira, M. G. (2006). Cortisol como uma variável em psicologia da saúde [Cortisol as a Variable in Health Psychology]. *Psicologia, Saúde & Doenças,* 7 (II): 165-177.

Spector, P. A. and O'Connell, B. J. (1994). The contribution of personality traits, negative affectivity, locus of control and Type A to the subsequent reports of job stressors and job strains. *Journal of Occupational & Organizational Psychology,* 67 (I): 1-12.

Stone, P. W., Mooney-Kane, C., Larson, E. L., Pastor, D. K., Zwanziger, J. and Dick, A. W. (2007). Nurse working conditions, organizational climate, and intent to leave in ICUs: an instrumental variable approach. *Health Services Research,* 42 (III): 1085-1104.

Stordeur, S. and D'Hoore, W. (2007). Organizational configuration of hospitals succeeding in attracting and retaining nurses. *Journal of Advanced Nursing,* 57 (I): 45-58.

Straub, R. O. (2005). *Psicologia da saúde*. Porto Alegre: Artmed. [*Health Psychology*. Porto Alegre: Artmed].

Tavares, M. L., Soares-Fortunato, J. M. and Leite-Moreira, A. F. (2000). Stress: respostas fisiológicas e fisiopatológicas [Stress: physiological and pathophysiological responses]. *Revista Portuguesa de Psicossomática,* 2 (II): 51-65.

Thatcher, J. and Day, M. C. (2008). Re-appraising stress appraisals: The underlying properties of stress in sport. *Psychology of Sport and Exercise,* 9: 318-335.

Tomaka, J., Blascovich, J., Kibler, J. and Ernst, J. M. (1997). Cognitive and physiological antecedents of threat and challenge appraisal. *Journal of personality and social psychology,* 73: 63-72.

Vaz Serra, A. (2007). *O stress na vida de todos os dias* (3ª ed.) [*Stress in everyday life* (3rd ed.)]. Coimbra: Autor.

Yildirim, D. and Aycan, Z. (2008). Nurses' work demands and work-family conflict: a questionnaire survey. *International Journal of Nursing Studies,* 45 (IX): 1366-1378.

In: Occupational Stress
Editors: N. Mucci, G. Giorgi et al.
ISBN: 978-1-53615-404-7

Chapter 2

WORK ANALYSIS AND THE RESOLUTION OF OCCUPATIONAL STRESS: THEORETICAL METHOD, MEASUREMENT AND APPLICATION

James Hunter
Employee Assistance Program, University of Missouri System
Columbia, Missouri, US

ABSTRACT

This abstract offers summary results from three recent applied work analysis projects. The first set of data are associated with an academic medical unit, the second data set is associated with an academic strategic marketing and communications unit and the third data set is connected to an academic international program.

In all projects; a seven-point; Likert-type scale was utilized to collect work analysis data by way of interviews with 7 representing the most important or intense factor. With regard to Project 1; mean values and standard deviations for each work analysis factor are depicted in the following chart.

Table 1. Medical unit

Work Analysis Domain	Mean	Standard Deviation
Essential Functions	6.84	.37
Required Training	5.69	1.10
Personality Characteristics	6.30	.94
Customer Service Requirements	6.53	.51
Values	6.53	.66
Organizational Linkage	6.15	.80
Tools – Machines	4.92	1.15
Work Standards	5.92	.95
Required Education	5.23	1.23
Critical Incidents	6.46	.77
Ultimate Criterion	4.53	1.50
Major Tensions	6.00	1.00

In Project 1; Cronbach's Alpha for the 12 item work analysis scale is of acceptable internal consistency: $\alpha = .73$.

In terms of validity analysis for Project 1; significant bivariate correlations exist among several items in the scale such as the following.

- Essential Functions is significantly correlated with Personality Characteristics: $r = .84$, $p = .00$
- Critical Incident is significantly correlated with Essential Functions: $r = .83$; $p = .00$
- Organizational Linkage is significantly correlated with Personality Characteristics: $r = .70$; $p = .00$
- Personality Characteristics is significantly correlated with Critical Incident: $r = .81$; $p = .00$
- Work Standards is significantly correlated with Organizational Linkage: $r = .78$; $p = .00$
- Critical Incident is significantly correlated with Work Standards: $r = .72$; $p = .00$

In Project 2; Cronbach's Alpha is of very good internal Consistency: $\alpha = .81$. The most intense intervention points across all work analytic domains for Project 2 are depicted below.

Table 2. Strategic marketing and communications

Work Analysis Domain	Mean	Standard Deviation
Customer Service Requirements	5.26	1.27
Critical Incident	5.20	1.47
Organizational Linkage	5.06	1.33
Work Standards	5.06	.88
Major Tensions	5.06	1.48
Ultimate Criterion	4.80	.86

In terms of validity analysis for Project 2; significant bivariate correlations exist among several scale items; the strongest of which are summarized here.

- Essential Functions is significantly correlated with Major Tensions; $r = .68$; $p = .00$
- Customer Service Requirements is significantly correlated with Major Tensions; $r = .66$; $p = .00$
- Work Standards is significantly correlated with Major Tensions; $r = .78$; $p = .00$

For Project 3; Cronbach's Alpha for the work analysis scale is of excellent internal consistency: $\alpha = .85$. Mean values and standard deviations are depicted in the following chart.

Table 3. International program

Work Analysis Domain	Mean	Standard Deviation
Essential Functions	6.8	.4
Required Training	5.7	1.0
Personality Characteristics	5.8	1.1
Customer Service Requirements	6.1	.7
Values	5.9	.7
Organizational Linkage	6.1	1.2
Tools - Machines	5.9	1.6
Work Standards	5.9	.9
Required Education	4.7	1.7
Critical Incidents	6.2	.9
Ultimate Criterion	5.4	1.5
Major Tensions	6.3	.8

In each Project; the most intense intervention points across all work analytic domains were utilized to initiate conflict resolution and the moderation of occupational stress.

INTRODUCTORY REMARKS

This text is an extension of the original manuscript published in Derailed Organizational Interventions for Stress and Well-Being: Confessions of Failure and Solutions for Success; Maria Karanika-Murray and Caroline Biron, Editors; Springer Science and Business Media Dordrecht (2015). The purpose of this report is to outline; posit an apparatus to assess, moderate and resolve conflict, tensions or stressors in work settings. A theoretical paradigm including options for measurement is put forth to illustrate the range, depth and utility of a work analytic instrument for organizations and its members. A primary aim of this document to is further amplify the salience and fit of work analysis as an essential device for stress management, conflict resolution and organizational effectiveness.

A few fundamental comments about conflict and stress are necessary at this juncture to transition readers into the proposed work analysis theoretical model. Conflict is natural, inevitable and even vital for individuals, teams and organizations. Conflict is often present at the intersection of one entity and another as each pursues specified objectives. Conflict may intensify when entities encounter competing aims, when resources are in short supply or when perceptions of transactional outcomes vary. Conflict may represent a dimension of drive or motivation that propels entities toward success. Stress is also inevitable, vital and natural for organizations, teams and individuals. Stress intensifies and proliferates when demands exceed entity capacity, as part of various boundary transactions, as a consequence of appraisal processes and in association with various ambient factors. Stress is also a factor that contributes to individual, team and organizational wellbeing. That is; many sources of stress are deemed as good; positive factors that enhance the human experience.

A primary task for all organizations is the effective management of conflict, tensions and stress. Work analysis is proposed herein as a key device for the successful management of these factors.

THEORETICAL PARADIGM

The effective management of workplace conflict, tension or stress is a requisite task for practitioners in the area of occupational health psychology, human resource management, employee assistance programs, organizational diagnosis and consultation and associated disciplines. Conflict or tension in work settings originate from various sources such as role overload, role ambiguity, change initiatives, work schedules, scarcity of resources, political behavior, role conflict, work design, union – management negotiations, the social context and during exchanges at boundaries with customers, intergroup associates and the external environment. Leaders of organizations employ various tools to manage conflict: mediation, organizational consultation and an array of employee relations interventions. This report posits that work analysis is an essential, additional device for the accurate appraisal and successful management of tensions or conflict within the workplace.

This treatise is designed to elucidate how various forms of organizational conflict are potentially remedied through work analysis. The ensuing comments attempt to identify a wide array of interactions and processes in organizations that may generate tension or conflict for employees, work groups or the larger enterprise. A far-reaching conceptualization of conflict is utilized herein. That is, the framework of conflict or tension referenced here is not inherently negative. For example, organizations must routinely manage a variety of tensions in their environments many of which are characteristically good such as increased customer requests for goods or services, employee suggestions for process improvements or technological shifts that require members to acquire additional knowledge, skills and abilities. In each of these examples work analysis may serve as a powerful, useful apparatus to appraise and settle conflict.

A brief investigation of the traditional use of work analysis will provide a channel to deeper inquiry into the utility of the procedure in resolving organizational conflict. Formal methodology for appraising key work domains as each potentially serves as a vector for conflict, including their intersections is also contained in this manuscript. Finally, this chapter provides a systematic and calibrated technique for using work analysis to assess and settle conflict within the work context.

Traditional Use of Work Analysis

Two founding contributors to I/O psychology; Frederick Taylor (scientific management) and Lillian Moeller Gilbreth (time and motion studies) used work analysis to increase organizational efficiencies (Muchinsky and Culbertson, 2016). These scholars and practitioners helped establish the platform for work analysis calibration. Furthermore; the practice of I/O psychology often requires the identification of standards or criteria for effective work performance. Such standards or criteria represent the foundation for personnel training and development programs, compensation decisions, employment (i.e., personnel selection, promotion and retention) decisions and the overriding legal basis for all employment conclusions. Further amplification of the traditional use of work analysis is listed here.

Work analysis is the foundation for every human resource management activity including recruitment and selection, classification, compensation, training and development, career management, organizational change, workforce planning, organizational consultation and broadly stated: the management of conflict in work settings. Work analysis is the systematic investigation of (a) work role (e.g., job and employee) requirements and (b) the broader context (organization – environment frameworks) within which work roles are enacted. Within the work analytic domain; a focus on work roles often alerts the analyst, role holder and organizational unit to contemplate how individual roles intersect with the broader array of roles within the organization and the inferences of these intersections for the specific role under consideration. Work analysis choices or options include but are not restricted to the descriptor type; the various features of work examined during a work analysis (Brannick et al. 2007); the use of rating scales (if utilizing a questionnaire methodology) and the sources of work analytic information. A brief summary of work analysis options is provided below to further amplify the utility of this tool.

Firstly, three major types of descriptors are used in work analysis: (1) the requirements of the work itself including activities performed by employees (Sackett & Laczo, 2003); (Fine & Getkate, 1995); (Cunningham, 1996); (Jeanneret, Borman Kubisiak & Hanson, 1999) and (Hunter 2015); (2) a consideration of the employee characteristics needed to successfully perform the work such as knowledge, skill, ability and other characteristics; KSAO (Sackett & Laczo, 2003); (Costanza, Fleishman, & Marshall-Miles, 1999); (Campbell, McCloy, Oppler & Sager, 1993); (Peterson et al., 2001); and (Hunter, 2015); and (3) the work context within which work is performed and roles are enacted (Johns, 2006); (Hattrup & Jackson, 1996); (Dierdorff & Morgenson, 2007); and (Hunter, 2015).

Next, the use of a questionnaire in work analysis is prevalent. Examples of the questionnaire approach include the task inventory (Gael, 1983); the PAQ (McCormick et al., 1972); and the O*NET (Peterson et al., 2001). This approach provides a systematic means to acquire large amounts of work-related information that is qualitatively summarized. Questionnaires typically use rating scales to depict the importance, frequency, consequence, intensity, difficulty or requirements within a work analytic decision frame (Fleishman, 1992); (Sanchez & Fraser, 1992); (Friedman, 1991); (Levine & Brannick, 2000); (Harvey, 1991); and (Hunter, 2015).

Sources of work analysis information include written documentation (existing job descriptions); role occupants (because of their familiarity with the role including specific knowledge about what is done on a day to day basis); supervisors (since they may have a broader perspective about the distinction of roles within a given work area including the attributes needed for role success); and work analysts (due to their skill in designing, administering, interpreting and evaluating work analytic techniques).

Work analysis documents content and competency requirements of jobs and roles in order to produce job descriptions or role profiles, generates data for organizational design – development and is useful for recruitment, selection, training and reward (Armstrong, 2003). Additionally, work analysis involves developing a detailed description of the tasks involved in a job, determining the relationship of a given job to other jobs and ascertaining the knowledge, skills and abilities necessary for an employee to perform the job successfully (Ghorpade, 1988). Next, work analysis is the study of what a jobholder does on the job, what must be known in order to do it, what resources are used in doing it, and perhaps the conditions under which it is to be done. When organizational needs require improved personnel decisions for people on specific positions, jobs, or groups of jobs, work analysis (or position analysis) is necessary. Jobs are analyzed to understand them clearly enough to know which variables or performance constructs should be predicted and to identify variables or constructs that might be effective predictors – that is, to develop predictive hypotheses. In work analysis, a job as a whole is analyzed into component parts; the level of detail can vary widely (Guion, 1998).

A primary function of HR management involves an identification of what tasks need to be done (that is, what are the specific job elements in positions), and what skills, knowledge, and abilities are necessary for the successful completion of the identified job elements. This identification is traditionally accomplished through work analytic procedures (Van De Water, 1997). In occupational health psychology and employee assistance programs, work analysis is used to analyze and map jobs or occupations for stress and identify variables that explain differences among job categories (Cooper, Dewe & O'Driscoll, 2003). With regard to instructional program design and evaluation, work analysis is an essential tool for use in identifying a wide variety of training needs for a cross-section of work roles and employees. For example, the purpose of a needs assessment is to provide information for the design of training programs and therefore it is necessary to analyze jobs in order to design relevant instruction (Goldstein & Ford, 2002).

Work analysis can provide all the information necessary to carry out the entire range of personnel functions (selection, training, performance evaluation, etc.). For example, job-oriented procedures describe the reasons for a job's existence and the conditions under which a job's purpose is fulfilled. Worker-oriented procedures describe the actual behaviors required of the job incumbent in order to accomplish the intended result. Trait-oriented procedures describe the human attributes that are prerequisite to performing those behaviors or activities (Saal & Knight, 1998). Work analysis is utilized to identify the criteria for effective execution of a job. It (work analysis) is the formal procedure by which the content of work is identified in terms of specific activities performed and the requisite attributes to perform the role successfully. Work analysis is a fundamental tool used to make compensation decisions. It sets the stage or platform for criterion development, performance appraisal, personnel training, wage and salary administration, placement and promotions.

Work analysis is a means to chronicle the quality of work life requirements of an organization. Quality of work life (QWL) is an area of organizational research that includes topics such as employee work and health outcomes, organizational processes and interventions and the system of work – life integration. QWL is acknowledged as a factor that significantly influences employee job satisfaction, team building and improved organizational performance. QWL is identified as a personal reaction to the work environment and an experience such as perceptions of control, involvement, commitment, work – life balance and well-being in relation to someone's job and organization. Interventions geared to enhance the quality of work life attempt to find ways to make the conduct of work (when and where it is performed) more compatible with the personal, family and organizational-context needs of employees (Hammer, L. B. & Zimmerman, K. L., 2011). A high quality of work life contributes to greater productivity of the organization and to the emotional and physical health of employees. Positive QWL outcomes are partially achieved through work analysis.

Finally; work analytic procedures provide a lens to illuminate or determine what work roles are jobs are most influenced by the occupational stressor: work – life conflict. Work – life conflict is a form of interrole conflict in which the role pressures from work and life (family or personal) domains are mutually incompatible in some respect. In work – life conflict, participation in the work role makes participation in the family or personal role more difficult. Work – life conflict can occur in two directions: work can interfere with family or personal pursuits = work to life conflict or life (family or personal) pursuits can interfere with the completion of work demands = life to work conflict (Frone, M. R. 2003). A variety of challenging individual and organizational consequences are linked to work – life conflict. At the individual domain, work – life conflict can generate or produce psychosomatic symptoms, depression, general psychological distress, medication use, drinking problems, substance dependence disorders, clinical mood disorders, clinical anxiety disorders, hypertension, obesity, high cholesterol, poor eating habits and decreased exercise. At the organizational level, work – life conflict can produce or generate low levels of job satisfaction, job distress, low levels of self-reported work performance, higher rates of absenteeism, low levels of organizational commitment, increased intent to find other work and greater need for work flexibility. At the family domain, work – life conflict can produce the following consequences: lower family (life) satisfaction, decreased performance in the family (life) role, increased family (life) related absenteeism and tardiness, increased parenting overload and receipt of less emotional support and instrumental assistance from family members (Senecal, C., Vallerand, R. J., & Guay, F., 2001). Effective organizations should have a variety of work – life balance initiatives in place for the workforce to moderate this stressor. An initial means to moderate the work – life stressor is work analysis.

THE NEXUS OF CONFLICT AND STRESS

Each of the aforementioned organizational, operational functions has the potential to serve as a conductor or vector of conflict or stress within the work context and the execution or administration of these work processes may actually produce conflict outcomes. For example, members of work organizations may perceive injustice during the process and implementation of organizational decisions associated with these procedures. Moreover, employees may link personally undesirable outcomes connected to these business activities to key organizational justice constructs (Gilliland & Chan, 2002), in particular distributive, procedural and interactional justice. For example, with regard to distributive justice; the fairness of a distribution relative to the distribution allocated to a comparison other, conflict or stress may surface when stakeholders perceive or find inequity in pay, training opportunities or performance feedback. In terms of procedural justice; the fairness of organizational processes used to produce outcomes, conflict or stress may emerge when employees sense or observe bias, inconsistency, inaccuracy or unethical behavior resulting in lost opportunities or decreased status. Finally, in relation to the concept of interactional justice; the quality of interpersonal exchange within the work context, conflict or stress is produced when members feel and notice disparate interactions that create potentially insurmountable barriers and a contaminated, damaged social context.

Notwithstanding the organizational justice frame being utilized, organizational members respond to associated outcomes in a feeling, cognitive and behavioral manner. The quality or character of each employee feeling, thought and behavior produces a physiological change and a specific level of stress, tension or conflict. This type of conflict is tangible and represents an intervention point for employees, administrators and the larger institution.

The traditional uses of work analysis are in essence systematic attempts to respond to stressors, demands, tensions or conflict within an organization. A broad conceptualization of stress and conflict is utilized in this regard to include any demand placed on employees, work units or the larger organization (Selye, 1974, Kahn, 1973, Kahn & Byosiere, 1992).

Table 4. Abbreviated taxonomy of occupational stressors, manifestations, moderators and researchers

Type of Stressor	Definition	Manifestation	Moderators – Interventions	Researchers
Organizational Role Stress	– Environmental demands, constraints and events that affect an individual's role fulfillment – Role stress emanates from the perceived expectations that others have for one's behavior or even one's own expectations for appropriate behaviors	– Role Conflict – two or more sets of incompatible demands concerning work issues – Role Ambiguity – the lack of specificity and predictability concerning an employee's job or role functions and responsibilities – an objective situation at work in which there is insufficient, misleading or restricted flow of information pertaining to one's work role – Role Overload – too much work, time pressures and deadlines, and lack of personal resources needed to fulfill duties, commitments and responsibilities	– Social support and job control – Assess need for clarity, hardiness, self-efficacy, internal locus of control, positive affectivity – Reduce exposure to the stressor – Modify perception and cognition	Beehr, T.A., & Glazer, S. (2005) Kahn, R.L., Wolfe, D, et. al. (1964) Hurrell, J.J., & Lindstrom, K. (1992)
Work Schedules	– Any schedule (shift work, staggered hours, time-autonomous, special leave) is a stressor if it does not conform to the needs of the individual worker	– Shift work – disturbed biological rhythms (circadian) caused by working at night or early in the morning – Social – family disturbance – Sleep disturbance – Long hours – increased fatigue, reduced motivation, prolonged exposure to work stressors, use of poor lifestyle habits such as smoking, lack of exercise and inadequate diet	– Modify the shift system – Reduce exposure to the stressor – Acknowledge individual differences with regard to their tolerance of shift work – Increase employee control over work schedules – Naps – Fitness programs – Behavior modification – Physician prescribed medications	Totterdell, P. (2005) Beers, T. (2000) Costa, G. (1996)

Type of Stressor	Definition	Manifestation	Moderators – Interventions	Researchers
Organizational Justice	– Stress or distress is experienced when employees perceive inequities in the distribution of organizational resources (the fairness of outcomes), procedural justice (the fairness of the process by which outcomes are assigned and interactional justice (the fairness of interpersonal transaction)	– Employee perception or actual inequitable distribution of a workplace resource relative to a comparison other – Employee perception or actual inequitable workplace process used to determine outcomes – Poor interpersonal exchange usually between authority and those subjected to their decisions	– Employee voice – Transparency in decision processes – Measures of fairness – Employee participation in decision procedures	Cropanzano, R., Goldman, B., & Benson, L. (2005) Adams, J. (1963) Edwards, J.R. (1992)
Poor Leadership	– Conditions at work in which leaders are abusive, aggressive or punitive and in which those in leadership roles lack appropriate leadership skills	– Abusive leadership – aggressive or punitive behavior toward employees – Passive leadership – no intervention until problems are brought to the attention of leadership or problems are serious enough to demand attention – Laissez-faire leadership – leaders avoid decision-making and the responsibilities associated with their position	– Idealized (positive) influence – Inspirational motivation – Intellectual motivation – Individualized consideration – Job control – Social support	Kelloway, E.K., Sivanathan, N., Francis, L., & Barling, J. (2005) Yukl, G. (1998)
Work – Life Conflict	– A form of inter-role conflict in which the role pressures from the work and family (life) domains are mutually incompatible in some respect	– The intersection of… – High number of work hours – Intense psychological involvement in work – Intense work demands, role overload, role ambiguity and job dissatisfaction with…	– Supportive workplace policy – Compassionate leadership – Use of positive help-seeking and direct-action coping styles – Social support from coworkers, family members and friends – Ecological assessments	Ballavia, G., & Frone, M. (2005) Kahn, R.L., Wolfe, D.M., et. al. (1964)

Table 4. (Continued)

Type of Stressor	Definition	Manifestation	Moderators – Interventions	Researchers
Work – Life Conflict (Continued)	– Participation in the work role is made more difficult by virtue of participation in the family (life) role	– Complex family demands such as those associated with childcare and household chores – Intense psychological involvement with family and life pursuits – Life – family stressors such as intense non-work role demands		Kelloway, E.K., Gottlieb, B.H., et. al. (1999)
Harassment and Discrimination	– Perceiving or receiving differential treatment in the workplace based on some biological, physical or social characteristic leading to the creation of an unwelcoming or hostile environment that can negatively affect targets' job satisfaction, mental and physical health and ability to do the job	– Unwelcomed verbal or physical conduct – Micro behaviors that cause harm to an individual in the workplace – Unequal treatment of a group or category of actual or potential employees	– No tolerance workplace policy – Individual voice (reporting, confronting, filing a complaint) – Behavioral – physical health interventions – Social support – Diversity management initiatives	Rospenda, K., & Richman, J. (2005) Antilla, S. (2002) Barling, J., Dekker, I., Loughlin, C.A., Kelloway, E.K., Fullagar, C., et. al. (1996)

Type of Stressor	Definition	Manifestation	Moderators – Interventions	Researchers
Workplace Aggression	– Efforts by individuals to harm others with whom they work, or have worked, or the organization in which they are presently, or were previously employed – Attempted injurious or destructive behavior initiated either by an organizational insider or outsider that is instigated by some factor in the organizational context – Behavior by an individual or individuals within or outside an organization that is intended to physically or psychologically harm a worker or workers and occurs in a work-related context	– Physical violence resulting in injury or death – Yelling – Swearing – Insults – Sarcasm – Spreading rumors	– No tolerance workplace policy – Social support (instrumental and informational) – Training – Modify job design – Crisis response	Schat, A., & Kelloway, E.K. (2005) Anderson, C.A., & Bushman, B.J. (2002) Fox, S., & Spector, P. E. (1999)
Physical Work Environment	– Physical or environmental demands that tax or exceed the adaptive capabilities of employees	– Poor person – environment fit with the specified organization – Aversive ambient conditions (illumination, heating, ventilation and sound)	– Measure the stressor – modify physical variables – Recognize individual differences – Employee voice	McCoy, J., & Evans, G. (2005) Jukes, J. (2000) Evan, G.W. (2001)

Table 4. (Continued)

Type of Stressor	Definition	Manifestation	Moderators – Interventions	Researchers
Workplace Safety	– Environmental conditions that affect the physical safety, working conditions and responsibility for the physical safety of others to include emotional employee well-being and psychological safety – Work-related environmental conditions, strains (physiological and psychological) reactions to work-related conditions and health status (long-term consequences of job stressors)	– Exposure to hazardous conditions – Inadequate or nonexistent adaptive equipment – Long hours – Role overload – Role ambiguity	– Measure the stressor – Provide adaptive equipment – Provide social support – Employee voice – Employee health initiatives (primary, secondary and tertiary) – Modify job design – Reduce exposure to the stressor	Barlow, L., & Iverson, R.D. (2005) Karasek, R.A. (1979) Quick, J.C. (1984)
Economic Stressors	– Objective (employment instability, economic deprivation) and subjective (employment uncertainty, economic strain) – aspects of one's life that create adverse conditions	– Unemployment – Underemployment – Job insecurity	– Job training – Self-efficacy – Transparent organizational decision-making – Career counseling	Probst, T. (2005) Kaufam, H. (1982)

Type of Stressor	Definition	Manifestation	Moderators – Interventions	Researchers
Technology	– Exposure to technological innovation, organizational use of computer monitoring software, computer viruses, unintended deletion of files and repetitive use of tools (mouse, keyboard) resulting in stress or distress for employees	– Ergonomic strain – Social isolation – Office noise and lighting – Electronic – performance monitoring	– On-the-job exercise programs – Ergonomic reviews – Training – Social support – Increase employee control and participation	Coovert, M.D., Thompson, L.F., & Craiger, J.P. (2005) Aiello, J.R., & Svec, C.M. (1993) Bohr, P.C. (2000)
Industrial Relations	– Any number of recurrent organizational demands such as recruitment and selection, strikes, compensation demands, working conditions, job demands and organizational policies and procedures that generate stress or distress in the workforce	– Labor – management conflict – Employee dissatisfaction with organizational decision procedures – Insufficient social context – Intense episodic work demands (time pressures) – Role demands	– Measure the stressor – Occupational stress training – Removal of stressors – Health and wellness initiatives – Employee counseling – Employee participation in policy development	Francis, L., & Kelloway, E.K. (2005) Barling, J. (1998) Blau, G. (1981)
Organizational Politics	– Actions by individuals which are directed toward the goal of furthering their own self-interests without regard for the well-being of others or the organization	– Lack of resources – Segmentation of information feedback – Ambiguous goals and roles – Advancement opportunities – Job autonomy – Skill variety – Organizational Climate – Interactions with coworkers and supervisors	– Create – maintain unambiguous work environments – Model positive behavior – Employee voice – Fair policies and procedures – Employee participation in goal setting	Harris, K. & Kacmar, K.M., (2005) Anderson, T.P. (1994) Vigoda, E. (2000)

Table 4. (Continued)

Type of Stressor	Definition	Manifestation	Moderators – Interventions	Researchers
Burnout	– Five (5) elements… – Dysphoric symptoms – emotional exhaustion – Accent on mental, behavioral and physical symptoms – Generally considered a work-related condition – Symptoms are observed in normal individuals – Decreased effectiveness and poor work performance occur because of negative attitudes and behavior	– Gloomy, tearful and depressed mood – Feelings of helplessness, hopelessness and powerlessness – Increased psychosomatic complaints – Absenteeism, job turnover and increased risk-taking behaviors – Decreased motivation, decreased enthusiasm and lack of interest	– Cognitive – behavioral treatment – Work – Life Balance initiatives – Exercise – Social skills and assertiveness training – Reduce role overload and role ambiguity – Job redesign – Social support	Kivimaki, M., & Lindstrom, K. (2006) Cummings, T. G., & Worley, C. G. (2005)
Social Context	– A chronic problem reflecting uneasy relationships between people and their work – A psychological syndrome comprised of three key dimensions: exhaustion-energy, – cynicism-involvement and inefficacy-efficacy	– Role overload or underload – Too little or too much job control – Lack of appropriate compensation or recognition for work – Lack of positive connections with colleagues – Organizational justice disparities – Ongoing value conflicts – Turnover intent – Organizational withdrawal – Back pain – Productivity decline – Workplace aggression	– Social support – Job variety – Employee participation in decision processes –	Leiter, M.P., & Stright, N. (2009) Andersson, L., & Pearson, C. (1999) Cropanzano, R., & Mitchell, M. (2005)

Type of Stressor	Definition	Manifestation	Moderators – Interventions	Researchers
Career Concerns	– Work-related or career stressors associated with advancement, security and motivation	– Poor person-job fit – Low stress tolerance for high-stress, demanding roles – Underload; (non-demanding jobs occupied by employees with a high need for stimulation, who look for challenges and possible high rewards – Overload; the inability of workers to meet unattainable performance targets, stay at work for long hours or work in hazardous or risky environments	– Personality assessment – Job design – Job rotation – Organizational career ladders – Social support – Lateral moves to create cross-functional experience – Assessment and development centers – Mentoring – Stress management programs – Succession planning – New psychological contracts	Baruch, Y. (2009) Clarke, S, & Cooper, C.L. (2004) Elsass, P.M., & Ralston, D.A. (1989)
Acute Stressors	– Extreme experiences during work such as confrontations with violence or accidents – Radical changes in organizational structure such as reorganization, collective discharge or bankruptcy resulting in a situation where employees suddenly lose their security with regard to work	– Employee reacts with disbelief and bewilderment – although usually acting reasonably adequate in terms of role performance – The employee processes a range of emotions subsequent to the event such as fear, anger, despair and self-blame. These emotions are often accompanied by physical reactions such as headache, trembling or nausea.	– Risk assessment – modification of organizational variables = primary prevention – Stress management training for employees and administrators focusing on specific acute stressors = secondary prevention	Clohessy, S. & Elders, A. (1999)

Table 4. (Continued)

Type of Stressor	Definition	Manifestation	Moderators – Interventions	Researchers
Acute Stressors (Continued)	– Extreme experiences in social networks such as loss of a team member – Extreme experiences from outside such as technical, natural and environmental catastrophes – The concept of acute means that the stressor occurs suddenly and taxes employees or work units beyond their ability to cope	– The employee alternates between two central psychological processes – intrusion and denial. – Intrusion refers to re-experiencing the traumatic event. It takes a number of forms, the most common being involuntary recollection of the stressor. A person continuously deals with what has happened. – Memories and emotions come up again and again. – Nightmares and repetitive dreams are also a common way in which thoughts, feelings and images related to the event are re-experienced. Finally, there are startle reactions in situations that resemble the original event. – The psychological process of denial has to do with a general numbing of psychic responsiveness. It is expressed by not wanting to talk about the event, by avoiding the physical location of where the event occurred, by diminished interest in significant activities and by emotional numbness.	– Individual interventions; counseling and community resource utilization by employees = tertiary prevention – Peer assistance and self-help mechanisms – Guided emotional ventilation	Dunning, C. (1988) Karasek, R. A., & Theorell, T. (1990)

Type of Stressor	Definition	Manifestation	Moderators – Interventions	Researchers
Acute Stressors (Continued)		– The employee searches for meaning. That is, the victim looks for a way to understand the situation by means of interpretations of what happened to them. "Why has this happened to me?" "How could this happen?" Employees may also blame themselves for having made mistakes. In these ways, employees attempt to regain control. In cognitive-oriented approaches to coping with traumatic stress, much attention has been paid to the process of attributing meaning and replacing old ideas with new ideas – meaning. – startle reactions in situations that resemble the original event. – The psychological process of denial has to do with a general numbing of psychic responsiveness. It is expressed by not wanting to talk about the event, by avoiding the physical location of where the event occurred, by diminished interest in significant activities and by emotional numbness.		

Table 4. (Continued)

Type of Stressor	Definition	Manifestation	Moderators – Interventions	Researchers
Acute Stressors (Continued)		The employee searches for meaning. That is, the victim looks for a way to understand the situation by means of interpretations of what happened to them. "Why has this happened to me?" "How could this happen?" Employees may also blame themselves for having made mistakes. In these ways, employees attempt to regain control. In cognitive-oriented approaches to coping with traumatic stress, much attention has been paid to the process of attributing meaning and replacing old ideas with new ideas – meaning. – The coping process influences the energy level of an employee. They become tired and exhausted after even small activities at work or home. The normal interest in significant others or activities decreases and minor problems in their ecological environment may easily result in impatience or aggression. – Complaints about the work context are aired with colleagues.		

Type of Stressor	Definition	Manifestation	Moderators – Interventions	Researchers
Acute Stressors (Continued)		– Hypervigilance and jumpiness after intense work stressors are other prominent reactions. – These are often of a specific nature – that is, they are connected with characteristics of the initial traumatic event. – Permanent psychological problems = major depression, post-traumatic stress disorder, substance abuse and burnout – Lowered self-care – Absenteeism – Sleep disturbance – Fatigue – Increased use of sick leave – Turnover intent		
Organizational Culture	– Pressures for goal attainment – Complexities associated with employee adaptation and integration – Latency and pattern maintenance	– Resistance to change – Lack of compatibility of values and goals – Orderliness (or lack thereof) of task environments – Safety – Social embedding (quality of social relationships)	– Employee voice and participation in decision processes – Safety climate analyses – On-boarding support – Social support and mutual trust – Reflective space and learning circles – Planned, sequential organizational change	Argyris, C. (1983) Chemiss, C. (1995) Goffman, E. (1971) Schabracq, M. (2003)

Table 4. (Continued)

Type of Stressor	Definition	Manifestation	Moderators – Interventions	Researchers
Gender Differences	– Social role expectations – Gender socialization – Gender segregation – Tokenism – Sexual harassment – Impact of family status on work circumstances	– Workplace psychological distress (anxiety and depression) – Workplace physical distress (muscle strain, injuries) – Work – life conflict	– Social support – Problem-focused coping – Emotion-focused coping – Job control	Desmarais, S., & Alksnis, C. (2005) Bandura, A. (1986) Bell, D. (1987) Frone, M. (2000)
Psychological Contract	– Implicit contract between a stakeholder and the organization specifying what each expects to give and receive from each other in the relationship – A set of unwritten reciprocal expectations between a stakeholder and the organization – A stakeholder's belief regarding the terms and conditions of a reciprocal exchange agreement between a focal person and another party	– Depression – Anger – Withdrawal – Job dissatisfaction – Hypertension – Lowered organizational citizenship behavior – Increased labor disputes – Work – life imbalance – Feeling devalued	– Use organizational justice constructs (distributive, procedural and interactional) – Individual stress management training – Examine – research the positive individual and organizational effects of the psychological contract – Identify antecedents of psychological contract violations – Increase employee control and autonomy	Arnold, J. (1996) Blau, P.M. (1964) Guest, D. (1998)

Type of Stressor	Definition	Manifestation	Moderators – Interventions	Researchers
Psychological Contract (Continued)	– A psychological contract emerges when one party believes that a promise of future returns has been made, a contribution has been given and thus, an obligation has been created to provide future benefits – The psychological contract is the perception of two or more stakeholders (i.e., employee and organizational representative) of reciprocal promises and obligations implied in their relationship – A stress – strain condition emerges when one party in a relationship perceives another to have failed to fulfill promised obligations – A stress – strain condition spirals when stakeholders experience feelings of injustice, betrayal and dissatisfaction connected to organizational decisions			

Table 4. (Continued)

Type of Stressor	Definition	Manifestation	Moderators – Interventions	Researchers
Psychological Contract (Continued)	– The condition worsens when stakeholders lose trust, faith and expectations of fair dealings with the organization			
Risk Management Concerns	– Lack of variety or short work cycles, fragmented or meaningless work, underuse of skills, high uncertainty, continuous exposure to people through work – Work overload or underload, machine pacing, high levels of time pressure, continuous exposure to deadlines Shift working, night shifts, inflexible work schedules, unpredictable hours, long or unsociable hours – Low participation in decision making, lack of control over workload, pacing, shift working, etc.	– Depression – Anxiety – Work – family conflict – Work injuries – Turnover intent – Organizational withdrawal – Damaged workplace social context	– Risk assessment – Translation, planning and implementation of interventions – Evaluation, feedback and organizational learning	Cox, T., Griffiths, A., & Randall, R. (2003) Spector, P.E. (1987) Warr, P.B. (1992)

Type of Stressor	Definition	Manifestation	Moderators – Interventions	Researchers
Risk Management Concerns (Continued)	– Inadequate equipment availability, suitability or maintenance, poor environmental conditions, such as lack of space, poor lighting, excessive noise – Poor communication, low levels of support for problem solving and personal development, lack of definition of, or agreement on organizational objectives – Social or physical isolation, poor relationships with superiors, interpersonal conflict, lack of social support – Role ambiguity, role conflict and responsibility for people – Career stagnation and uncertainty, under-promotion or over-promotion, poor pay, job insecurity, low social value to work – Conflicting demands of work and home, low support at home, dual career problems – Social or physical isolation, poor relationships with superiors, interpersonal conflict, lack of social support			

Table 4. (Continued)

Type of Stressor	Definition	Manifestation	Moderators – Interventions	Researchers
Risk Management Concerns (Continued)	– Role ambiguity, role conflict and responsibility for people – Career stagnation and uncertainty, under-promotion or over-promotion, poor pay, job insecurity, low social value to work – Conflicting demands of work and home, low support at home, dual career problems			
Work Design	– Poor physical conditions (excessive noise, inadequate lighting, insufficient ventilation) – Poor social relations	– Lowered job satisfaction – Decreased psychological wellbeing – Increased health care claims – Absenteeism – Cynicism – Burnout	– Job redesign – Skill variety – Task identity – Task significance – Autonomy – Employee feedback – Risk assessment – Use of person-job fit theory – Employee rewards	Kompier, M. (2003) Karasek, R.A. (1987) Kahn, R.L., & Byosiere, P. (1992)

Source: Hunter, James. University of Missouri – Employee Assistance Program (FY 2010); Revised (FY 2016). © Copyright – The Curators of the University of Missouri.

A multitude of stressors influence employees, work groups and organizations. Stressors are located in a variety of domains such as the workplace and its ambient environment, one's personal life, various social settings and in the complex configuration of spaces that link or adjoin work and life transactions. As utilized herein, a stressor is defined as stress-producing environmental circumstances or stress-producing events and conditions (SPECs); (1992; McGrath & Beehr, 1990). Stress; whether positive or negative requires an individual, team or organization to respond or adapt. Furthermore, stress is a nonspecific arousal reaction in response to all situations that require the mobilization of energy. The arousal aims at the facilitation of the body's attempts to make a physical effort. The bodily reactions aim at the avoidance of disturbing signals from the body (Selye, 1950). This physiological stress definition implies that stress is a reaction – what triggers the reaction is labeled a stressor. It also suggests that stress is a neutral concept. This manner of defining stress submits it is not inherently negative, although it may become negative during certain conditions. The definition of stress also implies that it is a natural and healthy reaction in all situations that require increased energy (Theorell, 2003). Good stress or eustress (Selye, 1976; Quick, Quick, Nelson & Hurrell, 1997) is desirable and associated with positive effects of an antecedent response; it is essentially good health and high performance. Distress (Simmons, 2000; Simmons & Nelson, 2001); by contrast, represents a negative psychological response to a stressor, as indicated by the presence of negative psychological states. An abbreviated taxonomy of occupational stressors, manifestations, moderators and researchers is depicted in Table 4 (Hunter, 2016).

Work analytic domains extend specifically to managing other forms of stress and conflict in organizations as the following discourse illuminates.

Use of Work Analysis to Manage Organizational Conflict

Conflict is an important variable in understanding human behavior in work settings (Katz & Kahn, 1978). Work groups encounter predictable differences in goals, perceptions, preferences and beliefs. There is a greater likelihood of conflict as groups increase in size and diversity. (Bolman & Deal, 2003). Conflict is found in every realm of organizational reality and the parties to conflict range in size from individuals, work groups, coalitions and the larger organization (Pruitt, 1998). Frequently, the origins of workplace conflict or stressors are too often located in or at the individual or interpersonal domain. As a consequence, concomitant stress and conflict management interventions lack a requisite systemic character. Herein, a paramount hypothesis is that work analysis is an essential, systematic and comprehensive tool for the effective appraisal and management of occupational stress and conflict.

Conflict emerges or exists when one entity within the work context perceives that another entity has negatively affected or is about to negatively influence something viewed as important (Thomas, 1992). Conflict behavior consists of opposing actions taken by two or more parties (Deutsch, 1973; Peterson, 1983), in pursuit of a variety of aims. Conflict at work may emerge due to: antecedent conditions to some overt struggle such as scarcity of resources; affective states such as tension or hostility; cognitive states, mainly the perception that some entity acts against another's interests; or verbal or nonverbal behavior, ranging from passive resistance to active aggression (Katz & Kahn). Stressors, stress, strain or conflict in organizations may also surface during union – management exchanges including those involving contract negotiations, the actual unionizing process or as part of overall workplace change initiatives that could involve job security, total compensation or work values (Barling, Fullagar & Kelloway, 1992). Individuals, groups and organizations confronted with threats to their wellbeing experience conflict and stress (Bass, 2008). Associated conflict symptoms include absenteeism, increased emotional arousal, frustration, defensiveness, faulty decision making and physiological symptoms such as sweating, heavier breathing and increased heart rate (Spielberger, 1972).

An additional paradigm of conflict; focal conflict theory, put forth by Whitaker and Lieberman (1964) is of utility in interpreting work-context conflict or tensions. The theorists posit that disturbing motives, reactive motives, enabling solutions and restrictive solutions characterize the sequence of conflict within groups. Specifically, disturbing motives are behaviors which break group equilibrium, violate norms or threaten its boundaries. As a consequence, the work group moves to generate a variety of solutions to conflict. An enabling solution incorporates work group creativity and acceptance of differences. Furthermore, enabling solutions employ group or team differences such as personality, values or the presenting problem as an opportunity or resource and therefore generates possibilities for individual, team or organizational expansion, growth and development. Reflective space (Krantz, 1998) by way of work analysis is one avenue by which a work group can effectively employ enabling solutions. By contrast, reactive motives seek to overcome the distress associated with group or team conflict often rooted in internalized feelings of being out of control, experiences of ridicule, criticism and the fear of abandonment. The employment of restrictive solutions often inhibits group or team potential and accomplishes little toward the comprehensive, effective resolution of existing conflict or tensions. Two fundamental types of restrictive solutions are applicable here: denial; the refusal to acknowledge an impulse-evoking fact, feeling or memory and displacement dynamics (blaming or scapegoating) which are shifting impulses aroused by one person or situation to a more convenient, safer target (Hampden-Turner, 1981, Klein, 1980 and Whitaker & Lieberman).

Other researchers (Kriesberg, 1982; Pruitt & Rubin, 1986; Rubin, Pruitt & Kim, 1994) refer to one or another source of conflict behavior, most commonly divergence of interest and annoyance that that is attributed to another party. Divergence of interest is found whenever parties have opposing preferences with respect to future events. Annoyance usually reflects relative deprivation, a perception that outcomes in some valued realm are inferior to a reasonable standard. Egoistic relative deprivation is an assessment of one's personal outcomes and often underlies interpersonal conflict. Fraternalistic relative deprivation is an assessment of the outcomes achieved by one's group or organization and appears to be the most important source of collective conflict (Brown, 1998). A parallel conceptualization of workplace conflict includes a sequence of events or episodes that occur between entities as the following model suggests.

Each episode of conflict within the work context has an internal logic, with each preceding event causing subsequent dynamics (Thomas). These episodes include the internal experiences of employees, work units, customers and the larger external environment. Every episode is immersed in a defined structural – organizational – cultural context that shapes the character of exchange between entities. This structural – organizational – cultural context includes properties of employees and parts of the system. The intersection of these structural – organizational – cultural components produces conflict outcomes – the consequences or results of conflict episodes. These consequences identify intervention points at various system levels: social, technical, structural and environmental; and thus work analysis provides a device for comprehensive appraisal and subsequent action.

Envision a work scenario where various tensions are present and the focal point of conflict is one employee. Reflect upon an incident at work in which an assortment of customers have substantial dissatisfaction with products or services emanating from a particular work group with associated ambiguity and political behavior blocking needed change. Consider an organizational scenario in which a defined process such as compensation analysis, performance management, recruitment, selection and placement or training and development has served to generate undesirable consequences. Cogitate working conditions such as hours of work, scheduling of breaks, production demands or the safety climate, where any or all of which serves as the basis for organizational conflict. Contemplate a case in a workplace where conflict or stressors are present, yet there is lack of clarity or consensus on what methods to employ to reestablish equilibrium. Imagine the stress and even distress experienced by employees and the organization in each situation. In these and other cases, work analysis is a useful mechanism to appraise and settle workplace stressors and conflict.

Work analysis is a multi-frame device to evaluate and resolve organizational conflict and stress. The technique is useful in managing potential errors and additional tensions created through decision shortcuts and diagnostic heuristics. Work analysis is a means to engage the workplace social context to appraise, reduce and put an end to conflict. The social context of work life (Leiter & Stright, 2009) is a critical channel through which many organizational outcomes such as teamwork, quality, productivity, and employee wellbeing are achieved and the methodology of work analysis put forth in this report sufficiently activates this important domain. This sphere of influence; the social context can provide data about a number of other key work analytic variables such as workload, control, rewards and values, as each serve as potential transfer agents of conflict.

Organizations may use work analysis as a reflective space (Krantz) apparatus for assistance in making optimal decisions. This notion of reflective space incorporates several diagnostic mechanisms including but not restricted to open system theory (Katz & Kahn), organization – environment relations (Davis & Powell, 1992 & Katz & Kahn), developmental theory of organizations (Berne, 1973), the double-task perspective (Bridger, 2001), role analysis (Krantz & Maltz, 1997 & Levinson, 2004) and organization as a whole (Levinson, 2004). The calibrated, systemic use of work analysis by way of reflective space allows organizations to pause long enough to appraise transactions in their environments and learn from their experiences. Work analysis clarifies, defines and manages key operational boundaries. It generates data, produces interpretations and provides the basis for needed recommendations and associated change. It (work analysis) is a fundamental means to manage conflict and stress within the work context. Finally, work analytic procedures may serve to engender a degree of symbiosis (Kulas, Haynes, Kalten, Hopp & Duffala, 2002) among the job holder, work role, team, larger organization and external environment. This type of interdependence can nurture organizational interventions constructed from comprehensive analyses, which are also designed to produce positive, system-wide outcomes to focus on a comprehensive set of variables and stakeholders. The effective use of work analysis may address and integrate individual, work role, team and organizational vision or goals.

MEASUREMENT – APPLICATION

All behavior exists in some capacity and is therefore subject to measurement (Thorndike, 1949). If work analysis is a practical strategy to appraise and settle stress or conflict in organizations, what specific work analytic techniques are employed to bring about effective change and to restore equilibrium? The following applied methodology has been devised for use in attending to workplace conflict. The aim here is to engage in conflict management through a systematic, calibrated and reflective process. Five features, facets or building blocks are included as part of this analytic technique: (1) the type of information collected, (2) the source of information utilized, (3) the technique of collecting information, (4) the level of analysis or detail observed during the analytical process, and (5) the approach to storing, retrieving and distributing data (Sanchez & Levine, 2001). This work analytical procedure focuses on twelve (12) key domains of work. These domains including their comparative character and utility are listed here and in the following grid.

Essential Functions – key role responsibilities

Required Training – requisite training for role success

Personality Characteristics – personality characteristics needed for role effectiveness

Customer Service Requirements – key customer service requirements for the role holder

Values – key values that should guide efforts of the employee in role

Organizational Linkage – key work units to which the role is linked

Tools – Machines – technologies and tools necessary for work role effectiveness

Work Standards – essential work standards such as accuracy

Required Education – formal education necessary for role success

Critical Incident – transactions or critical events that create lasting impressions of the role

Ultimate Criterion – assess the relevant, deficient or contaminated nature of performance criterion

Major Tensions – identify major tensions associated with the work role

Note: Physical Work Environment *- noise, lighting, vibrations, ventilation, ergonomics, radiation, occupational dermatoses, crowding and an array of other factors (in some cases; inclusion of this 13th factor may have utility in the assessment and moderation of organizational conflict or stress)*

These 12 domains of work represent key diagnostic and intervention points toward the moderation or resolution of organizational conflict or stress. The salience and fit of each domain for use in assessing and resolving organizational conflict or stress is summarized here.

First, substantial organizational conflict may surface and proliferate when the essential functions of a job are too heavy, unclear or negatively intersect with other jobs or responsibilities, potentially resulting in role overload, ambiguity or conflict. Next, organizational training activities position job holders and work units to effectively and efficiently respond to environmental demands. Insufficient or missing training programs may serve to generate organizational conflict. With regard to personality characteristics, Argyris (1957, 1964) posited a basic conflict between human personality and how organizations were typically structured and managed. Argyris noted person-structure conflict as built into traditional principles of organizational design and management. The structural concept of task specialization defines jobs as narrowly as possible to improve efficiencies. A potential consequence of this organizational design strategy is the emergence of conflict when specific features of personality such as introversion, extraversion, agreeableness, openness to experience, emotional stability or conscientiousness intersect with the previously referenced principles of work design and administration. In terms of customer service requirements, a deep understanding of theories of consumer behavior and work motivation, and the effective application of concomitant rules and techniques can serve to mitigate conflict at work. Next, organizational conflict is often value laden. For example, espoused values are those beliefs or concepts that are specifically endorsed by management or the organization at large. Enacted values are those that are converted into employee behavior. A perceived difference between espoused and enacted values can be a source of cynicism and conflict among employees (Muchinsky). Moreover, values represent basic convictions that a specific mode of conduct or end-state of existence is personally or socially preferable to an opposite or converse mode of conduct or end-state of existence (Rokeach, 1973). They contain a judgmental element in that they carry an individual's ideas as to what is right, good or desirable. Values have both content and intensity attributes. The content attribute says that a mode of conduct or end-state of existence is important. The intensity attribute specifies how important it is (Robbins, 2003). Stress and conflict may emerge in work settings during transactions that involve competing individual or group values. With regard to organizational linkage, the science of linkage analysis (Muchinsky) is one method to gain a greater understanding of a job. The procedure unites two basic types of work analysis information: task-oriented (i.e., work activities) and worker-oriented (i.e., human attributes). A linkage analysis examines the relationship between KSAOs and tasks performed. The results of this analysis reveal which particular KSAOs are linked to the performance of many important and frequently performed tasks. In a related vein, the open system model (Katz & Kahn) is a useful apparatus to appraise vital links among organizational subunits. The open system model is very useful to analysts and stakeholders as they identify and assess tensions or conflict at the input, conversion or output boundaries ultimately providing salient organizational linkage information. Similarly, organization – environment relations (Davis & Powell; and Katz & Kahn) is a useful paradigm to understand various forms of organizational conflict and focuses on the functional relationships that organizations establish with different sectors of the environment. The environment must be taken into account to explain the behavior in organizations, including the uncertain array of exchange activities within the organization – environment context that may precipitate conflict. Any of these tools; linkage analysis, the open system model or organization – environment relations may provide key information toward the management and resolution of organizational conflict. With regard to tools and machines, key technologies frequently serve to enhance organizational operations. When these tools or machines are inadequate or unavailable productivity is potentially lowered, product quality is theoretically compromised and substantial conflict may appear. Work standards or job performance criteria (Muchinsky) such as objective performance criteria (i.e., a set of factors used to assess job performance that are relatively factual in character) and subjective performance criteria (i.e., a set of factors used to assess job performance that are the product of someone's judgment of these factors) can serve to produce conflict within the work context. Specific criteria in this regard include production, sales, tenure or turnover, absenteeism, accidents, theft, deviant workplace behavior, emotional labor and adaptive citizenship behavior. The presence and ongoing measurement of these criteria may produce considerable conflict at work; especially if the criteria are beyond an employee's ability to effectively and efficiently respond to these demands. In consideration of required education, the EEOC has produced the Uniform Guidelines on Employee Selection Procedures for organizations to follow in making employment decisions. Hiring and promotional decisions linked to educational criteria can produce extreme turbulence or conflict in work settings as reflected by the large volume of associated major court cases (i.e., Griggs v. Duke Power Company; Albemarle v. Moody; Bakke v. University of California; Watson v. Fort Worth Bank & Trust; and Ricci v. Destefano). Critical incidents: events that create lasting impressions of the role holder, work unit or organization; especially if negative, can generate intense conflict. In some cases, these events are extremely difficult to overcome and result in diminished relations, tarnished reputations and lost revenue. Based on one's position in a work setting; job holder or key stakeholder, beliefs will vary regarding the ultimate criterion or criteria to use in the determination of success or failure at work. This type of fundamental disparity will likely produce conflict or tension at work. It is vital that the criterion or criteria used to make evaluative decisions are relevant, ample and free of contamination. Finally, organizational political behaviors (i.e., resource allocation, self-serving behavior, and how decisions are made in general) are likely to produce a variety of major tensions, associated conflict scenarios, and the effective management of these political dynamics is likely to moderate conflict at work.

This particular method of work analysis allows the jobholder or work unit around which workplace tensions are located to select two (or more) stakeholders to submit diagnostic and problem-solving data. The analyst; one well-trained in work analysis, interviews the job holder or work unit representative, designated stakeholders, assembles qualitative and quantitative data, forms impressions in each domain, and synthesizes the total results into recommendations, ultimately positioning a work unit or larger organization to render a most advantageous decision toward conflict resolution and stress reduction or elimination. Job incumbents and other subject matter experts are vital partners in the collection, analysis and interpretation of the work analytic data emerging from this technique. An additional source of information is the existing classification specification for the work role. The fundamental nature of this process includes interviews, direct observation and a structured questionnaire. This procedure positions an organization to examine the interactional complexity and transactional nature among the multifaceted array of (12) key work domains. During this process, stakeholders also rank the intensity of each factor or stressor as each may potentially contribute to stress, tension or conflict. An exclusively qualitative approach or option is also available using this model as well as a model using the job holder and work analyst as he primary sources of data for the work analysis grid. This model is adaptable to include fewer feedback loops. That is; subsequent to the consulting entry phase; in collaboration with organizational leadership the work analyst may select to interview fewer stakeholders to complete the project.

This procedure delivers a variety of key information regarding individual attributes requisite for job success, essential organizational support necessary for achievement of desired outcomes and the existing stressors that may impede successful task completion. Additionally, this technique is utilized to help stakeholders answer questions about the job, its requirements, and needed change and may serve as a reference point to resolve future challenges connected to training, classification, selection, performance appraisal, compensation and reengineering pursuits.

Table 5. Work analysis analytical grid

	Job Holder Response	**Stakeholder I Response**	**Stakeholder II Response**	**Intensity of Factor 7 = Very Intense, 6, 5, 4, 3, 2, 1 = Of Little Intensity**	**Analyst Impressions**
Essential Functions Identify essential functions of the position.				Job Holder ___ Stakeholder I___ Stakeholder II___	
Required Training What training programs are required to position the job holder to succeed?				Job Holder ___ Stakeholder I___ Stakeholder II___	
Personality Characteristics List the personality characteristics needed for role effectiveness. (introversion-extraversion, agreeableness, openness to experience, emotional stability, conscientiousness)				Job Holder ___ Stakeholder I ___ Stakeholder II___	
Customer Service Requirements What are key customer service requirements for the job holder to consider? (flexibility, professionalism, responsiveness, subject matter expert, etc.)				Job Holder ___ Stakeholder I___ Stakeholder II___	

Table 5. (Continued)

	Job Holder Response	Stakeholder I Response	Stakeholder II Response	Intensity of Factor 7 = Very Intense, 6, 5, 4, 3, 2, 1 = Of Little Intensity	Analyst Impressions
Values Identify values that should guide efforts of the job holder. (honesty, respect, etc.)				Job Holder ___ Stakeholder I___ Stakeholder II___	
Organizational Linkage List key work units or departments to which the job or role is linked.				Job Holder ___ Stakeholder I___ Stakeholder II___	
Tools – Machines Identify tools and technology need for role effectiveness.				Job Holder ___ Stakeholder I___ Stakeholder II___	
Work Standards (Quality – Quantity) Identify essential work standards. (timeliness, accuracy, neatness, error-free)				Job Holder ___ Stakeholder I___ Stakeholder II___	

	Job Holder Response	Stakeholder I Response	Stakeholder II Response	Intensity of Factor 7 = Very Intense, 6, 5, 4, 3, 2, 1 = Of Little Intensity	Analyst Impressions
Required Education What education must the job holder contain in order to succeed?				Job Holder ___ Stakeholder I___ Stakeholder II___	
Critical Incident Describe critical incidents that may contribute to lasting impressions of the role and work unit.				Job Holder ___ Stakeholder I___ Stakeholder II___	
Ultimate Criterion Assess whether the criterion or criteria used to make evaluative decisions are relevant, deficient or contaminated.				Job Holder ___ Stakeholder I___ Stakeholder II___	
Major Tensions Discuss major tensions associated with the job or work role such as role overload, role ambiguity, role conflict or organizational politics.				Job Holder ___ Stakeholder I___ Stakeholder II___	

The method described herein also delivers essential work analytic data connected to conceptual criterion; the theoretical standard to understand and actual criterion; the operational or actual standard to measure or assess, as well as criterion deficiency; the degree to which the actual criteria fail to overlap the conceptual criteria; that is, how deficient the actual criteria are in representing the conceptual ones, criterion relevance; the degree to which the actual criteria and the conceptual criteria coincide and criterion contamination; the part of the actual criteria that is unrelated to the conceptual criteria (Muchinsky).

The criterion question is fundamental in the resolution of multifarious demands, stressors or conflict within work settings. Criterion provides the basis for measurement and successful interactions across a vast assortment of workplace domains. As utilized here, criterion assists employees, managers, work groups and the larger institution to specify far-reaching performance standards and to determine the utility of the criterion over time. Resolving the criterion question positions the larger enterprise to engage in higher-order interactions and transactions through multiple boundaries and lessens the intensity of focus on a single unit of analysis; the individual. A fundamental assertion at this juncture is that resolution of the criterion question is essential in the appraisal and solution of many forms of conflict in work settings.

Conclusion

Work is a changing entity. As time elapses on the job, one's work may shift because tasks become obsolete, new requirements are added by leadership or the jobholder modifies the way work is completed in response to environmental demands. These changes may generate stress or conflict as the work and role intersects with the larger ambient environment. In addition to all that has been tried; alongside of other alternatives, work analysis is a legitimate approach to the appraisal and resolution of organizational stress and conflict. The technique described herein represents a form of discovery and is posited as something that will make a positive difference in organizations and for their members.

This work analytic procedure combines central elements of the organizational diagnostic process: systematic collection and evaluation of qualitative and quantitative measures and consequently balances stakeholders and diagnosticians throughout the intervention and change process. This technique amply illuminates workplace here-and-now data while concurrently generates essential information for use in long range strategic plans and concomitant interventions. The method detailed in this report is dynamic and flexible and thereby accommodates shifting organizational scenarios and structures. This technique works well when one or more conflict resolution strategies such as coaching, mediation, performance management, employee training or even broad-based strategic design and formulation have been utilized yet stress, conflict or workplace tensions remain. This procedure produces relevant, context-specific, wide-ranging data for use in subsequent decision making. It has the capacity to pinpoint key workplace variables in need of modification. Organizational points of intervention such as essential functions, values, customer service requirements, organizational linkage or ultimate criterion are likely to vary based upon the interactional complexity among key variables that are linked to stress and conflict.

This applied methodology is one option for effective stress and conflict management in work settings. Inclusion of an additional domain into this paradigm; the physical work environment may prove useful during the comprehensive appraisal, reduction or elimination of stressors or conflict at work and shall incorporate key elements such as noise, lighting, vibrations, ventilation, ergonomics, radiation, occupational dermatoses, crowding and an array of other factors. The methodology summarized herein has been utilized numerous times within a university setting with a wide range of work units and during independent, external consulting activities. Outcomes are characteristically positive with an ease in employee role pressures, lessened negative attributions directed at the job holder and administrators acquiring influential qualitative and quantitative data to generate systematic decisions. Future research into this topic and subsequent revision of this manuscript will focus more on the interaction among observation, measurement and interpretation with a desired end of methodological precision. The quest for precision is essential as is the process of examining key questions germane to this construct.

In the complex configuration of spaces among employees, work units, transactions, stress and conflict; work analysis can provide vital information for effective decision making.

REFERENCES

Adams, J. S. (1963). Toward an understanding of inequity. *Journal of Abnormal and Social Psychology, 47*, 422-436.

Aiello, J., R., & Svec, C., M. (1993). Computer monitoring of work performance: Extending the social facilitation framework to electronic presence. *Journal of Applied Social Psychology,* 23, 537-548.

Albemarle Paper Co. v. Moody - 422 U.S. 405. (1975). Retrieved January 17, 2013 from http://supreme.justia.com/cases/federal/us/422/405.

Anderson, C. A., & Bushman, B., J. (2002). Human Aggression. *Annual Review of Psychology,* 53, 27-51.

Anderson, L. M., & Pearson, C. M. (1999). Tit-for-tat? The spiraling effect of incivility in the workplace. *Academy of Management Review,* 24, 452-471.

Anderson, T. P. (1994). Creating measures of dysfunctional office and organizational politics: The DOOP and short for DOOP scales. *Psychology,* 31, 24-34.

Argyris, C. (1983). *Strategy, Change and Defense Routines.* Boston, MA: Pitman.

Argyris, C. (1957). *Personality and Organization.* New York: Harper-Collins.

Argyris, C. (1964). *Integrating the Individual and the Organization.* New York: John Wiley.

Armstrong, M. (2001). *Handbook of Human Resource Management Practice.* Kogan-Page LTD.

Aronson, E. (1972). *The Social Animal.* (2nd ed.) W. H. Freeman and Company. San Francisco.

Aycan, S. (2008). Cross-cultural approaches to work – family conflict. In K. Korabik, D. S. Lero, & D. L. Whitehead (eds.), *Handbook of Work – Family Integration: Research, Theory and Best Practices* (pp. 353-370). London: Elsevier. doi:10.1016/B978-012372574-5.50022-3

Bandura, A. (1986). *Social Foundations of Thought and Action: A Social Cognitive Theory.* Englewood Cliffs: NJ: Prentice Hall.

Barling, J., Fullagar, C., & Kelloway, E. K. (1992). *The Union and Its Members: A Psychological Approach.* Oxford University Press. New York.

Barling, J. (1998). Industrial relations: A "blind spot" in teaching, research, and practice of industrial/organizational psychology. *Canadian Psychology,* 29, 103-108.

Barling, J., Dekker, I., Loughlin, C. A., Kelloway, E. K., Fullagar, C., & Johnson, D. (1996). Prediction and replication of the organizational and personal consequences of workplace sexual harassment. *Journal of Managerial Psychology,* 11 (5), 4-25.

Barlow, L., & Iverson, R. D. (2005). Workplace Safety. In *Handbook of Work Stress,* pp. 247-265. Julian Barling, E. Kevin Kelloway & Michael Frone, (eds.).

Baruch, Y. (2009). Stress and Careers. In *International Handbook of Work and Health Psychology,* (3rd ed.), pp. 197-220. C. L. Cooper, J. C. Quick and M. J. Schabracq (eds.).

Bass, B. (2008). *Stress Effects.* In *The Bass Handbook of Leadership: Theory, Research & Managerial Applications*, pp. 812-839. Free Press: New York.

Bates, C. A., Bowes-Sperry, L., & O'Leary-Kelly, A. M. (2006). Sexual Harassment in the Workplace: A Look Back and a Look Ahead. In *Handbook of Workplace Violence,* pp. 381-415. E. Kevin Kelloway, Julian Barling & Joseph Hurrell, Jr. (eds.).

Beehr, T. A., & Glazer, S. (2005). Organizational Role Stress. In *Handbook of Work Stress*, pp. 7-34. Julian Barling, E. Kevin Kelloway & Michael Frone, (eds.).

Beehr, T. A., King, L. A., & King, D. W. (1990). Social support and occupational stress: Talking to supervisors. *Journal of Vocational Behavior, 36,* 61-81.

Beers, T. (2000, June). Flexible schedules and work shifts: Replacing the 9-to-5 workday? *Monthly Labor Review.*

Bell, D. (1987). Gender differences in the social moderators of stress. In R. C. Barnett, L. Biener, & G. K. Baruch (eds.), *Gender and Stress,* pp. 257-277. New York: free Press.

Bellavia, G. M. & Frone, M. R. (2005). Work-Family Conflict. In *Handbook of Work Stress,* pp. 113-147. Julian Barling, E. Kevin Kelloway & Michael Frone, (eds.).

Berne, E. (1973). *The Structure and Dynamics of Organizations and Groups.* Ballantine Books.

Berridge, J., & Cooper, C. L. (1983). Stress and coping in US organizations: The role of the employee assistance programme. *Work and Stress, 7,* 89-1-2.

Berridge, J., & Cooper, C. L. (1994). The employee assistance programme: Its role in organizational coping and excellence. *Personnel Review, 23,* 4-20.

Berridge, J., Cooper, C. L., & Highley, C. (1997). *Employee Assistance Programmes and Workplace Counseling.* Chichester UK: John Wiley.

Blau, G. (1981). Organizational investigation of job stress, social support, service length and job strain. *Organizational Behavior and Human Performance,* 27, 279-302.

Bohr, P., C. (2000). Efficacy of office ergonomic education. *Journal of Occupational Rehabilitation.* 10, 243-255.

Bowman, L. G., & Deal, T. E. (2003). *Reframing Organizations: Artistry, Choice, and Leadership.* (3rd ed.) Jossey-Bass.

Bridger, H. (2001). Courses and Working Conferences as Transitional Learning Institutions. In: E. Trist and H. Murray, *The Social Engagement of Social Science. A Tavistock Anthology, Vol. 1: The Socio-Psychological Perspective.* The University of Pennsylvania Press, Philadelphia, PA.

Caplan, G. (1964). *Principles of Preventive Psychiatry.* New York: Basic Books.

Cherniss, C. (1995). *Beyond Burnout.* New York: Routledge.

Clarke, S., & Cooper, C. L. (2004). *Managing the Risk of Workplace Stress.* London: Routledge.

Coffey, A., & Atkinson, P. (1996). *Making Sense of Qualitative Data: Complementary Research Strategies.* Thousand Oaks, CA: Sage.

Commission on Chronic Illness. (1957). *Chronic Illness in the United States* (Vol. 1). Cambridge, MA: Harvard University Press.

Cooper, C. L., Dewe, P., & O'Driscoll, M. (2003). *Employee Assistance Programs.* In Handbook of Occupational Health Psychology, pp. 289-304. James Campbell Quick and Lois E. Tetrick, (eds.).

Cooper, C., Sloan, S. J., & Williams, S. (1988). *Occupational Stress Indicator.* London: NFER-Nelson.

Coovert, M., D., Thompson, L., F., & Craiger, J. P. (2005). *Technology.* In Handbook of Work Stress, pp. 299-324. Julian Barling, E. Kevin Kelloway & Michael Frone, (eds.).

Costa, G. (1996). The impact of shift and night work on health. *Applied Ergonomics, 27*, 9-16.

Cropanzano, R., Goldman, B. M., & Benson III, L. (2005). *Organizational Justice.* In Handbook of Work Stress, pp. 63-87. Julian Barling, E. Kevin Kelloway & Michael Frone, (eds.).

Cropanzano, R. & Mitchell, M. (2005). Social exchange theory: an interdisciplinary review. *Journal of Management,* 31, 874-900.

Cummings, Thomas G., & Worley, Christopher G. (2005). *Organization Development and Change*, 8th (ed.). Thompson/Southwestern.

Daniels, K. (1996). Why aren't managers concerned about occupational stress? *Work and Stress, 10,* 352- 366.

Davis, G. F., & Powell, W. W. (1992). *Organization – Environment Relations.* In M. D. Dunnette, and L. M. Hough, (eds.), Handbook of Industrial & Organizational Psychology, Vol. 3, pp. 315-375. Palo Alto CA: Consulting Psychologists Press.

Desmarais, S., & Alksnis, C. (2005). *Gender Issues.* In Handbook of Work Stress, pp. 455-485. Julian Barling, E. Kevin Kelloway & Michael Frone, (eds.).

Deutsch, M. (1973). *The Resolution of Conflict.* New Haven, CT: Yale University Press.

Edwards, J. R. (1992). A cybernetic theory of stress, coping, and well-being in organizations. *Academy of Management Review, 17,* 238-274.

Elsass, P. M., & Ralston, D. A. (1989). Individual responses to the stress of career plateauing. *Journal of Management,* 15, 35-47.

Employee Assistance Professionals Association (EAPA). (1999). *Standards of Practice and Professional Guidelines for Employee Assistance Programs.* London: Author.

Evan, G. W. (2001). Environmental Stress and Health. In A. Baum, T. Revenson, & J. Singer (eds.). *Handbook of Health Psychology,* pp. 365-385. Mahwah, NJ: Lawrence Erlbaum.

Francis, L., & Kelloway, E. K. (2005). *Industrial Relations.* In Handbook of Work Stress, pp. 325-352. Julian Barling, E. Kevin Kelloway & Michael Frone, (eds.).

Fox, S., & Spector, P. E. (1999). A model of work frustration-aggression. *Journal of Organizational Behavior,* 20, 915-931.

Frone, M. R. (2003). Work-family balance. In J. C. Quick & L. E. Tetrick (eds.), *Handbook of Occupational Health Psychology* (pp. 143-162). Washington, DC: American Psychological Association.

Frone, M. R. (2000). Work-family conflict and employee psychiatric disorders: The national comorbidity survey. *Journal of Applied Psychology,* 85, 888-895.

Geurts, S. & Demerouti, E. (2003). *Work/Non-Work Interface: A Review of Theories and Findings.* In The Handbook of Work and Health Psychology (2nd edition), pp. 279-312. Marc J. Schabracq, J. A. M. Winnubst & C. L. Cooper (eds.).

Gilliland, S. W., & Chan, D. (2002). *Justice in Organizations: Theory, Methods and Applications.* In Handbook of Industrial, Work & Organizational Psychology, pp. 143-165. Neil Anderson, Deniz S. Ones,

Handan Kepir Sinangil & Chockalingam Viswesvaran, (eds.). Sage Publications.

Goffman, E. (1971). *Relations in Public.* New York: Harper & Row.

Gordon, R. S., Jr. (1983). An operational classification of disease prevention. *Public Health Reports, 98,* 107-109.

Greenley, P. & Burgess, W. A. (1999). *Philosophy and Management of Engineering Control.* In Handbook of Occupational Safety and Health, Second Edition, pp. 1029-1080. Louis J. DiBerardinis (ed.).

Griggs v. Duke Power Co. - 401 U.S. 424. (1971). Retrieved January 17, 2013 from http:// supreme.justia.com/ cases/ federal/ us/ 401/ 424/ case. html.

Ghorpade, J. V. (1988). *Job Analysis: A Handbook for the Human Resource Director.* Prentice Hall: Englewood Cliffs, NJ.

Gilliland, S. W., & Chan, D. (2002). Justice in Organizations: Theory, Methods and Applications. In: *Handbook of Industrial, Work & Organizational Psychology*, pp. 143-165. Neil Anderson, Deniz S. Ones, Handan Kepir Sinangil & Chockalingam Viswesvaran, (eds.). Sage Publications.

Greenley, P. & Burgess, W. A. (1999). *Philosophy and Management of Engineering Control.* In Handbook of Occupational Safety and Health, Second Edition, pp. 1029-1080. Louis J. DiBerardinis (ed.).

Goldstein, I. L., & Ford, K. (2001). *Training in Organizations: Needs Assessment, Development and Evaluation.* Cengage Learning.

Guion, R. M. (1998). *Assessment, Measurement, and Prediction for Personnel Decisions.* Mahwah, NJ. Lawrence Erlbaum.

Hamborg, K., & Greif, S. (2003). *New Technologies and Stress.* In Handbook of Work and Health Psychology (2nd edition), pp. 209-235. Marc J. Schabracq, J. A. M. Winnubst & C. L. Cooper (eds.).

Hammer, L. B. & Zimmerman, K. L. (2011). Quality of work life. In S. Zedek (ed.), *APA Handbook of Industrial and Organizational Psychology, Volume 3* (pp. 399-431). doi: 101177/1046496408326575

Hampden-Turner, C. (1981). *Maps of the Mind.* Macmillan: New York.

Harris, K., & Kacmar, K. M. (2005). *Organizational Politics.* In Handbook of Work Stress, pp. 353-374. Julian Barling, E. Kevin Kelloway & Michael Frone, (eds.).

Harrison, M. I. (1994). *Diagnosing Organizations: Methods, Models and Processes* (2nd ed.). Sage Publications.

Hunter, J. (2008). *EAP Stress Analysis Questionnaire.* University of Missouri.

Hunter, J. (2010). *Taxonomy of Occupational Stressors, Manifestations, Moderators & Researchers: Abbreviated.* University of Missouri.

Hunter, J. (2013). Work Analysis and the Resolution of Organizational Conflict: Theoretical Method, Measurement and Application. In *Derailed Organizational Stress and Well-Being Interventions: Confessions of Failure and Solutions for Success.* Caroline Biron & Maria Karanika-Murray, (eds.). Nottingham Trent University, UK: Springer Publications. (2015).

Hurrell, J. J., & Lindstrom, K. (1992). Comparison of job demands, control and psychosomatic complaints at different career stages of managers in Finland and the United States. *Scandinavian Journal of Work, Environment & Health,* 18, 11-13.

John, Oliver P. (1999). The Big-Five Trait Taxonomy: History, Measurement, and Theoretical Perspectives. In L. Pervin and O. P. John (eds.), *Handbook of Personality: Theory and Research* (2nd ed.). New York: Guilford.

Jukes. J. (2000). Optimizing the working environment. In D. Clements-Croome (ed.), *Creating the Productive Workplace.* London: E&FN Spon.

Kaufman, H. (1982). *Professionals in Search of Work.* New York: Wiley.

Kahn, R. L., & Byosiere, P. (1992). Stress in organizations. In M. D. Dunnette & L. M. Hough (eds.), *Handbook of Industrial and Organizational Psychology* (Vol. 3, pp. 571-650). Palo Alto, CA: Consulting Psychologists Press.

Kahn, R. L. (1973). Conflict, Ambiguity, and Overload: Three Elements in Job Stress. Occupational Health, No. 3, pp. 2-9. In *Handbook of Human Factors and Ergonomics*, G. Salvendy, Editor. (2006).

Kahn, R. L., Wolfe, D. M., Quinn, R. P., Snoek, J., D., & Rosenthal, R. A. (1964). *Organizational Stress: Studies in Role Conflict and Ambiguity.* New York: Wiley.

Karasek, R. A. (1979). Job demands, job decision latitude, and mental strain: Implications for job redesign. *Administrative Science Quarterly,* 24, 285-307.

Katz, D., & Kahn, R. L. (1978). *The Social Psychology of Organizations* (2nd ed.) New York: Wiley.

Kelloway, E. K., Sivanathan, N., Francis, L., & Barling, J. (2005). *Poor Leadership.* In Handbook of Work Stress, pp. 89-112. Julian Barling, E. Kevin Kelloway & Michael Frone, (eds.).

Kivimaki, M., & Lindstrom, K. (2006). Psychosocial Approach to Occupational Health. In *Handbook of Human Factors and Ergonomics* (3rd ed.). John Wiley.

Klein, M. (1980). *Envy, Gratitude and Other Works.* Hogarth: London.

Kompier, M. (2003). Job Design and Well-Being. In *The Handbook of Work and Health Psychology*, pp. 429-454. Marc J. Schabracq, J. A. M. Winnubst & C. L. Cooper (eds.).

Kulas, J. T., Haynes, B. A., Kalten, S. M., Hopp, P. J., & Duffala, R. L. (2002). Integrating, individual assessment, position requirements, team-based competencies, and organizational vision: Roles for consulting psychologists. In R. L. Lowman, (ed.), *Handbook of Organizational Consulting Psychology*, pp. 450-465. Jossey-Bass.

Krantz, J., & Maltz, M. (1997). A Framework for Consulting to Organizational Role. *Consulting Psychology Journal, Practice and Research*, Volume 49, Number 2, Spring, 1997, an American Psychological Association Publication.

Krantz, J. (1998). Anxiety and the New Order. In E. Klein, F. Gabelnick and P. Herr (eds.). *Leadership in the 21st Century.* Madison, CT: International Universities Press.

Lanza, M. (2006). Violence in nursing. In *Handbook of Workplace Violence*, pp. 147-167. E. Kevin Kelloway, Julian Barling & Joseph Hurrell, Jr. (eds.).

Lazarus, R. S., & Folkman, S. (1984). *Stress, Appraisal, and Coping.* New York: Springer.

Lehto, M. R., & Nah, F. (2006). Decision-making model and decision support. In: *Handbook of Human Factors and Ergonomics.*

Leiter, M. P., & Stright, N. (2009). The social context of work life: Implications for burnout and work engagement. In *International Handbook of Work and Health Psychology* (3rd ed.), pp. 25-47. C. L. Cooper, J. C. Quick and M. J. Schabracq (eds.). Levinson, H. (2004). *Organizational Assessment: A Step–By–Step Guide to Effective Consulting.* American Psychological Association, Washington, DC.

Lewin, K. (1947). Group decision and social change. In I. Newcomb & E, Hartley (eds.). *Readings in Social Psychology.* New York: Holt.

Likert, R. (1932). A Technique for the Measurement of Attitudes. *Archives of Psychology* 140: 1–55.

Maxcy, K., F., Rosenau, J., M., Last, J., M., & Wallace, R. B. (1998). *Public Health & Preventive Medicine, 14th (ed.).* McGraw-Hill.

McCall, Jr., M., W., & Bobko, P. (1992). Research methods in the service of discovery. In M. D. Dunnette, and L. M. Hough, (eds.). *Handbook of Industrial & Organizational Psychology,* Volume 1, pp.381-418. Consulting Psychologists Press.

McCoy, J., & Evans, G. (2005). Physical work environment. In *Handbook of Work Stress,* pp. 219-243. Julian Barling, E. Kevin Kelloway & Michael Frone, (eds.).

McGrath, J. E., & Beehr, T. A. (1990). Time and the stress process: Some temporal issues in the conceptualization and measurement of stress. *Stress Medicine, 6,* 93-104.

McCrae, R. R., & Costa, P. T. (1987). Validation of the five-factor model of personality across instruments and observers. *Journal of Personality & Social Psychology, 56,* 585-595.

Morgan, G. (1997). *Images of Organization,* (2nd ed.). Sage Publications: Thousand Oaks, CA.

Muchinsky, P. M., & Culbertson, C. (2016). *Psychology Applied to Work: An Introduction to Industrial and Organizational Psychology, 11th Edition.* Hypergraphic Press, Summerfield, NC.

Nelson, D. L., & Simmons, B. L. (2003). Health psychology and work stress: A more positive approach. In *Handbook of Occupational Health Psychology*, pp. 97-119. James Campbell Quick & Lois E. Tetrick (eds.).

Paugh III, James J. (1999). Managing worker's compensation. In *Handbook of Occupational Safety and Health, Second Edition*, Louis J. DiBerardinis (ed.).

Peterson, D. R. (1983). Conflict. In H. H. Kelley, E. Berscheid, A. Christensen, J. H. Harvey, T. L. Hutson, G. Levinger, E. McClintock, L. A. Peplau, & D. Peterson, *Close Relationships* (pp. 360-396). New York: Freeman.

Probst, T. M. (2005). Economic stressors. In *Handbook of Work Stress*, pp. 267-297. Julian Barling, E. Kevin Kelloway & Michael Frone, (eds.).

Pruitt, D. G. (1998). Social conflict. In *The Handbook of Social Psychology, Volume 2,* (4th ed). The McGraw Hill Companies, Inc.

Quick, J. C., & Quick, J. D. (1984). *Organizational Stress and Preventive Management.* New York: McGraw Hill.

Regents of University of California v. Bakke. (1978). Retrieved January 17, 2013 from http:// www.pbs.org/ wnet/ supremecourt/ rights/ landmark_ regents.html.

Ricci v. Destefano. (2008). Retrieved January 17, 2013 from http://www. supremecourt.gov/opinions/08pdf/07-1428.pdf.

Robbins, S. P. (2003). *Organizational Behavior,* (10th ed.). Prentice Hall.

Rokeach, M. (1973). *The Nature of Human Values.* New York: Free Press.

Rospenda, K., M., & Richman, J., A. (2005). Harassment and discrimination. In *Handbook of Work Stress*, pp. 148-185. Julian Barling, E. Kevin Kelloway & Michael Frone, (eds.).

Saal, F. E., & Knight, P. A. (1988). *Industrial/Organizational Psychology: Science & Practice.* Brooks/Cole Publishing Company. Pacific Grove, California.

Sanchez, J. I., & Levine, E. L. (2001). The analysis of work in the 20th and 21st centuries. In *Handbook of Industrial, Work and Organizational Psychology, Volume 1, Personnel Psychology*, pp. 71-89. Neil

Anderson, Deniz S. Ones, Handan Kepir Sinangil and Chockalingam Viswesvaran (eds.).

Schabracq, M. J. (2003). Organisational culture, stress and change. In *The Handbook of Work and Health Psychology*, pp. 37-62. Marc J. Schabracq, J. A. M. Winnubst & C. L. Cooper (eds.).

Schat, A., C., & Kelloway, E., K. (2005). Workplace aggression. In *Handbook of Work Stress*, pp. 189-218. Julian Barling, E. Kevin Kelloway & Michael Frone, (eds.).

Schaufeli, W. B., & Buunk, B. P. (2003). Burnout: An overview of 25 years of research and theorizing. In *The Handbook of Work and Health Psychology*, pp. 383-425. Marc J. Schabracq, J. A. M. Winnubst & C. L. Cooper (eds.).

Selye, H. (1950). *The Physiology and Pathology of Exposure to Stress.* Montreal Canada: Medical Publishers, Acta.

Selye, H. (1974). *Stress without Distress.* Philadelphia: J. B. Lippincott Co.

Spielberger, C. D. (1972). Anxiety as an emotional state. In C. D. Spielberger (ed.), *Anxiety: Current Trends in Theory and Research*, Vol. 1. New York: Academic Press.

Spielberger, C. D., & Reheiser, E. C. (1995). *Measuring occupational stress: The job stress survey*. In *Occupational Stress: A Handbook.* R. Crandall, and P. Perrewe', (eds.), pp. 51-69. Taylor and Francis, Publishers.

Terkel, S. (1974). *Working: People Talk About What They Do All Day and How They Fell About What They Do.* New York: Pantheon/Random House.

Thomas, K., W. (1992). Conflict and negotiation processes in organizations. In *Handbook of Industrial & Organizational Psychology, Second Edition, Volume 3*, pp. 651-717. Marvin D. Dunnette and Leaetta M. Hough (eds.) Consulting Psychologists Press.

Thorndike, R. L. (1949). *Personnel Selection: Test and Measurement Techniques.* New York: John Wiley.

Totterdell, P. (2005). Work schedules. In *Handbook of Work Stress*, pp. 35-62. Julian Barling, E. Kevin Kelloway & Michael Frone, (eds.).

Van De Water, T. J., (1997). Psychology's Entrepreneurs and the Marketing of Industrial Psychology. *Journal of Applied Psychology*, 82, 486-499.

Vigoda, E. (2000). Stress-related aftermaths to workplace politics: the relationships among politics, job distress, and aggressive behavior in organizations. *Journal of Organizational Behavior,* 23, 571-591.

Watson v. Fort Worth Bank & Trust – 487 U.S. 977. (1988). Retrieved January 17, 2013 from http:// supreme.justia.com/ cases/ federal/ us/ 487/977/case.html

Whitaker, D., & Lieberman M. A. (1964). *Psychotherapy through the Group Process*. London: Tavistock.

Yukl, G. (1998). *Leadership in Organizations.* (4th ed.). Upper Saddle River, NJ: Prentice Hall.

In: Occupational Stress
Editors: N. Mucci, G. Giorgi et al.
ISBN: 978-1-53615-404-7

Chapter 3

BURNOUT: THE GOOD, THE BAD AND MOVING FORWARD

Shailesh Kumar*[*] *and Rishi Kumar
Waikato Clinical Campus, University of Auckland,
Auckland, New Zealand

ABSTRACT

The term burnout was first introduced in the 70s. Since then scientific publications on this topic have proliferated. Human services professions have been identified as a group vulnerable to developing burnout due to significant degree of interpersonal contact with troubled client population. Burnout has significant impact on the delivery of service, the quality of service, the emotional and physical health of the person experiencing it and their interpersonal/social functioning. There is also some evidence to suggest burnout may have protective effects on the psyche of the person experiencing it. Burnout serves as an emotional brake by slowing down the working and thus scope of further strain on the person. Distancing oneself from demanding work situations may also be protective against emotional drain and depletion of empathy. Key lessons from opinions and research studies on the prevention and management of burnout are reviewed in this

[*] Corresponding Author's E-mail: Shailesh.kumar@waikatodhb.health.nz.

chapter. Active screening of burnout, helping employees develop resilience and positive coping and developing a strong organizational culture of tackling burnout early are methods which can help prevent this global problem from developing further. A combination of intensive individual or group therapy sessions based on cognitive behavioral principles along with booster sessions appears to be most effective in managing burnout once it has developed. Treatment interventions for reducing scores on the three dimensions of burnout have also been identified.

BURNOUT: CONCEPTUAL EVOLUTION

Burnout is now widely accepted as a health consequence of working in situations involving high levels of stress especially with direct human interactions. Freudenberger first introduced the concept of burnout [1]. Since then, various definitions of burnout have emerged. Kuremyr et al. (1994) defined burnout as “an experience of physical, emotional and mental exhaustion caused by long-term involvement in situations that are emotionally demanding” [2]. Lee and Asforth (1990) defined burnout as “a syndrome of emotional exhaustion, depersonalization and feelings [3].” This definition was based on Maslach’s and Jackson’s (1986) work who used “emotional exhaustion” (tiredness, somatic symptoms, decreased emotional resources and a feeling that one has nothing left to give to others) [4], to mean people feeling emotionally over extended and exhausted by their work, “depersonalization” when people develop negative, cynical attitudes and impersonal feelings towards their clients, treat them as objects, and “reduced personal accomplishments” (feeling a loss of incompetence, inefficiency and inadequacy) to mean when people feel their work has low productivity and they are achieving little. The latter definition of burnout has been widely used in scientific literature [4]. Common to all these definitions is the central metaphorical implication that somebody could only burn out if they were “burning” before making engagement. Just like a candle that burns and then runs out of wick, professionals burn with enthusiasm and interest in their job and with exposure to stress and over time they burnout [5].

Why is Burnout Higher among Human Services Workers?

It is no coincidence that burnout has been most extensively studied in what is described as human services professions. Such professions include health care, social work, psychotherapy, legal services, and police work who are required to work, face to face, with needy, demanding and often troubled people [6]. They invariably use themselves as "tools" in their work, at great emotional cost [7] which may leave them feeling emotionally depleted. Having had the advantage of the vocabulary to articulate emotions, and the ability to express how their relationships with people affected them subjectively would have made it easier to study burnout in this group [6]. It is also worth acknowledging that those who suffer from burnout show overly high commitment to, and a personal investment in, their work [3] rendering them particularly vulnerable to stress and feelings of exhaustion at work [8] [9]. It is, therefore, understandable that the topic of burnout among human services professions has received much and well-deserved attention. Up to 6000 publications were published over a 35-year period since its inception in the scientific literature, majority of which had been from the human services profession although reports of burnout among managers, entrepreneurs, and white- and blue collar workers have also emerged [6].

There also seems to be a steady growth in the prevalence of burnout, so much so that in certain professions it is reported to have reached "epidemic proportions [6] [10]. Various societal changes may have contributed to this steady growth. A progressive weakening in the professional authority of certain groups, including doctors, nurses, teachers, social workers and police officers with diminution of the traditional prestige of these professionals may have displaced the inherent joy such professions derived from serving others [6]. Among this group, doctors have to work in an increasingly litigious and unforgiving environment [11]. Bureaucratic requirements imposed upon them are increasing and medical knowledge is advancing rapidly with which doctors have to constantly keep in touch [12]. Globally doctors are practicing in an environment of limited resources, micro-management, sensationalist media reports of medical errors and unethical physician conduct, or challenges to their authority and skills by patients and other healthcare providers' [13]. Service delivery is changing from an office-based model to a population-based health model. Doctors have to fulfil administrative duties, such as dealing effectively with workforce issues, often in addition to their significant clinical commitments [12]. Fulfilling unaccustomed tasks creates stressors and it would appear that constantly changing work environment predisposes doctors to experiencing high levels of stress [14]. Job efforts have increased globally and job rewards in the form of recognition and gratitude decreased in last four decades, thus creating the perfect Petri dish environment for breeding burnout [6]. It is in this context that the topic of burnout has become more important than ever in the health care setting.

BURNOUT: THE BAD ASPECTS

Burnout develops in an individual but affects the entire system. Consequences of burnout have been categorized in professional (poor decision making leading to medical errors, hostile attitude toward pati8ents, adverse patient events, reduced commitment to productivity and providing safe clinical care, strained collegial relationships and disengagement) and personal (depression, anxiety, sleep disturbance, fatigue, strained partner relationships, alcohol and drug abuse, divorce, premature retirement and suicide) groups [15].

Negative patient and workplace centered consequences of burnout are well-documented in the literature. At a systems level it is associated with suboptimal patient care, poorer collegial relationship [16] [17] absenteeism, productivity problems, job dissatisfaction, lower quality of care, adverse work environment, lowered retention of skilled staff and patient dissatisfaction [18] [19] [20] [21].

Noting such associations between burnout and adverse client outcomes we need to understand better whether specific dimensions of burnout affect specific aspects of healthcare delivery. There is some evidence to suggest the three dimensions of burnout may impact different aspects of burnout. Emotional Exhaustion is considered to be the most important predictor of absenteeism, Depersonalization predicts retention and Personal Accomplishment predicts client satisfaction [22]. Such relationships need to be investigated further and may help service planners develop strategies specific to the issues the organization may be facing i.e., absenteeism, poor retention or low levels of satisfaction among clients. Attention is being given to positive organizational behavior of employees and wellness rather than focusing on the negative aspects of burnout. Such shift in focus may help us answer some questions that need our attention e.g., what does it mean to be well- fewer episodes of burnout or shorter recovery time or building resilience [23]?

The impact of demotivation and exhaustion at work spans beyond patient care. It affects family life, inter-personal work relationships of the person experiencing it. At an individual level burnout is reported to increase the risk of depression and anxiety [16] [17]. A direct consequence of burnout could be on professional idealism and coping mechanisms. Golliher et al. (1995) hypothesized that as clinical experience increases, idealism and stress decrease, and the use of coping mechanisms increases [24]. They designed a study to clarify the nature of the hypothesized relationship between the three variables across three levels of experience: low, medium and high experience levels. First year psychiatric residents and first year clinical psychology doctoral students (low experience level), third year residents and clinical psychology interns (medium experience level) and clinical psychologists and psychiatrists (high experience level) were surveyed to determine their attitudes towards the mental health profession. Their answers were analyzed through analysis of variance by level of experience and discipline (clinical psychology or psychiatry) to determine significant differences in idealism, burnout levels, and coping mechanisms. As predicted, the low experience level group was more stressed, more idealistic and used fewer coping techniques than the high experience level group. The results for the medium experience group were equivocal. Significant differences between clinical psychology and psychiatry included higher stress for psychiatrists and differences in the areas in which clinical psychologists and psychiatrists were idealistic. Significant interactions between level of experience and discipline suggested a different progression through the three levels of experience for clinical psychology than for psychiatry [24].

It is not surprising, therefore, to see intervention or prevention studies of burnout have incorporated strategies for enhancing coping, stress management and resilience building. Unfortunately, the evidence base for the effectiveness of stress management training interventions on job stress and to prevent burnout among healthcare workers beyond the intervention is insufficient [25]. A recent systematic review and meta-analysis has however found *evidence that both individual focused and structural or organizational strategies can result in clinically meaningful reductions in burnout among physicians* [10]. Whether these findings may extend to other professional groups needs to be seen.

In developing intervention strategies, the issue of stigma and barriers to help seeing does need to be considered. Despite such wide-ranging implications and onset being imbedded in the work context, burnout is perceived as an individual's problem so the person experiencing it should be "fixed" [26]. The person experiencing burnout is often afraid of being seen as weak and such stigma often acts as a barrier against help seeking. In the context of physicians, a group predisposed to experiencing burnout [27], the addition of "internal and external barriers" to treatment contributes to deeply worrying trend of twice the rate of suicides than the general population, increased risk of alcohol and drug abuse, divorce and physician attrition [28]. The direct effects of burnout may be equally bad as the more indirect effect associated with stigma.

Being exposed to greater and chronic stress does have its consequences and burnout may not be the only outcome. Doctors as a group have higher prevalence of depression and burnout than the general population and indeed many other professional groups. One interesting finding about depression in doctors is that many of the risk factors associated with depression in the general population are not applicable to them. Such risk factors include low female gender, socio-economic status, low education, and unemployment. A random cross-sectional French study of 1,200 health care professionals reported the prevalence of burnout to be 15.7% among women, and 22% among men [29]. A similar study from rural British Columbia reported that 80% of physicians suffered from moderate-to-severe emotional exhaustion, 61% suffered from moderate-to-severe depersonalization, and 44% had moderate-to-low feelings of personal accomplishment [19]. Most prominent are the imbalance between demands and resources at work, and the conflict between values (i.e., between personal values and those of the organization, and between the officially stated organizational values and the values in action [6].

It is also important to highlight while burnout may be associated with depression but the relationship between the two is complex. A significant overlap exists between the two constructs because the symptoms of depression resemble those of burnout, the two are not necessarily the same. Burnout occurs in the context of anger, it is situation specific- affects work & often spares personal lives. Depression is the opposite as it is often due to internal or biochemical factors, affects wide range of situations including family lives and work [30]. The distinction between burnout and depression became clearer from a Canadian study that reported a statistically significant correlation between depression and emotional exhaustion ($P < .0001$), a weaker correlation between depression and depersonalization and no correlation between depression and sense of personal accomplishment [19]. Similarly, stress also needs to be distinguished from burnout – burnout is the consequence of being stressed at work, having no way out, over a protracted period of time – a phenomenon described by Farber (1983) as "the final step in a progression of unsuccessful attempts to cape with a variety of negative stress conditions" [9]. Stress is the first step in the process which by becoming chronic and enduring causes burnout.

But is Burnout All Bad?

Burnout has multiple negative health, social and occupational implications. It, also, has some positive implications which are often not acknowledged. Burnout symptoms may appear in order to protect human psyche against further damage in the face of ongoing stress. Like physical pain stops a person from further exposure to trauma, burnout does the same with emotional trauma and depletion. Emotional exhaustion acts as a "brake" to stop burnt out individuals who may not know how or when to slow down. Freudenberger (1983) described depersonalization as a means of protection against further emotional drown or a homeostatic mechanism in an emotionally exhausted worker [1]. Negative changes in attitude (reduced work goals, loss of idealism, heightened self-interest, increasing detachment from clients have been described [30] as a form of coping. Huggard (2003) has suggested that even though disengagement and distancing is often employed as a coping mechanism by people facing burnout, it leads to a reduction in empathy [31]. At least for some, detachment from emotional engagement with patients can be beneficial offering benefits such as protection against burnout, better concentration, sustained impartiality and objectivity and better time management [32].

The relationship between empathy, an effective therapeutic tool doctors routinely use, and burnout is worth investigating. Doctors are said to express their empathy at two levels -deep and surface [33]. At a deeper level, doctors generate consistent emotional and cognitive reactions before and during empathic interactions with the patient, similar to the method used by some stage and screen actors. At a surface level of expressing empathy doctors demonstrate empathic behaviors toward the patient without consistent emotional and cognitive reactions. Although deep acting is preferred, doctors rely on surface acting when immediate emotional and cognitive understanding of patients is impossible. By consciously choosing between deep and surface acting to empathize with their patients doctors may become more effective in their roles as healers [33]. In certain situations outright detachment rather than controlled empathy may be essential to protect doctors from experiencing compassion fatigue [34]. A degree of detachment and finding a balance between empathy and detachment can be effective coping mechanism in clinical practice [35] and may indeed prevent burnout [31] [32]. Burnout, in its early stages, fosters detachment and thus prevents deterioration in forging empathic relationship between doctors and patients. In advanced stages of burnout, as depersonalization, cynicism and treating people as objects develop empathy is lost [18] making professionals either less effective or even harmful in their work.

Research Agenda for the Future: Learnings from the Good and the Bad

Increasingly burnout is being seen as a gradual process in which "an erosion of engagement" occurs [6]. The process of an engaged clinician slowly becoming unengaged has always been recognized as being at the core of the concept of burnout but this is being given more importance with the recent advent of Positive Psychology movement, whose purpose "*is to begin to catalyze a change in the focus of psychology from pre-occupation only with repairing the worst things in life to also building positive qualities"* [36]. Shifting focus to the process of engagement rather than emotional exhaustion is helpful in developing strategies for developing strengths that can prevent burnout. Accepting burnout as an erosion of engagement may also help us shift from seeing burnout as an "individual issue" that needs to be fixed, to that of a systems issue which can be prevented by enhancing worker engagement. The future may see burnout being accepted as the negative pole of a continuum of employee well-being and work engagement constituting the opposite positive pole of burnout.

The complex relationship between burnout and engagement can be understood from the Job Demands Resources model [37]. Irrespective of the type of job, its characteristics fall into two groups: Job resources and Job Demands [37] [38] Physical, psychological, social or organizational aspects of a job that are able to reduce costs and demands of the job, help achieve work goals and enhance personal growth and learning, all constitute job resources. Job demands on the other hand incorporate those aspects of the job that require sustained physical and psychological efforts from the worker. In other words, job resources refer to what the worker gets out of the job or how they reduce the job demands. The greater the job resources, the greater the work engagement, which in turn predicted organizational commitment whereas job demands predicted burnout and depression [39]. These authors proposed "*by integrating both human thriving and ill-health in the same model, the JD-R model may help bridge the gap between negative and positive psychology.* A central tenet of this model is the expectation that a more engaged worker is less likely to experience burnout with the likely corollary that by enhancing work engagement organizations can prevent burnout. Some authors have conceptualized engagement as a direct antithesis of burnout. Thus, the three dimensions of burnout become polar opposites to three dimensions of engagement: vigor is the opposite of emotional exhaustion, dedication that of cynicism [40] [41].

While such bipolar representations of burnout and engagement may appear logical, research on *affect* also tells us that the relationship between opposite poles of an *emotion* such as happiness and sadness are not necessarily linear. Low scores on sadness scale do not correlate with high scores on happiness i.e., less happy does not necessarily translate in to a state of happiness. Modifications in a measurement scale and research method will need to be more sophisticated before a negative construct like burnout can be accepted as the opposite pole of engagement and starts drawing conclusions that a more engaged employee is a less burnt out one [42] [43].

In addition to the conceptual issues with job engagement there may be the need to introduce additional parameters to understand the relationship between engagement and burnout. A Norwegian study of 439 employees from different occupational backgrounds with an exceptionally long follow up of 11 years that examined reciprocal and reversed causality between work characteristics and mental health parameters found job demands alone were not significantly associated with poor mental health. Low job control with high job demand on the other hand had negative effect on mental health suggesting having control over one's job has "buffering effect" on mental health [43]. As well as the two dimensions of job demands, and job resources job control may be a significant determinant of work engagement, there may be similar other determinants who need investigations.

Past research has been immensely helpful in raising awareness of burnout as a concept. Measurement tools for burnout have become sophisticated and at least three are in wide use: Maslach Burnout Inventory

[18], Burnout Measure [45] by and Copenhagen Burnout Inventory [46]. We need to do better in screening for burnout in order to facilitate early detention and offer early intervention to those who are experiencing it. Screening may help raise awareness of burnout and enable open discussions on it. Such organizational culture may break some of the resistance and stigma issues.

When it comes to specific intervention strategies, once burnout has developed there is evidence to suggest long-term intervention may have more prolonged effects for reducing burnout than short term intervention and yield permanent behavioral changes, especially for coping skills [47]. Professional experiencing more severe burnout are likely to require a longer period of supervision, monitoring, support and feedback. Individuals at risk of developing burnout will benefit from a multi-pronged approach that addresses factors, within the individual and their environment [48]. The key, when it comes to focus on employee engagement and enhancing control over one's job is to make culture changes within organizations.

Finally, positive psychology enthusiasts may offer the concept as panacea for all human suffering. It is worth considering one size does not fit all. Looking for a positive emotional state may take us to a point of having to choose one of two schools of thought: the hedonic and the eudemonic [49]. The former is invested in the goal of maximizing happiness, reducing pain and enhancing subjective wellbeing whereas the eudemonic school focusses on contentment, being satisfied and on a more stable sense of being well. Both schools of thoughts are effective and have stood the test of time. Rather than favoring one over other is preferable to pursue the school that suits one's personality and individual outlook to life.

CONCLUSION

Individuals working in the human services professions, often dealing with close person to person contact, which requires an empathetic communication, are at a higher risk of burnout than the general population. Depersonalization, disengagement and emotional exhaustion are all consequences of this chronic exposure to stress, which can affect quality of care, interpersonal relationships and future longevity. While these are negative aspects of burnout, the 'emotional brake' caused can act as a preventative measure towards future burnout. Promoting work engagement and satisfaction amongst health professionals may prevent burnout. This can be facilitated through models that incorporate job demands resources and control as well as or other organizational measures, which focus on positive psychology school of thought. It remains vital that we treat each situation individually that is causing burnout, assess the needs of the individuals within a particular environment and develop preventative and/or management plans accordingly.

REFERENCES

[1] Freudenberger, H. Staff Burn-Out. *Journal of Social Issues.*, 1974 January, 30(1), 159-165.

[2] Kuremyr, D; Kihlgren, M; Norberg, A; Aström, S; Karlsson, I. Emotional experiences, empathy and burnout among staff caring for demented patients at a collective living unit and a nursing home. *J Adv Nurs.*, 1994 April, 19(4), 670-679.

[3] Lee, R; Ashforth, B. A further examination of managerial burnout: Toward an integrated model. *Journal of Organizational Behavior.*, 1993 January, 14(1), 3-20.

[4] Maslach, C; Jackson, SE. *Maslach Burnout Inventory Manual.* 2nd ed. Palo Alto: Consulting Psychologists Press, 1986.

[5] Korunka, C; Temet, S; Zdrehus, C; Borza, A. Burnout: definition, recognition and prevention approaches: *BOIT - Burnout Intervention Training for Managers and Team Leaders*, 2010.

[6] Schaufeli, W; Leiter, M; Maslach, C. Burnout: 35 years of research and practice. *Career Development International.*, 2008 November, 14(3), 204-220.

[7] Carson, J; Maal, S; Roche, S; Fagin, L; De Villiers, N; O'Malley, P; et al. Burnout in mental health nurses: much ado about nothing? *Stress Medicine.*, 1999 April, 15(2), 127–134.

[8] Salmela-Aro, K; Nataanen, P; Nurmi, JE. The role of work-related personal projects during two burnout interventions: a longitudinal study. *Work & Stress.*, 2004, 18(3), 208- 230.

[9] Farber, B. Introduction: A critical perspective on burnout. In Farber B, editor. *Stress and Burnout: The Human Service Professions*. New York: Perganon, 1983.

[10] West, CLND; Erwin, P; Shanafelt, T. Interventions to prevent and reduce physician burnout: a systematic review and meta-analysis. *Lancet.*, 2016 November, 388(10057), 2272-2281.

[11] Myers, M. Physician impairment: is it relevant to academic psychiatry?. *Academic Psychiatry.*, 2008 January, 32(1), 33-43.

[12] Hughes, D; Burke, D; Hickie, I; Wilson, A; Tobin, M. Advanced training in adult psychiatry. *Australasian Psychiatry.*, 2002 March, 10(1), 6-11.

[13] World Medical Association (WMA) *Medical Ethics Manual*. [Online], 2009 [cited 20111 March 24. Available from: (http://www.wma.net/en/30publications/30ethicsmanual/pdf/chap_6_en.pdf).

[14] Kumar, S. Burnout and psychiatrists: What do we know and where to from here? *Epidemiology and Psychiatric Sciences.*, 2011 December, 20(4), 295-301.

[15] Balch, CM; Freischlag, JA; Shanafelt, TD. Stress and burnout amongst surgeons: understanding and managing the syndrome and avoiding the adverse consequences. *Archives of Surgery.*, 2009 April, 144(4), 371-6.

[16] Privitera, M; Rosenstein, A; Plessow, F; LoCastro, T. Physician Burnout and Occupational Stress: An inconvenient truth with unintended consequences. *Journal of Hospital Administration.*, 2014 December, 4(1), 1-9.

[17] Cocker, F; Joss, N. Compassion Fatigue among Healthcare, Emergency and Community Service Workers: A Systematic Review. *Int J Environ Res Public Health.*, 2016 June, 13(6), 1-18.

[18] Maslach, C; Jackson, S; Leiter, M. Maslach *Burnout Inventory Manual.* 3rd ed. Palo Alto: Consulting Psychologist Press, 1996.

[19] Thommasen, H; Lavanchy, M; Connelly, I; Berkowitz, JGS. Mental health, job satisfaction, and intention to relocate. Opinions of physicians in rural British Columbia. *Canadian Family Physician.*, 2001 April, 47, 737-744.

[20] Hannigan, B; Edwards, D; Coyle, D; Fothergill, A; Burnard, P. Burnout in community mental health nurses: findings from the all-Wales stress study. *Journal of Psychiatric & Mental Health Nursing.*, 2000 April, 7(2), 127-134.

[21] Vaccaro, J; Clark, G. A profile of community mental health center psychiatrists: results of a national survey. *Community Mental Health Journal.*, 1987, 23, 282-289.

[22] Schaufeli, W; Enzmann, D. *The Burnout Companion to Study and Practice: A Critical Analysis.* London, Taylor and Francis, 1998.

[23] Eckleberry-Hunt, J; Van Dyke, A; Lick, Tucciarone D; Tucciarone, J. Changing the Conversation From Burnout to Wellness: Physician Well-being in Residency Training Programs. *Journal of Graduate Medical Education.*, 2009 December, 1(2), 225-30.

[24] Golliher, E. *The relationship of job satisfaction to level of experience of clinical psychologists and psychiatrists.* Dissertation Virginia Consortium For Professional Psychology, Old Dominion University, 1995.

[25] van Wyk, B; Wyk, PV. Preventive staff-support interventions for health workers. *Cochrane Database of Systematic Reviews*, 2010 Mar, 17(3), 1-34.

[26] Maslach, C. Finding solutions to the problem of burnout. *Consulting Psychology Journal: Practice and Research.*, 2017, 2, 143-152.

[27] Ey, S; Moffit, M; Kinzie, JM; Brunett, PH. Feasibility of a Comprehensive Wellness and Suicide Prevention Program: A Decade of Caring for Physicians in Training and Practice. *J Grad Med Educ.*, 2016 December, 8(5), 747–753.

[28] Lacy, B; Chan, J. Physician Burnout: The Hidden Health Care Crisis. *J Grad Med Educ.*, 2016 March, 16(3), 747–753.

[29] Martin, F; Poyen, D; Bouderlique, E; Gouvernet, J; Rivet, B; Disdier, P; et al. Depression and Burnout in Hospital Health Care Professionals.

International Journal of Occupational and Environmental Health., 1997 July, 3(3), 204-209.

[30] Benbow, S; Jolley, D. Old age psychiatrists: what do they find stressful? *International Journal of Geriatric Psychiatry.*, 1997 September, 12(9), 879-882.

[31] Huggard, P. Secondary traumatic stress: Doctors at risk. *New Ethicals Journal.*, 2003, 6(9), 9-14.

[32] Halpern, J. *From Detached Concern to Empathy: Humanizing Medical Practice.* Oxford: Oxford University Press, 2001.

[33] Larson, EB; Yao, X. Clinical empathy as emotional labor in the patient-physician relationship. *JAMA.*, 2005 March, 293(9), 1100-6.

[34] Kumar, S. Psychiatrists in Distress: When Work Becomes A Problem. In Figley C, Huggard P, Rees C, editors. *First Do No Self Harm: Understanding and Promoting Physician Stress Resilience*. Oxford: Oxford University Press, 2013.

[35] Austen, L. Increasing emotional support for healthcare workers can rebalance clinical detachment and empathy. *Br J Gen Pract.*, 2016 July, 66(648), 376-7.

[36] Seligman, M; Csikszentmihalyi, M. Positive psychology: An introduction. *American Psychologist.*, 2001 January, 56(1), 5-14.

[37] Schaufeli, W; Bakker, A. Job demands, job resources, and their relationship with burnout and engagement: a multi-sample study. *Journal of Organizational Behaviour.*, 2004 March, 25(3), 293-315.

[38] Demerouti, E; Bakker, A; Nachreiner, F; Schaufeli, W. The job demands-resources model of burnout. *Journal of Applied Psychology.*, 2001 July, 86(3), 499-512.

[39] Hakanen, J; Schaufeli, W; Ahola, K. The Job Demands-Resources model: A three-year cross-lagged study of burnout, depression, commitment and work engagement. *Work & Stress.*, 2008 July, 22(3), 224-241.

[40] Maslach, C; Leiter, MP. *The Truth about Burnout: How Organizations Cause Personal Stress and What to do about It.* San Francisco: Jossey-Bass, 1997.

[41] Schaufeli, W; Salanova, M; González-Romá, V; Bakker, A. The Measurement of Engagement and Burnout: A Two Sample Confirmatory Factor Analytic Approach. *Journal of Happiness Studies.*, 2002 March, 3(1), 71-92.

[42] Schaufeli, W; Salanova, M. Efficacy or inefficacy, that's the question: Burnout and work engagement, and their relationships with efficacy beliefs. *Anxiety, Stress, and Coping.*, 2007 June, 20(2), 177-196.

[43] González-Romá, V; Schaufeli, W; Bakker, A; Lloreta, S. Burnout and work engagement: Independent factors or opposite poles? *Journal of Vocational Behavior.*, 2006 February, 68(1), 165-174.

[44] Dalgard, O; Sørensen, T; Sandanger, I; Nygård, JF; Svensson, E; Reas, DL. Job demands, job control, and mental health in an 11-year follow-up study: Normal and reversed relationships. *Work & Stress.*, 2009 October, 23(3), 284-296.

[45] Pines, A; Aronson, E. *Career Burnout: Causes and Cures.* New York: Free Press, 1988.

[46] Kristensen, T; Borritz, M; Villadsen, E; Christensen, K. The Copenhagen Burnout Inventory: A new tool for the assessment of burnout. *Work & Stress.*, 2005, 19(3), 192-207.

[47] Rowe, MM. Four-year Longitudinal Study of Behavioral Changes in Coping with Stress. *American Journal of Health Behavior.*, 2006, 30, 602-612.

[48] McLeod, H; Densley, L; Chapman, K. The effects of training in behaviour modification strategies on stress, burnout, and therapeutic attitudes in frontline inpatient mental health nurses. *The Australian Journal of Rehabilitation Counselling.*, 2006, 12(1), 1-10.

[49] Schwarz, N; Strack, F. Reports of Subjective Well-Being: Judgmental Processes and Their Methodological Implications. In Kahneman D, Diener E, Schwarz N, editors. *Well-Being: The Foundations of Hedonic Psychology*. Russell-Sage, 1999, p. 61-84.

In: Occupational Stress
Editors: N. Mucci, G. Giorgi et al.
ISBN: 978-1-53615-404-7

Chapter 4

Occupational Stress Related: Adrenal Fatigue, Hormonal Imbalance and Prevention through Bio-Identical Hormones Approach

Antara Banerjee[1,*], PhD, Yashna Chabria[1], MSc, Francesco Marotta[2,†], MD, PhD, Annabella Campiotti[3], MD, Matteo Mantovani[4], Pharm D and Surajit Pathak[1], PhD

[1]Faculty of Allied Health Sciences, Chettinad Academy of Research and Education, Kelambakkam, India

[2]ReGenera ReGenera R&D International for Aging Intervention, Milano-Beijing, Italy and VCC Preventive Medical Promotion Foundation, Beijing, China

[3]San Babila Clinic, Vitality Therapeutics, Milano, Italy

[4]San Carlo Phamacy and Lab, Ferrara, Italy

[*] Corresponding Author's E-mail: antara.banerjee27@gmail.com.

[†] Corresponding Author's E-mail: fmarchimede@libero.it.

ABSTRACT

This chapter focuses on adrenal fatigue and hormonal imbalance induced by work related stress. Occupational stress can be described as work associated stress, which brings about drastic variations in the physical, emotional and mental responses of an individual when exposed to excessive work and pressures that challenges their abilities. During a stressful event, the hypothalamus sends signals to the adrenal glands to dispense, epinephrine and nor epinephrine into the bloodstream, in order to exert the fight or flight response effectively. With further increase in time, the adrenal glands begin to release excessive cortisol into the circulation which in turn escalates the blood glucose levels and eventually leads to adrenal fatigue or adrenal exhaustion. Stress has been found to be a critical factor in several health conditions ranging from cardiovascular damage to digestive impairment as well as immune suppression. Elevated production of stress hormones (adrenaline and cortisol) has been found to have a predominant contribution in several medical complications. Adrenal fatigue indicates a substantial decline in the optimal cortisol levels, due to sub optimal functioning of the adrenal glands under stress. In this chapter, we discussed about the stress induced adrenal fatigue and hormonal imbalance, and the use of bio-identical hormones to prevent and replenish the activity of the adrenal glands. This overview of stress induced adrenal fatigue and hormonal imbalance and its associated treatment using bio-identical hormone therapy, when properly formulated, tested as for stability and optimal sublingual absorption, will give us a better knowledge about the dysfunction and its concomitant therapeutic and preventive measures.

Keywords: occupational stress, adrenal fatigue, cortisol, bio-identical hormones

1. INTRODUCTION

Occupational stress also well known as work associated stress can be circumscribed as the physical, mental and emotional responses of workers towards their excessive work demands and pressures which challenge their abilities and thereby lead to several health complications [1]. Work place health and stress associated dysfunction have become a great topic of concern over the last decade. Manifold factors have been recognized to play a prominent role in work place stress, these mainly include, negative workload, isolation, difficult relationships with administrators and/ or co-workers, types of hours worked, role of conflict, toxic work environment, role ambiguity, career development barriers, managerial bullying [2]. There are different types of stress these mainly include acute stress, post-Traumatic stress and chronic stress. Acute stress can be defined as the sudden onset of anxiety or stress response in the presence of a stressor, this mainly occurs during a conflict or an argument at workplace. In acute stress, a person's arousal state escalates distinctly and begins to descent. When the occurrences at the work front are life threatening such as accidents, disasters, robberies then the substantial levels of stress are maintained commonly known as post-traumatic stress. Depression and anxiety are the main health conditions associated with post-traumatic stress. The accumulation of manifold stressful events over a long period of time leads to chronic stress. Chronic stress contrary to acute stress is enduring and presents with multitudinal physical and psychological complications such as hypertension, heart dysfunction, depression, adrenal fatigue, anxiety disorder and cognitive impairment. Such unresolved stressful conditions maintains the body in a state of activation for a long time leading to fatigue and affects the body's defense mechanism profoundly [3]. Stressor is the main cause of stress; it can be anything that elicits a stressful reaction or response. Stress has been recognized as an essential factor involved in several medical conditions including cardiovascular damage, neurological disorders, immune deficiencies, hormonal imbalance and digestive impairment. Workers exposed to chronic work stress have mainly been found to suffer from escalated cholesterol levels; erratic blood pressure changes, diabetes, ulcers, substance abuse and clinical depression. The impact of these medical conditions has been found to have adverse effects on the organizations such as, low morale, antipathy at workplace, enmity, reduced productivity and enhanced absenteeism [2]. In a stressful situation, the 'fight or flight' mechanism is a normal body response in order to confront the impending danger effectively. However prolonged periods of stress response also known as chronic stress can lead to excessive deterioration of both physical and mental health [4].

2. Stress Associated Complications

Long term exposure to stressors leads to several health complications due to excessive stimulation of the body to maintain the stress response. The most common mental disorders and physical disorders are listed in the figure below (Figure 1).

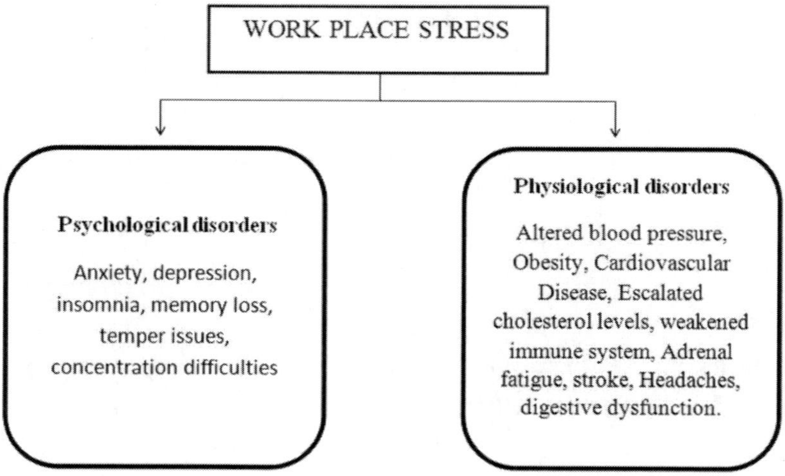

Figure 1. Disorders due to workplace stress.

2.1. Adrenal Fatigue

Chronic stress leads to consistent stimulation of the adrenal glands to release the stress hormone cortisol which is critical to elicit the fight or flight response. However, excessive stimulation of the adrenals leads to the exhaustion of the adrenals which in turn abates the secretions of the steroid hormones leading to a condition known as hypoadrenia (hypo-'less' and adrenia- 'adrenal functioning'). The most common form of hypoadrenia is known as adrenal fatigue or non-Addison's hypoadrenia [5]. James L. Wilson initially put forward the term adrenal fatigue. It is commonly caused by some form of stress. Stress can either be physical, emotional, psychological, environmental, infectious, or an aggregate of these. Melby and Spink in 1958 [6] were the first to analyze the response of the adrenal glands to stress. The cortisol production in the body is produced in a diurnal pattern where in its levels are escalated in the morning and at night with a minimal hike in the afternoon. Impaired adrenal leads to the disruption of this cycle either due to increased cortisol secretion during the stressful event or during the abated levels when the glands are exhausted [7]. Depleted adrenal function profoundly alters metabolism, cardiovascular activity, electrolyte balance as well as reproductive functions. Adrenal fatigue is predominantly associated with hypoglycemia, allergic reactions and diminished immune responses. Adrenal fatigue was previously not considered as a medical condition by most of the medical practitioners and was referred as a common dysfunction sickness as the adrenal glands were normal but with low production of cortisol into the bloodstream. Adrenal fatigue is commonly mistook as Addison's disease which is an auto-immune disorder also referred to as primary adrenal insufficiency leading to diminished steroid hormone production [8]. The preeminent factors contributing to the onset of adrenal fatigue include, unhealthy diet, Consumption of food stimulants such as certain foods and beverages when exhausted, excessive exertion, depleted power, lack of relaxation and rejuvenating activities, etc. The common signs and symptoms of adrenal fatigue include chronic fatigue, reduced memory, difficulty in losing weight, exorbitant craving for salt and sugar, insomnia, decreased productivity, hypoglycemia, fibromyalgia, chronic fatigue syndrome, excessive allergic reactions, depression, severe anxiety and difficulty in performing day-to-day activities [9].

2.2. Hormonal Imbalance

The adrenal glands are known to secrete minimal yet precise quantities of steroid hormones. However, several factors including physical, emotional and physiological stress influence the functioning of the adrenal glands. During a stressful event the adrenal glands rapidly secrete exorbitant quantities of norepinephrine and epinephrine into the blood stream to effectuate the fight or flight response. Prolonged secretions of the adrenal glands due to chronic stress results in intricate interactions between the nervous and the endocrine systems which in turn results in the release of cortisol in substantial amounts into the circulation. Stress results in excessive reaction of the sympathetic nervous system that escalates the secretion of stress hormones such as cortisol and epinephrine [4]. Stressors excite the hippocampus, which in turn stimulates the hypothalamus leading to the activation of the hypothalamic-pituitary-adrenal axis [10]. The hypothalamic-pituitary-adrenal axis plays a significant role in the body's ability to deal with several stressors such as hypertension, infections,

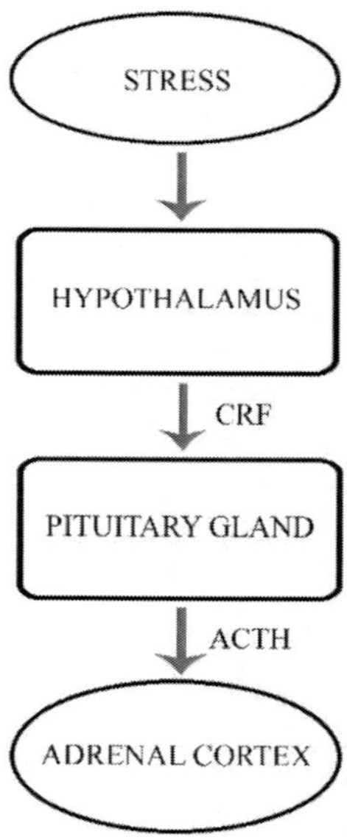

Figure 2. Effect of stress on HPA axis.

surgery, etc. [11]. The hypothalamus is the main centre that releases corticotrophin releasing factor (CRF) which in turn signals the pituitary gland to dispense adrenocorticotropic hormone (ACTH) which stimulates the adrenal glands to produce elevated levels of cortisol. Upon provocation of this pathway, the body initiates an alarm response. Sustained alarm response, results in impaired and desensitized hippocampus receptors which alter the negative feedback mechanism evoking a feed-forward overproduction of cortisol. Escalated cortisol levels have adverse effects on growth hormone, reproductive hormones and thyroid hormone levels [10]. Eventually the exhausted adrenals do not produce the essential precise amounts of cortisol leading to chronic fatigue several other health complications (Figure 2).

3. Diagnosis of Adrenal Fatigue

Hypoadrenia is generally associated with hypotension. Abated blood pressure levels indicate reduced function of the adrenals. Postural blood pressure levels have also been found to be predominantly decline indicating their role in the determining the function of the adrenal glands. The most common and effective diagnostic measure for determining adrenal fatigue is salivary hormone testing. The hormone levels of the body are measured by testing the saliva of the patient instead of blood or urine. This test is more suitable as the hormone levels in the saliva are indicative of the quantity of the hormone present inside the cells rather than that circulating outside the cells in the blood stream. Extremely low functioning of the adrenals is depicted as the Addison's syndrome and excessive output from the adrenals is indicative of Cushing's syndrome [8].

4. Therapeutic Regimens

The most predominantly recommended therapies for adrenal fatigue include, appropriate nutrition, physical interventions that include yoga and simple exercises to restore the adrenal function, sufficient rest, prescriptive intake of adaptogenic herbs, as well as stress management strategies such as meditation and psychological counseling [12].

4.1. Dietary Interventions

Routine dietary and lifestyle practices may have a profound effect on the adrenal health, therefore healthy alterations can aid in reduced adrenal fatigue. Hypoglycemia promotes release of cortisol and therefore skipping meals or excessive consumption of carbohydrates takes a toll on adrenal health. Several chemical stressors such as drugs as well as caffeine should be avoided as they induce the release of cortisol for prolonged time periods. The response of adrenal glands to stress results in escalated metabolism rates leading to severe decline in the nutrients in essential for the body. Insufficient intake of proteins, fats and carbohydrates and irregular meals worsen the condition of the adrenals. The dietary intake of about 30-40% of whole grains, 10-15% of beans, seeds and nuts, 5-10% of fruits, 30-40% of vegetables and 10-20% of animal foods predominantly dairy products have been found the most efficient dietary supplementation to combat adrenal fatigue [8]. Supplementing the regular diet with soluble and fermented fibers along with phytonutrients enhance the insulin sensitivity. Adequate levels of vitamins and minerals also play a critical role in promoting adrenal function and preventing HPA axis dysfunction effectively [13]. Therefore a balanced diet along with abstinence from caffeine, soft drinks, alcohol and other CNS stimulants is essential to prevent adrenal exhaustion [10].

4.2. Exercises

Exercise being a common stressor itself has been known to restore the cortisol levels in the body. It is an ancient and eminent practice known to ameliorate physical and mental health. Studies carried out on the athletes indicated elevated levels of cortisol and speedy recovery when compared to the individuals not exposed to any physical activity. Reduced inflammatory state is observed I the body due to immune suppression brought about by the exercise induced cortisol escalation [10]. Yoga has been observed to have a profound ablative effect on the HPA/SNS axis response to stressors [14]. Along with decreased levels of fatigue several other beneficial measures

recover. However, equine-derived hormone therapy was found to give rise to cancers in menopausal women due to their structure not being recognized by the human body. They can also lead to severe cardiovascular damage and alterations in the lipid profile. This in turn leads to reduced metabolism and escalated toxic and carcinogenic effects of the synthetic hormone. Several limitations of the conventional hormone therapy gave rise to the need of an alternative treatment with more effective and physiological pharmaceutical formulation [23].

5.3. Routes of Hormone Administration

There are several routes for the administration for the BHT. These mainly include transdermal, vaginal, oral, and sublingual (beneath the tongue or between the internal part of the cheek and the controlateral gum) and rectal administration. Among these, the sublingual bioidentical hormone therapies have been found to have more beneficial therapeutic effects in comparison to the oral and dermal topical administration. The limitations of the topical administration can be mainly attributed to its pharmacokinetic profiles. The compounded hormone can be supplemented in the form of oil, emulsions, and pellets. The main advantage of the sublingual route is its ability to bypass the upper gastrointestinal tract enzymatic attack and its ability to avoid first pass metabolism. The first pass metabolism is the critical mechanism involved in the abated bioavailability of the orally supplemented hormone [24]. The sublingual supplementation of the bioidentical hormone has been found to ameliorate mood and vasomotor functioning in menopausal women [25]. The implementation via the sublingual route is constantly growing worldwide. It is now regarded as the most effective method to yield a direct absorption of the hormones. It also permits the physician to govern and personalize the drug doses [26].

5.4. BHT for Adrenal Fatigue

The conventional medications used for maintaining the cortisol levels are corticosteroids and prednisone, which have their own adverse effects such as escalated blood sugar levels, blood pressure, weight gain and shortness of breath. Therefore, the alternative approach for the treatment of adrenal fatigue can be brought about by implementation of bioidentical hormones. Hydrocortisone the bioidentical cortisol that is commercially available is the preferred for replacement therapy for adrenal fatigue [27].

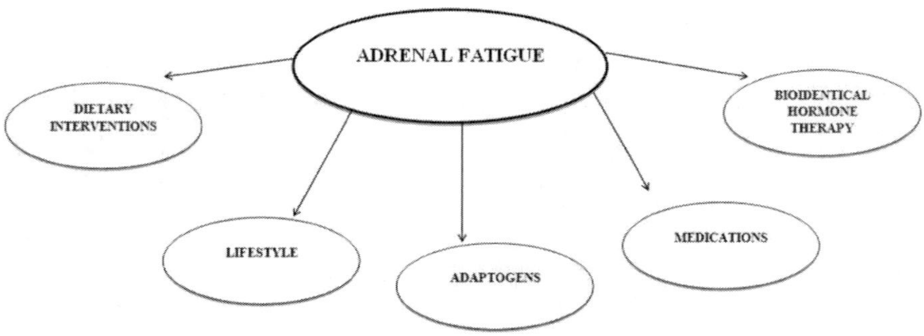

Figure 3. Therapeutic Regimens for adrenal fatigue.

The glucocorticoids in the body are produced in a pulsatile and circadian manner, with escalated levels in the morning and night. The plasma life of hydrocortisone is limited due to which multiple doses of hydrocortisone should be administered throughout the day. The uptake of 15-25mg/d of hydrocortisone has been found to mimic the endogenous cortisol levels [28]. Studies have been carried out which have indicated that low dose administration of hydrocortisone in chronic fatigue patients, increase the overall cortisol throughput as confirmed by higher urinary cortisol levels, thereby highlighting the alterations in the HPA- axis dysfunction in the fatigue patients [29]. The use of cortisone acetate for effective treatment requires the conversion of the compound into cortisol by 11β-hydroxysteroid dehydrogenase (type 1). Most of the adrenal fatigue patients also suffer from abated levels of DHEA. Therefore, supplementation of bioidentical DHEA can also be useful to restore the adrenal function.

Pregnenolone, another stress hormone precursor can also be administered to ameliorate the symptoms in the adrenal fatigue patients. The efficacy of the replacement therapy is mainly determined by monitoring clinical manifestations before and after treatment such as glucose levels, obesity, ability to handle daily stress and associated fatigue. Excessive administration of these glucocorticoids can lead to osteoporosis, substantial morbidity and obesity (Figure 3).

6. Future Aspects

Adrenal fatigue has been known to have manifold effects on the individual such as altered blood sugar levels, altered blood pressure and chronic fatigue. Thus the adrenals should be rejuvenated in order to secrete required levels of steroid hormones. Treatment with bioidentical hormone therapy has come forward as a potent therapeutic regimen. The treatment with bioidentical hormones directly replaces the abated hormones. This treatment when combined with conventional therapies such as special dietary and physical regimens which will help repair the glands naturally and the required hormone levels can be maintained by administration of hydrocortisone, which will not only maintain the required hormone levels but also stimulate the glands to produce endogenous hormones effectively. Such combined interventions may have profound and rapid effects on the treatment of adrenal fatigue.

Conclusion

Adrenal fatigue has come forward as a critical disorder which though not recognized by medical practitioners as a health disorder has the ability to cause serious health implications. Several therapeutic regimens have been administered for the restoration of adrenal function. Effective treatment of adrenal fatigue in the early stages can be effectively brought about by simple alterations such as dietary interventions, lifestyle changes, meditations and physical exercises. However as the disease progresses, these conventional treatments are not very fruitful. For treatment of extreme cases of adrenal fatigue leading to adrenal insufficiency, synthetic hormonal therapy was utilized extensively. This therapy had its own limitations as the compounds administered were found to have toxic and carcinogenic effects. This gave rise to an alternative approach for effective treatment of adrenal fatigue, known as the bioidentical hormone approach. These hormones have been observed to be very useful and effective as they have the molecular structure similar to the endogenous hormones. Thus, this treatment has come forward as a new hope for the treatment of adrenal fatigue.

Conflict of Interest

The authors reported no potential conflict of interest.

Acknowledgments

The authors are thankful to Chettinad Academy of Research and Education (CARE), Chennai, India, for the research facilities and support.

Funding Resources

This study was partially financially supported by grants from Chettinad Hospital & Research Institute (CHRI), Chettinad Academy of Research and Education (CARE), Kelambakkam, Chennai-603103, India and by San Babila Clinic, Vitality Therapeutics, Cellular-Energy Metabolomics Unit, Corso Matteotti, 1/A, 20121, Milano.

Author Contribution

Yashna Chabria, Antara Banerjee wrote the MS. Surajit Pathak and Francesco Marotta designed and revised the MS.

References

[1] *Workplace health and safety Queensland* (2011).

[2] Colligan, T. W., Higgins, E. M. (2006). Workplace stress: Etiology and consequences. *Journal of Workplace Behavioral Health*, 21(II): 89-97.

[3] Kendall, E., Murphy, P., O'Neill, V., and Bursnall, S. (2003) *Occupational Stress: Factors that Contribute to its Occurrence and Effective Management: A Report to the Workers' Compensation and Rehabilitation Commission, Western Australia.* Centre for Human Services. Griffith University.

[4] Head, K. A., Kelly, G. S. (2009). Nutrients and Botanicals for Treatment of Stress: Adrenal Fatigue, Neurotransmitter Imbalance, Anxiety, and Restless Sleep. *Alternative Medicine*, 14(II).

[5] Yehuda R., Giller E. L., Southwick S. M., Lowy M. T., Mason J. W. (1991). Hypothalamic-Pituitary-Adrenal Dysfunction in Posttraumatic Stress Disorder. *Biol Psychiatry*, 3 0:1031-1048.

[6] Melby, J. C., Spink, W. W. (1958). Comparative studies in adrenal cortisol function and cortisol metabolism in healthy adults and patients with shock due to infection. *J Clin Invest*, 37:1791-1797.

[7] Loriaux, D. L., Fleseriu, M. (2009). Relative adrenal insufficiency. *Current opinion in Endocrinology, diabetes and obesity*, 16:392-400.

[8] Wilson, J. L. (2001). *Adrenal Fatigue the 21st Century Stress Syndrome.* Smart Publications.

[9] Lee, D. J. (2010) Adrenal Fatigue Syndrome Part 1: Pathophysiology and Diagnosis. *Human Kinetics*, 15(I): 28-31.

[10] Anderson, D. C. (2008). Assessment and Nutraceutical Management of Stress-induced Adrenal Dysfunction. *Integrative Medicine,* 7(IV).

[11] Oelkers, W. (1996). Adrenal insufficiency. *The New England Journal of Medicine,* 335:1206-1212.

[12] Liebert, M. A. (2014). Selected Treatment Options for Adrenal Exhaustion. *Alternative and Complementary Therapies*, 20(V).

[13] Guilliams, T. G., Edwards, L. (2010) Chronic Stress and the HPA Axis: Clinical Assessment and Therapeutic Considerations. *The Standard*, 9 (II).

[14] Ross A., Thomas S. (2010). The Health Benefits of Yoga and Exercise: A Review of Comparison Studies. *The Journal of alternative and Complementary Medicine,* 16(I):3-12.

[15] Edmonds M, McGuire H, Price J. Exercise therapy for chronic fatigue syndrome. *Cochrane Database of Systematic Reviews* 2004;3(3):1-28.

[16] Fulcher K. Y., White P. D. (2008) Randomized controlled trial of graded exercise in patients with chronic fatigue syndrome. *BMJ*, 314:1647.

[17] Panossian, A. G. (2003) Adaptogens. *Natural Pharmacy*, 7(IV):1, 19–20.

[18] Stoica, Mihaela & Buicu, Florin. (2010). Occupational Stress Management. *Management in Health.* 14. 7-9.

[19] Panigrahi, A. (2016). Managing Stress at Workplace. *Journal of Management Research and Analysis,* 3 (IV):154-160 154.

[20] Leka, S., Griffiths, A. Cox, T. (2004) *Work, Organization & Stress.* World Health Organization.

[21] Santoro N., Braunstein G. D., Butts C. L., Martin K. A., McDermott M., Pinkerton J. V.. (2016) Compounded Bioidentical Hormones in Endocrinology Practice: An Endocrine Society Scientific Statement. *J Clin Endocrinol Metab*, 101(IV):1318–1343.

[22] Deborah, C. (2011). *Bioidentical Hormone Therapy.*

[23] Files, J. A., Ko, M. G., Pruthi, S. (2011). Bioidentical Hormone Therapy. *Mayo Clin Proc*, 86(VII):673-680.

[24] Ruiz, A., Daniels, K. (2011). *Bioidentical Hormones: Advances in Research and What to Ask Your Provider*. Retrieved from https://

www. obgyn. net/ menopause/ bioidentical- hormones- advances-research-and-what-ask-your-provider

[25] Boothby L. A., Doering P. L, Kipersztok S. (2004). Bioidentical hormone therapy: a review. *Menopause,* 11:3.

[26] Ruiz, A. D., Daniels, K. R. (2014). The effectiveness of sublingual and topical compounded bioidentical hormone replacement therapy in postmenopausal women: an observational cohort study. *Int J Pharm Compd*, 18(I):70-7.

[27] Robert, F. BHRT- Sublingual Vs Transdermal.

[28] Mah P. M., Jenkins R. C., Rostami-Hodjegan A., Newell-Price J., Doane A., Ibbotson V., Tucker G. T., Ross R. J. (2004). Weight-related dosing, timing and monitoring of hydrocortisone replacement therapy in patients with adrenal insufficiency. *Clinical Endocrinology,* 61:367-375.

[29] Bornstein S. R., Allolio B., Arlt W., Barthel A., Don-Wauchope A., Hammer G. D., Husebye E. S., Merke D. P., Murad M. H., Stratakis C. A., Torpy D. J. (2016). Diagnosis and Treatment of Primary Adrenal Insufficiency: An Endocrine Society Clinical Practice Guideline. *J Clin Endocrinol Metab*, 101(III):364–389.

[30] Cleare, A. J., Miell, J., Heap, E., Sookdeo, S., Young, L., Malhi, G. S., O'Keane, V. Hypothalamo-Pituitary-Adrenal Axis Dysfunction in Chronic Fatigue Syndrome, and the Effects of Low-Dose Hydrocortisone Therapy. *The Journal of Clinical Endocrinology Metabolism.* 2001. 86(8):3545–3554.

In: Occupational Stress
Editors: N. Mucci, G. Giorgi et al.
ISBN: 978-1-53615-404-7

Chapter 5

ENVIRONMENTAL AND DIETARY METABOLIC STRESS IN WORKERS: NOVEL AVENUES IN ORAL HEAVY METAL CHELATION AND FATTY LIVER AIDS

Surajit Pathak[1], Sruthi K. Hari[1], Sathya Priya Thandavan[1], Yuki Sato[2], Vladimir Tsepkolenko[3], Masahiro Taki[2], Roberto Catanzaro[4], Hala Sweed[5], Francesco Marotta[6,*], Aldo Lorenzetti[6] and Antara Banerjee[1,†]

[1]Faculty of Allied Health Sciences,
Chettinad Academy of Research and Education, Kelambakkam, India
[2]Taki Dental Clinic,
Ichinomiya and Taki Medical Salon Natural Dentistry, Kyoto, Japan
[3]Virtus Medical Center,
Ukraine Institute of Dermatology and Healthy Aging, Odessa, Ukraine
[4]Dept of Clinical and Experimental Medicine,
Section of Gastroenterology, University of Catania, Catania, Italy

[*] Corresponding Author's E-mail: fmarchimede@libero.it.
[†] Corresponding Author's E-mail Antara.banerjee27@gmail.com.

[5]Geriatrics and Gerontology Department –Faculty of Medicine, Ain-Shams University, Egypt
[6]ReGenera R&D International for Aging Intervention, Milano-Beijing, Italy-China and VCC Preventive Medical Promotion Foundation, Beijing, China

ABSTRACT

Metals are commonly prevalent in the body along with various other fundamental molecules. However, an alteration in their concentration may damage vital physiological functioning. Several toxic metals may be predominant contributing factors in the occurrence of several chronic diseases which often produce only subtle clinical signs leading to misdiagnosis or being left undetected. The terminology "heavy metal" is referred to a toxic metal which does not normally belong to our biological system and is harmful when accumulated in the body. The accumulation of these heavy metals is more prominent in industrial workers. The toxic effects of heavy metals which have entered our body can be effectively counteracted by utilizing natural substances such as "Zeolites" which assist our organs to gradually cleanse and discard the toxic metals. Although natural zeolites were discovered over 250 years ago, people have begun to realize the true potential and capabilities of zeolite only in recent times. Zeolites, due to their specific internal structure, are able to trap heavy metals, mainly by their ability to exchange inherent cations for other cations on the basis of ion selectivity mechanisms. Novel studies have indicated that not all zeolites possess the same "trapping ability." In this chapter, specific studies have been highlighted that exhibit a new class of zeolites that are far more effective than the ones that are currently available.

Metabolic syndrome and various other associated cardiovascular and neurological complications, affects various social classes, mainly the workers under stressful conditions, invariably tend to be forced towards more detrimental dietary and lifestyle attitudes (pre-cooked food in company cafeteria, junk food, night shifts, lack of exercise, limited inclination to healthy food choices, eating while commuting etc. to mention some). This opens the way to a creeping, silent fatty liver infiltration (NAFLD) which is far more than a simple excess fat accumulation, but it does represent the first step leading to a much worse cascade of events. NAFLD at the moment has a prevalence of 23-34% in USA, China (with reports up to 46%) and alarmingly rising in Middle-East too. Patients with T2DM and NAFLD have a 2-3 fold higher incidence of acute myocardial infarction than those without NAFLD. In this regards,, late in 2004, some research studies had been done on a promising mixed herbal compound made in China (YHK) with a number of positive experimental and scanty clinical reports, following some empirical observational data. Further studies making pure extracts of the main ingredients together with inner enrichment of specific bioactive fraction (FOLHK) proved through very stringent, either in vitro or in vivo animal studies and clinical trials its effectiveness. This was shown to be significantly better over the common silymarin-based liver protectors as well surpassing the benefit of the initial prototype formulas while confirming its safety. While better working environment, healthy food and attitudes maintain their fundamental role as main pillars of health and disease prevention, the above non-chemical interventions may represent a convenient aid to support health protection.

Keywords: metal toxicity, environmental pollution, metal chelation, chemical agents, zeolites, molecular seivers, Chinese herbs, YHK, FOLHK, detoxification

1. Introduction

Heavy metal toxicity is a very common condition that affects many different species like plants, animals and human being leading to ecotoxicity. The heavy metal toxicity is interchangeably termed as heavy metal poisoning. Industrial pollution and environmental pollution are main reason which causes heavy metal toxicity (Tchounwou et al., 2012). A normal human body contains very low concentration of metal elements and which are described as trace elements according to the periodic table. Their atomic density is 5 times greater than water (Environ Chem Lett., 2010). These trace elements are very much essential for the normal metabolism to take place and for the growth of the body. The accretion of heavy metals in high amount in the tissue will lead to the oxidative stress which in turn causes cellular damage. Heavy metals are naturally present in the environment in the earth's crust. The non-degradable nature of the heavy metals imparts them stability and toxicity. Some of the naturally obtained heavy metals are mercury, zinc, arsenic, lead, magnesium, silver, gold, bismuth, copper, platinum, cadmium, aluminum, nickel, chromium and cobalt (Oghenerobor B. A et al., 2014).

Volcanic eruption, soil erosion, aerosol particles and forest fire are the main reasons of the environmental heavy metal toxicity. During volcanic eruption, the heavy metals from the earth's crust are released in the lava or through the smoke produced during the eruption. The common heavy metals produced during volcanic eruption are mercury, lead, magnesium, aluminum and zinc. Water and wind are important cause of soil erosion. The eroded soil sediments along with the heavy metals get mixed with the river water and soil. This pollutes the water and soil with toxic heavy metals (Igwe J. C and Abia A. A., 2006). The forest fire will also release high amount of toxic fumes into the atmosphere which have carbon dioxide, carbon monoxide, hydrogen sulphide etc. The smoke clouds will have colloidal particles and the heavy metals together will form aerosol droplets in the air, this can be inhaled easily and thereby causing disease (Sharma R. K and M Agrawal M., 2005). In plants the heavy metals can cause inhibition of photosynthesis, reduced rate of seed germination, low level of plant growth and enzyme activity and decreased lipid content. In humans and animals, heavy metal toxicity can lead to cancer, organ damage and growth development and in rare cases death (Nagajyoti P. C. et al., 2010). The other main reason for heavy metal toxicity is due to the industrial pollution. This include human factors such as textile, power plants, electroplating process, high tension lines, nuclear power, microelectronics, metal fishing, and plastics, coal burning power plants, mining extraction operation and paper processing plants.

2. Heavy Metal Toxicity Occurrence and Cause

The sedimentation of heavy metal is a threat to biological ecosystem since the heavy metal will get accumulated in all the forms such as water, soil, air etc. Basaltic igneous, granite igneous, shale and clays, black shale and sand stone emits the heavy metals and their sedimentation takes place. Magnesium, Cobalt, Nickel, Copper and Zinc are released in ample by igneous rocks like olivine, augite, and hornblende. The limestone and sandstone also release considerate amount of heavy metal in to the soil

Table 1. Different types of the heavy metals, its source and disease caused and its mechanism.

Heavy metal	Occurrence	Route of exposure	Mechanism	Effects
Iron:	J metal plating	Oral route Inhalation Maternal route	Acts as intercalating agents Activates pathways for carcinogenesis	Iron toxicosis GI hemorrhage Hypotension Lethargy Tachycardia Hepatic necrosis Metabolic acidosis
Zinc:	Refineries Brass manufactures Metal plating Plumbing	Dermal Oral route Inhalation		Affects the skins Damages the nervous mechanism
Cadmium:	Weathering river transport Mining Smelting Tobacco smoking Incineration of municipal waste Fertilizers	Smoking Oral route Inhalation Maternal route	Not very much understood Cytotoxic to through ROS activity Activates different stress responses	Bone mineralization Renal dysfunction Hypercalciuria Osteoporosis
Arsenic:	Volcanic eruption Pesticides Wood preservatives Dyes	Oral route Inhalation Dermal contact Parental route	Binds with the thiol and spreads throughout the body which involves different pathways	Cardiovascular disease Arsenicosis Skin disorder Neurologic disorders Diabetes hearing loss portal fibrosis hematologic disorders cancer
Lead:	Paint Gasoline Toys Household dust Cosmetics	Inhalation Oral route Dermal contact	Binds with the thiol	Abdominal pain, Renal dysfunction, Vertigo, Arthritis, Psychosis Autism, Dyslexia, Kidney damage
Chromium:	Metal coatings, plating and alloys Magnetic tapes Paint pigments Rubber Cement Paper Wood preservatives	Inhalation Dermal contact	Binds with the thiol and the production of reactive oxygen species	Ulcers DNA damage
Mercury:	Pharmaceuticals Paper and pulp preservatives	Inhalation, Oral route, Dermal contact	Changes the cell structure	Acrodynia or pink disease Brain damage

6. MECHANISM OF METAL CHELATION

Chelating is the process where the chelating agents will bind or cover the metal without letting the metal ions to react with other compound. It is like a protective covering or a layer over the metal. There are different types of chelating agents like monodentate ligands, bidendate ligands and polydentate ligands. The properties of the chelating agents are those that have good affinity towards the metal and there should less to no toxicity production by the chelating agents. They should have the capacity to collide with the natural chelators. It should be soluble in water. There are many chemical agents used in the chelating process for different metal ions (Flora S. J. S and Pachauri V., 2010). These are shown in the Table 2.

Table 2. Heavy metals and its chemical chelating agents. This table represents the chemical metal chelating agents used to chelate excess the metal ions in body which is causing the toxicity

S. No	Toxic element	Chelation agent
1.	Arsenic	dimercapol
2.	Lead	Ethylenediamine tetraacetic acid (EDTA)
3.	Mercury	2,3,dimercaptosussinic acid (DMSA), 2,3-dimercapto-propane-1-sulfonate(DMPA)
4.	Iron	Desferrioxamine Deferiprone
5.	Lead	Calcium disodium ethylenediamine tetraacetic acid (Ca2Na2 EDTA)
6.	Cobalt and Zinc	Calcium Triosoduim diethylene triaminepenta acetate (CaNa DTPA)
7.	Copper	β-β-dimethyl cysteine (DPA) or 3-mercapto-D-valine tetra-methylene-tetraamine (TETA)
8.	Calcium	Nitrito triacetic acid (NTA)

7. INTRODUCTION TO ZEOLITES

Zeolites are hydrated aluminum silicates composed of oxygen, aluminum and silicon. They occur naturally in crystalline form with collection of cavities and channels that contains cations, water and or small molecules which helps them to serve as an effective catalyst and as an absorbent (Baerlocher C et al., 2007). They are also synthesized chemically for various applications in industry and medicine. The term "Zeolite" is derived from Greek meaning "boiling stone" because of its unique property of releasing steam when it is heated. Generally Zeolites have large empty spaces, or cages, within their structures so that they can accommodate large cations, such as Na^+, K^+, Br^+, andCa_2^+, and also it can trap comparatively large molecules and cationic groups, such as water, ammonia, carbonate ions, and nitrate ions. The basic structure of zeolites is biologically neutral (Ribeiro F. R. et al., 1984).

Recent survey says there are about 40 naturally occurring zeolites including *chabazite, clinoptilolite* and *mordenite* are available and mined from volcanic and sedimentary rocks and also about 150 synthetic zeolites were designed for various industrial tenacities among them the most predominantly used ones are zeolite A (detergent), zeolite X and Y (catalytic crackers)and ZSM-5 (petroleum catalyst) practices. However, *mordenite* is not advised for human use, given the asbestosis risk of its easily volatile fibers.

8. SYNTHETIC ZEOLITES

Synthetic zeolites are commonly synthesized by two methods

(a) Hydrothermal Crystallization of aluminosilicate gels.
(b) Solutions in a basic environment.

There are few major factors that influence the synthesis of zeolites and product formation. These include composition of the reaction mixture, nature of reactants and their pre-treatments, temperature of the process, reaction time, pH of the reaction mixture and also either it has continuous or semi continuous mode of operation (Cundy C. S., Cox P. A., 2003).

9. Industrial Application of Zeolites

At first zeolites were introduced as absorbents in industries for separation and purifications. Later its application in all sectors was found, verified and used widely.

9.1. As Molecular Sievers

Zeolites are also known as molecular sievers since it serves as effective cleanser of heavy metals as they have the ability to trap the metal ions inside them because of their distinctive internal structure. Moreover, since it is a negatively charged molecule it has higher affinity towards positively charged molecules (toxins) and free radicals that helps them to bind with toxins and trap and detoxify (Davis M. E et al., 1988). The complete detoxification process take place about 6-9 weeks depending upon the bodies physical condition, lifestyle and also depends upon diet and age of the person. Flowers J. L et al., (2009) provided clinical evidence that supported *Clinoptilolite*, a natural zeolite has the capability of eliminating toxic heavy metals (like mercury, lead, arsenic and cadmium) and also it eliminated pesticides and antibiotics present in the body without disturbing the vital electrolytes (Natural Zeolites, 2017, ReGenera Research Group).

9.2. As Water Softeners

Zeolites plays major role in water purification sectors due to its porous composition and trapping ability. It is mainly utilized to remove the calcium ions present in water. Calcium ions, when it comes in contact with soap it form a scum. It is mandatory to avoid scum formation to maintain the purity of the water which is universally eliminated by treating it with sodium bearing zeolites. When the water is fully cleansed off then the zeolites are rejuvenated by using the brine solution and it can be reprocessed (Chang, Luke L. Y. 2002).

9.3. As Pollutant Filters

Zeolites are the most effective filters of sulfur dioxide (SO_2), a pollutant produced in enormous amount while burning high-sulfur coal and found to be a major cause for acid rain. Natural zeolites are found to confiscate the sulfur dioxide that is present in the natural gas and many studies reported that so far no other filters showed higher removal rate of SO_2 as much as natural zeolites (Townsend R. P., Coker E. N. 2001).

9.4. As Chelator

Zeolites, reservoir to their specific internal structure, have ability to trap inside heavy metals through series of selective mechanisms. This has been confirmed recently in heterotrophic biomass with a reduction of heavy metals noxious effects between 25% to 70% by the Environmental Science and Technology, School of Chemical Engineering, National Technical University of Athens. (2012). Various Studies have been conducted in comparison with GSH and Chabasite-phillipsite-based chelator and to prove the efficacy of natural zeolites over other chelators have been studied using faecal ammonia analysis that showed neither GLU-9599 nor i.v. GSH administration changed the gut extraction of ammonia but On the other hand, the oral Chabasite-phillipsite-based chelator brought about a significantly decreased concentration already at 1-month observation ($p < 0.001$ vs. baseline) and this effect was maintained also at the end of the study. (Figure 4, $p < 0.001$) (Natural Zeolites, 2017, ReGenera Research Group). Makita k et al., (2011) developed a new type of hydrophilic membrane which is composed of zeolite MCM-22 was synthesized by hydrothermal synthesis method on a porous -alumina support. MCM-22 which was synthesized predicted to have high acid proof properties due to the high Si/Al ratio in its framework. The precursor used for MCM-22 (MCM-22 (P)) synthesis was composed of layered aluminosilicate with a high content of silanol groups at the surfaces. The MCM-22 zeolite structure is formed by calcination of MCM-22 (P) through the condensation of silanol groups. MCM-22 was calcinated at relatively low temperatures (300–450◦C) to make sure to retain sufficient silanol groups on their surfaces, which proved the hydrophilic properties on its internal surfaces.

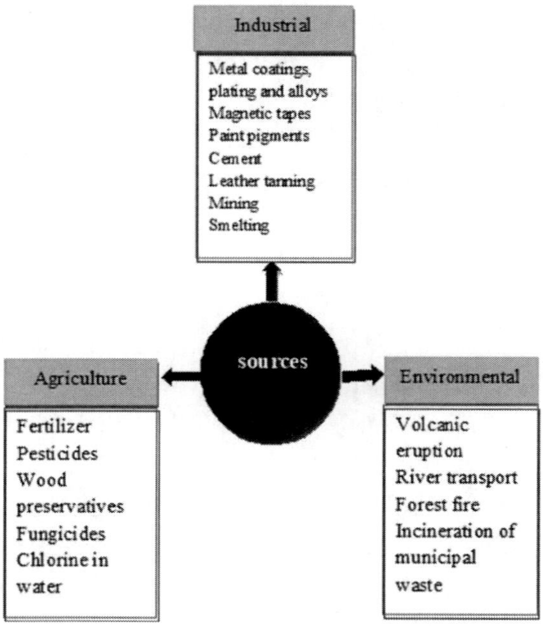

Figure 1. Source of the heavy metals.

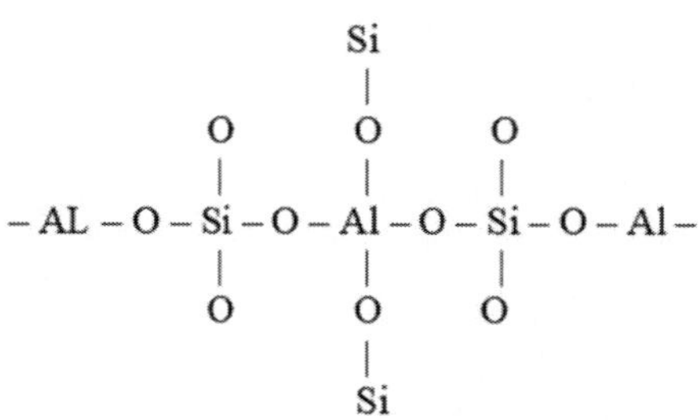

Figure 2. Structure of zeolites.

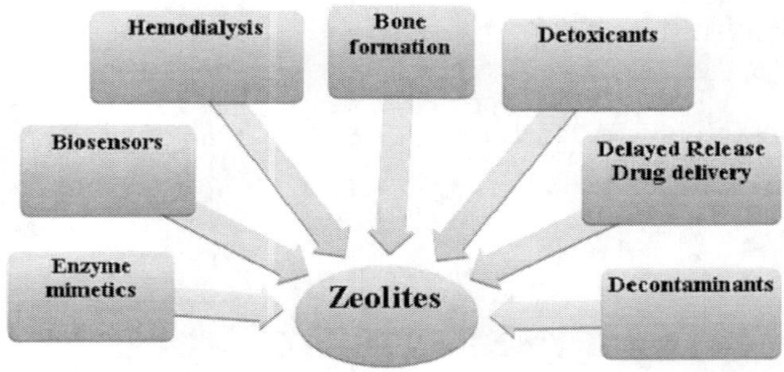

Figure 3. Medical uses of zeolites.

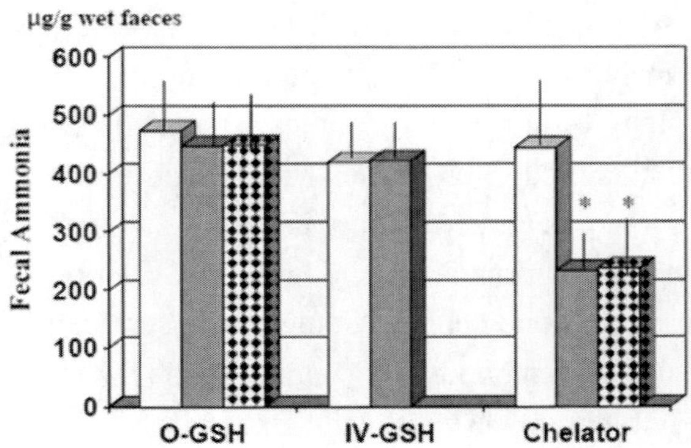

Figure 4. Faecal ammonia analysis: Effect of oral and I. V (GSH vs Zeolites); White Bar: Baseline; Grey Bar: one month treatment, Dotted Bar: two month treatment.

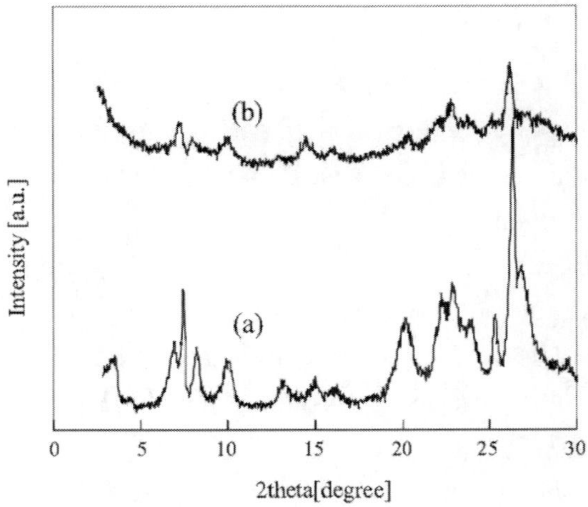

Figure 5. XRD patterns of (a) MCM-22 and (b) ITQ-2 seed crystals.

9.5. As Catalytic Crackers

In petroleum industries zeolites are used to break down large molecules present in the petrol into smaller molecules to produce gasoline.

10. Health Benefits of Zeolites

Zeolites are used as dietary supplements for major diseases such as cancer, heart diseases, lyme's disease and liver disease and also used to evacuate heavy metals that are accumulated in the body due to its peculiar structural "trapping" arrangement. Zeolites have also been being used as anti-oxidant and alkalinizing properties have also been reported. It is also used as additive in concentrated animal breeding facilities improving feed conversion, reducing airborne ammonia up to 80%, acting as a mycotoxin binder, and improving bone density. Some of the surface modified natural zeolites remove toxic compounds from animal food (Natural Zeolites, 2017, ReGenera Research Group, in-house lab data).

10.1. As Detoxifier (Heavy Metal Treatment)

The most emerging and life threatening pollution is the accumulation of heavy metals in the environment which leads to aggregate effects along the food chain. Natural zeolites such as clinoptilolite, phillipsite, and chabazite generally showed phenomenal activity towards eliminating the aluminum and also other heavy metals such as Cd_2^+, Pb_2^+, Zn_2^+, Cu_2^+, and partly, Cr_3. In particular, clinoptilolite showed highly effective activity towards the heavy metals since it stays stable even in the acidic environment and it also showed high affinity towards many heavy metals (PavelicK, Hadzija M. 2015).

Mercury is one of the commonest heavy metal releases in major industries and it is also used in many industrial processes such as pigments, batteries, etc. The most efficient method so far found to remove mercury accumulation is usage of the zeolites such as NaCl pre-treated pure heulandites crystals and NaCl pre-treated clinoptilolite containing rock samples. These zeolites trap the mercury together and eliminate them by ion exchange adsorption and surface precipitation process (Pavelic K, Hadzija M. 2015).

Organophosphate poisoning is another menacing heavy metal accretion which is highly toxic and affects the ecosystem. The substances that cause the poisoning affects human body by inhibiting the enzyme activity of cholinesterasein erythrocytes (RBCs) and also in major organs such as liver, stomach and brain. Intoxication of organophosphate poisoning is obligatory, in order to inhibit its effect. Zeolite is used to detoxify the organophosphate poisoning and its observed success rate is found to be significant when compared to other methods of intoxication. One such zeolite compound that prevented and eradicated this poisoning effectively is Zeolite tuff, which is composed of 61% clinoptilolite. Zeolite tuff is predominantly used along with arsenal of coherent prevention and therapy of organophosphate poisoning. We conclude that in future Zeolites may be the most effective and non-invasive way to remove heavy metal toxicity and can be used along with herbals. Synthetic Zeolites with special properties such as more pore size and specificity towards particular metal can be included so that the efficacy of the Zeolites will be upgraded (Pavelic K, Hadzija M. 2015). However, this avenue has to be taken with great caution and long-lasting studies as well stringent safety tests have to be carried out before human use can be envisaged, Some specific Italian natural Zeolites such as chabasite /phillipsite /analcime based food supplement, washed with volcanic water and non-chemically treated so to reach talc-size consistency are indicated for chelating intestinal ammonia-based toxins and heavy metals. In specific, these Zeolites show significant properties such as detoxifying, adsorbent, absorbent and antioxidant functions in the gastrointestinal tract better than other available zeolites. (Natural Zeolites, 2017, ReGenera Research Group, in-house data). Some recent clinical trials comparing them to oral and intravenous glutathione as well as a powerful natural antioxidant, have proven their significantly higher heavy metal and gut ammonia trapping ability as well as gut antioxidant property. (Makida Y. 2016) and these beneficial effects were followed up to two years (Marotta F, 2017).

11. Innovative Research Studies on Phytochemical Addressing Liver Protection from Metabolic Stress: *FOLHK*

Marotta's research team, late in 2004 conducted studies on a promising herbal compound *YHK*, made in China and manufactured in Japan which claimed to have a number of positive clinical reports, although unpublished and empirically done. His team set up a number of both in vitro and *in vivo* animal studies proving its effectiveness over the common silymarin-based liver protectors and for this being awarded two national prizes by JSH (Japan Society of Hepatology). These works were followed by a Canadian group which later published another biopsy-proven study on this compound in NASH patients. (Stefano JT et al., 2007). However, this pricy compound had no longer clinical testing from independent sources and this triggered some concerns about a reliable batch-to-batch quality control and also constant herbal extraction methodology procedure as well as safety profile while, at the same time, claiming questionable "curing" properties. Thus, starting in 2010 a new set of research work was started by making pure extracts of the main ingredients of the original Asian formula by sophisticated technologies (LC-ESI-Q-TOF -MS/MS- analysis) unavailable by the original prototype formula maker. As a result, the old rough formula has been further significantly strengthened and expanded in its mechanisms of action (FOLHK, experimental code). *FOLHK*, is composed of oleanolic acid and saponins-rich ginsenosides, lignans, phenolics and steroids-rich Eucommiaceae extract, Selenium, corosolic acid, N-acetyl cysteine, glucosinolate-derived compounds. This underwent, an intense research activity and its composition was more recently modified. A safety analysis was also done by an independent ISO-authorized laboratory. *FOHK* contains a number of proprietary SBF-Specific Bioactive Fractions and from bench studies to in vivo and pilot studies confirms the net superiority over the prototype formula YHK, while maintaining a strict pharmaceutical-grade biochemical stability. During 2013-2017 prof. Marotta's team together with other independent hepato-gastroenterology teams moved to clinical trials. In particular, these are taking place in Italy (significant decrease/normalization of liver enzymes in NASH subjects), Ukraine (biopsy-proven, preliminary positive data on inflammatory and fibrosis changes, ongoing), Japan (completed beneficial gene expression modulation on mitogen-activated protein kinase signalling, MicroRNA 122, chemerin receptor, chemokine-like receptor 1 and Cellular repressor of E1A-stimulated genes in healthy subjects), Egypt (ongoing clinical trial in overweight NASH subjects) and Malesya (completed in-house observational studies in over 60 subjects, $p < 0.05$ vs initial prototype YHK compound). Interestingly, most of the afore-mentioned beneficial gene expression modulating properties exerted by modified formula FOLHK was not expressed or only at a not significant level by the prototype formula YHK which shared some, albeit not highly purified, components with FOLHK.

FOLHK is predominantly amenable to treat NAFLD and NASH patients and it also bids liver protection against toxicants, heavy metals included and medication-induced liver metabolic burden (cardiovascular drugs, antibiotics, antifungal, anti-tuberculosis etc.).

CONCLUSION

Heavy metal toxicity is currently the life threatening issue faced in most of the countries and it is found to be the causes of major fatal and non-curable diseases such as cancer, heart diseases, liver problems, kidney problems etc. in most of the species like plants, human being, animals etc. These heavy metals are majorly the by-products and are dumped as wastes in the environment through various procedures. It affects integrity of land, air as well as water. So it is predominantly spread and entered the ecosystem and food chain. Many methods are adopted so far to detoxify the heavy metal accumulation but all the methods is not that efficient and also have many drawbacks. One of the most efficient and safe ways found to remove heavy metal accretion in body is by using Zeolites. Zeolites are non-absorbable alumino silicate minerals, which exerts their beneficial activity due to its unique structure. It has the ability to trap the metal ions and therefore they can be eliminated later with physiological stool discharge. Zeolites can be taken as oral supplements which will detoxify the body system by this gut cleansing but also by further intraluminal osmotic transfer of heavy metal stored in body organs. Such detoxifying action is further corroborated by highly effective liver protectors as shown in our ongoing studies with FOLHK. Moreover, these kind of hepatoprotective compounds are very amenable to be used not only to treat NAFLD and its possible progression to NASH, but also as a preventing protective strategy in impending cases or healthy cases falling into risk factor clustered category.

Acknowledgments

The authors are thankful to Chettinad Academy of Research and Education (CARE), Chennai, India for the research facilities and support.

Funding

This study was partially financially supported by grants from Chettinad Hospital & Research Institute (CHRI), Chettinad Academy of Research and Education (CARE), Kelambakkam, Chennai-603103, India whereas all all studies on FOLHK were supported by ReGenera R&D International for Aging Intervention, Milano, Italy.

Conflicts of Interests

No potential conflict of interest was reported by the authors.

Author Contribution

Sruthi K. Hari., Sathya Priya Thandavan, Antara Banerjee wrote the Manuscript. Antara Banerjee, Surajit Pathak, Francesco Marotta designed and revised the Manuscript. Vladimir Tsepkolenko, Roberto Catanzaro and Aldo Lorenzetti contributed by providing ongoing in-house clinical data and took care proof the whole experimental and clinical trials logistics and quality control at the production site.

References

Akpor, O. B., Ohiobor, G. O., and Olaolu, T. D. (2014). Heavy metal pollutants in wastewater effluents: sources, effects and remediation. *Advances in Bioscience and Bioengineering*, 2(4): 37-43.

Baerlocher, C., Meier W. H., Olson D. H. (2007). *Atlas of zeolite framework types. 6th Edition*, Elsevier, (http://www.iza-structure.org/databases/).

Bryan, G. W., (1971). The effects of heavy metals (other than mercury) on marine and estuarine organisms. *Proceedings of the Royal Society of London. B, Biological sciences,* 177(1048):389-410.

Chibuike, G. U. and Obiora, S. C. (2014). Heavy metal polluted soils: effect on plants and bioremediation methods. *Applied and Environmental Soil Science,* 2014:1-12.

Chande N, Laidlaw M, Adams P, Marotta P. Yo Jyo Hen Shi Ko (YHK) improves transaminases in nonalcoholic steatohepatitis (NASH): a randomized pilot study. *Dig Dis Sci.* 2006; 51(7):1183-9.

Cundy, C. S., and Cox, P. A. (2003). The hydrothermal synthesis of zeolites: history and development from the earliest days to the present time. *Chemical Reviews*, 103(3): 663-702.

Davis, M. E., Saldarriaga, C., Montes, C., Garces, J., & Crowdert, C. (1988). A molecular sieve with eighteen-membered rings. *Nature,* 331:698-699.

Duruibe, J. O., Ogwuegbu, M. O. C., and Egwurugwu, J. N. (2007). Heavy metal pollution and human biotoxic effects. *International Journal of Physical Sciences*, 2(5):112-118.

Flanigen, E. M., Patton, R. L., and Wilson, S. T. (1988). Structural, synthetic and physicochemical concepts in aluminophosphate-based molecular sieves. *Studies in Surface Science and Catalysis*, 37:13-27.

Flora, S. J., and Pachauri, V. (2010). Chelation in metal intoxication. *International Journal of Environmental Research and Public Health,* 7(7):2745-2788.

Flowers, J. L., Lonky, S. A., and Deitsch, E. J. (2009). Clinical evidence supporting the use of an activated clinoptilolite suspension as an agent to increase urinary excretion of toxic heavy metals. *Nutrition and Dietary Supplements*, 1:11-18.

Govind, P., and Madhuri, S. (2014). Heavy metals causing toxicity in animals and fishes. *Research Journal of Animal, Veterinary and Fishery Sciences*, 2(2): 17-23.

Igwe, J., and Abia, A. A. (2006). A bioseparation process for removing heavy metals from waste water using biosorbents. *African Journal of Biotechnolog*y, 5(12): 1167-1179.

Jaishankar, M., Tseten, T., Anbalagan, N., Mathew, B. B., and Beeregowda, K. N. (2014). Toxicity, mechanism and health effects of some heavy metals. *Interdisciplinary Toxicology*, 7(2): 60-72.

Luke, L., and Chang, Y. (2002). *Industrial Mineralogy: Materials, Processes, and Uses.* Upper Saddle River, NJ: Prentice Hall. (http://www.chemistryexplained.com/Va-Z/Zeolites.html#ixzz4zbLA0QD6).

Lukkari, T., Taavitsainen, M., Väisänen, A., and Haimi, J. (2004). Effects of heavy metals on earthworms along contamination gradients in organic rich soils. *Ecotoxicology and Environmental Safety*, 59(3): 340-348.

Makida, Y., He, F., Mohania, D., Balieiro-Neto, G., Alagozlu, H**.,** Pathak, S., Naito, Y., Lorenzetti, A., Takadanohara, H, Cervi, J and Marotta, F. (2016) Effect of a Novel GSH-based Compound and Chabasite-phillipsite-based Chelator in Environmentally-exposed Poor

Detoxifiers: An Adjuvant Hepatoprotective Treatment for Poly-drug Users? *Metabolomics* (Los Angel) 6:185.

Makita, K., Hirota, Y., Egashira, Y., Yoshida, K., Sasaki, Y., & Nishiyama, N. (2011). Synthesis of MCM-22 zeolite membranes and vapor permeation of water/acetic acid mixtures. *Journal of Membrane Science*, 372(1):269-276.

Marotta, F., Marcellino, M., Solimene, U., Cuffari, B., Yadav, H., Khokhlov, A. N., Lorenzetti, A., and Catanzaro, R. (2017) A 2-year Double-Blind RCT Follow-up Study with Fermented Papaya Preparation (FPP) Modulating Key Markers in Middle-Age Subjects with Clustered Neurodegenerative Disease-Risk Factors. *Clin Pharmacol Biopharm* 6:170.

Martin, S., and Griswold, W. (2009). Human health effects of heavy metals. *Environ Sci Technol Brief Cit*, 15: 1-6.

Minerals Yearbook: Volume I. *Metals and Minerals*: Zeolites, 2008.

Mishra, V. K., Upadhyaya, A. R., Pandey, S. K., and Tripathi, B. D. (2008). Heavy metal pollution induced due to coal mining effluent on surrounding aquatic ecosystem and its management through naturally occurring aquatic macrophytes. *Bioresource Technology*, 99(5): 930-936.

Nagajyoti, P. C., Lee, K. D., and Sreekanth, T. V. M. (2010). Heavy metals, occurrence and toxicity for plants: a review. *Environmental Chemistry Letters*, 8(3): 199-216.

Natural Zeolites Brochure, 2017. *Science of Living*.

Pavelic, K., and Hadzija., M. (2015). *Medical Applications of Zeolites*. Zeolite in human health.

Ribeiro F. R., Rodrigues A. E., Rollmann L. D., (1984). Naccache C. *Zeolites: Science and Technology*. Martinus Nijhoff Publishers, the Hague.

Reglero, M. M., Taggart, M. A., Monsalve-Gonzalez, L., & Mateo, R. (2009). Heavy metal exposure in large game from a lead mining area: effects on oxidative stress and fatty acid composition in liver. *Environmental Pollution*, 157(4):1388-1395.

Sethy, S. K., and Ghosh, S. (2013). Effect of heavy metals on germination of seeds. *Journal of Natural Science, Biology, and Medicine*, 4(2): 272-275.

Sha S., Marotta F., (2006). *United States Patent Application Publication*. Pub. No. US 2006/0105061 A1.

Sharma R. K and Agrawal M., Biological effects of heavy metals: an overview. *J Environ Biol.* 2005; 26:301-13.

Sharma, R. K., and Agrawal, M. (2005). Biological effects of heavy metals: an overview. *Journal of Environmental Biology*, 26(2): 301-313.

Singh, R., Gautam, N., Mishra, A., and Gupta, R. (2011). Heavy metals and living systems: an overview. *Indian Journal of Pharmacology*, 43(3): 246-253.

Stefano JT, de Oliveira CP, Corrêa-Giannella ML, de Lima VM, de Sá SV, de Oliveira EP, de Mello ES, Giannella-Neto D, Alves VA, Carrilho FJ. Nonalcoholic steatohepatitis (NASH) in ob/ob mice treated with yo jyo hen shi ko (YHK): effects on peroxisome proliferator-activated receptors (PPARs) and microsomal triglyceride transfer protein (MTP). *Dig Dis Sci.* 2007 Dec;52(12):3448-54.

Townsend, R. P., and Coker, E. N. (2001). Ion exchange in zeolites. *Studies in surface science and catalysis*, 137: 467-524.

In: Occupational Stress
Editors: N. Mucci, G. Giorgi et al.
ISBN: 978-1-53615-404-7

Chapter 6

BIOMARKERS OF EARLY EFFECTS FOR OCCUPATIONAL EXPOSURE

Vivian F. Silva Kahl[1,2,*], Ana Letícia Hilário Garcia[1], Melissa Rosa de Souza[1], Daiana Dalberto[1], Arielly F. Bento de Oliveira[1] and Juliana da Silva[1]

[1]Laboratory of Genetic Toxicological,
Lutheran University of Brazil (ULBRA), Canoas, RS, Brazil
[2]Telomere Length Regulation Unit, Children's Medical Research Institute (CMRI), Westmead, Sydney, NSW, Australia

ABSTRACT

Occupational exposure to different hazards is thought to be one of the greatest health challenge in the contemporary era. Although many studies are performed with animal models and *in vitro* evaluating the toxicity of single compounds, the real exposure occurs through the use of mixtures of different chemicals, establishing a complex scenario in occupational risk assessment. The use of biomarkers of early effects is a major tool in approaching the occupational exposure to complex mixtures, helping to

* Corresponding Author's E-mail: vivian.kahl@gmail.com.

increase risk prediction. The most significant use of biomarkers in occupational health have been in biological monitoring of workers from different areas: industry, primary production, agriculture, and urban workers, as some examples. This review will discuss the three major biomarkers of early effect used in the last few years by our research group: (1) Comet assay, which evaluates genotoxicity, being a versatile and sensitive method for measuring single- and double-strand DNA breaks; (2) Micronucleus assay, which can be applied to both lymphocytes and buccal cells; it is a mutagenic test that evaluates different chromosomal aberrations and cell death and can provide information of cytostasis; and (3) telomere length (TL) quantification, a relatively new method applying for identification of chromosomal instability linked to accelerated cellular senescence, several age-related diseases and neoplasia. The use of those three biomarkers has been proven useful in the assessment of occupational risk of individuals exposed to pesticides, coal, polycyclic aromatic hydrocarbon, lead, solvents, traffic air pollution, among other xenobiotics. Those tests may characterize the exposed from non-exposed individuals. Data from literature has shown that demographic characteristics, such as age, gender, and period and time of exposure may alter individual's response to chemicals. Additionally, lifestyle habits, as alcohol consumption, hours of sleep, smoking habits and dietary intake may also play a significant role in occupational risk evaluations. As human inter-individual variability is a major source of uncertainty in risk assessment, this review will also address those factors. Finally, in order to understand how biological systems and processes interact, System Biology tools are being used to integrate biological data. This approach is based on consideration of common biological processes and how chemicals may disrupt them, allowing to observe the interaction between the xenobiotic agent and the mechanisms of damage. This review will investigate the use of System Biology for connection of biomarkers of early effect to adverse outcomes as regard occupational risk concern. Biomarkers of effect indicates the biochemical or functional alterations including a wide range of biological responses; they are mainly used as group indicators, being sensitive but not specific, and aiming to decrease the inter-individual differences. As those biomarkers are recognized to have an association with several diseases, including cancer, they may help in early detection and prevention of such pathologies. Given this, studies in occupational exposure area are discussed in this chapter, approaching the use and the importance of such biomarkers as key strategies to help in management decisions.

Introduction

Occupational exposure evaluation is a tool for human biomonitoring that investigates human exposure to different xenobiotics and both effects and susceptibility factors to such agents (Manno et al., 2010). Occupational risk related to professional tasks stems from unhealthy activities, whose nature, conditions or working methods, as well as control mechanisms on chemical, biological, physical and mechanical agents of the environment can cause adverse effects to the worker's health (Angerer et al., 2007; Manno et al., 2010). Human biomonitoring includes main three different levels of assessment: a) internal exposure: dosage of toxins and metabolites; b) biochemical effects, such as protein and DNA adducts; and c) biological effects, such as cytogenetic and immunological parameters. The individual habits and susceptibility can influence in each of those three levels' responses (Angerer et al., 2007).

Different approaches are used to assess the effects and risks of exposure to chemical, physical and biological agents during the working routine. Biomarker is a general term for specific measures of interaction between a biological system and an environmental agent (Manno et al., 2010). There are three classes of biomarkers widely used in occupational risk evaluations: a) biomarker of exposure; b) of effect; and c) of susceptibility. Biomarkers of exposure involve exogenous substances or its metabolites or the product of an interaction between a xenobiotic agent and some target cell or molecule. Among the most used biomarkers of exposure, it is possible to highlight the Comet assay that detect intercellular differences of DNA damage or repair in any eukaryotic cell population (Collins, 2004); and the PIXE technique, based on X-ray particle emission, identifying inorganic elements in biological samples (Da Silva, 2016; Kahl et al., 2016a, 2018a,b). Biomarkers of effect are biochemical, physiological or behavior or other alterations within the organism, which depending the extension, may be associated with a disease or a potential risk to develop it. The Micronucleus assay is a biomarker of effect related to mutagenicity (Fenech, 2007), and other examples of this kind of biomarker are hematological parameters and oxidative stress levels (Silins and Hogberg, 2011). Susceptibility biomarkers refer to an inherited or acquired ability of an organism in respond to exposure changes to specific xenobiotic substances (Bonassi and Au, 2002). Metabolizing or detoxification enzymes are a group of susceptibility biomarkers with a toxicokinetic mechanism for use in human studies (Manno et al., 2010).

It is important to note that biomarkers of exposure indicate the current exposure, the biomarkers of effect predict the current risk of pathologies, while the susceptibility biomarkers suggest the modifications of this risk. Assigning a marker to one or the other type sometimes depends on its toxicological significance and the context in which the test is being used (Manno et al., 2010). In this chapter, we will discuss the three biomarkers most used by our research group in the last years, along with results from other groups using the same or similar methods: Comet assay, Micronucleus Test and Telomere Length (TL) measurement. Additionally, we will approach the main susceptibility factors that may alter individual's response to the biomarkers used and exposure suffered. Finally, we will investigate the use of System Biology for connection of biomarkers of early effect to adverse outcomes as regard occupational risk concern.

Comet Assay

The Single Cell Gel Electrophoresis (SCGE) method, more commonly known as Comet assay, has been presented as one of the most complete genotoxicity screening method. The assay can detect single-strand DNA breaks, alkali labile sites, (apurinic/apyrimidic (AP) sites), crosslinks, and incomplete DNA repair sites in individual cells (Valverde and Rojas, 2009). It can be applied to cells *in vitro*, *in vivo*, in human biomonitoring (including occupational exposure), molecular epidemiology, ecogenotoxicity, among other applications (Collins, 2004; Moller, 2018).

The Comet assay allows the identification of intercellular differences to assess DNA damage and possible repair in virtually any population of eukaryotic cells, as well as in other organisms. The test is already used to assess DNA damage or repair in human leukocytes, salivary gland tissue, and buccal, colon, epithelial, brain and sperm cells, different cancer cell lines (such as HT29, LT97, HepG2), as well as plant cells, yeast cells and also *Drosophila melanogaster* (Glei et al., 2016). The Organization for Economic Co-operation and Development (OECD, 2014) has adopted test guidelines for the Comet assay in 2014 for *in vivo* mammalian evaluations. The assay is recognized worldwide and nowadays is the accepted method for human biomonitoring according to FDA and WHO guidelines (Singh, 2016).

The standard Comet assay detects different lesions that are converted to DNA strand breaks under the alkaline conditions of the assay (Moller, 2018). The test is based on the relaxation of DNA bound to the nuclear matrix after cell lysis and histone looseness by rupturing the single or double strand, allowing the DNA loop to be free to move to a halo around the nucleus. After suffering electrical current, in which the pH may differ in the used buffer, the damaged DNA is attracted to the anode and migrates providing an image similar to a "comet tail." A reasonable explanation of the appearance of this tail is that it consists of DNA loops which have relaxed supercoiling by virtue of to break. The result is to evaluate the tail through microscopy: when increasing the DNA breaking frequencies increases the amount of fragmented DNA outside the nucleus thus demonstrating the induced damage (Azqueta et al., 2014; Collins 2015).

In the Comet assay the DNA is visualized by microscopy after staining with dyes that bind to DNA. The most commonly used staining are silver nitrate ($AgNO_3$), ethidium bromide (EtBr) and 4,6-diamidino-2-phenylindole (DAPI). After staining, visualization of the comet cells can be through optical microscopy when silver nitrate is used, or by fluorescence microscopy when either EtBr or DAPI are the choice for coloring slides. For fluorescence analysis, a few software packages to choose from will compute fluorescence parameters for comets selected by the operator. The most commonly used parameters is percentage of DNA in tail. Evaluation of DNA damage is also possible without sophisticated imaging programs. The optical microscopy allows the human eye to be easily trained to discriminate degrees of damage according to the appearance of each comet. Comets can be marked visually and classified into five classes (from no damage = 0 to maximum damage = 4) according to tail size and shape. The damage index (DI) varies from 0 (totally intact or undetectable tails: 100 cells × 0) to 400 (with damage: 100 cells × 4); consequently, the total comet score (DI) will be between 0 and 400 arbitrary units. The damage frequency (DF) is calculated for each sample based on the number of cells with tail versus those without tail and is presented as percentage. Both DI and DF are parameters used to assess DNA damage (Collins, 2004; Collins et al., 2008). International guidelines and recommendations for the Comet assay consider that visual comet scoring is a well-validated assessment method. Additionally, there is equivalence of visual scoring and image analysis (Dusinska and Collins, 2008).

As the damages observed through the Comet test are the result of transient injuries, they may be amenable to repair. The repair processes form AP sites, which in turn are converted into DNA breaks for the removal of the oxidized bases. Thus, in order to obtain more specificity and sensitivity in the application of the Comet assay, protocols were developed for the use of DNA repair enzymes, since the sites generated serve as an enzymatic substrate. In this context, the assay can be considered a confirmatory biomarker of oxidative damage (Collins, 2014; Moller, 2018). The enzyme endonuclease III was the first incorporated in the assay, allowing the detection of single-strand breaks at sites of oxidized pyrimidines. The enzymes formamidopirimidina DNA glicosilase [FPG (detecting 8-oxoguanine and other purine oxidation products)], T4 endonuclease V (for UV-induced dimerized pyrimidines), Alk (dramatically increasing the yield of DNA breaks in cells treated with methylmethanesulphonate) and 8-oxoguanine glycosylase [hOGG1 (with a rather higher specificity for 8-oxoguanine)] were also included in adapted protocols for detection of their specific damage substrates (Azqueta et al., 2013; Collins, 2004; Collins et al., 2008). Mainly, such protocols include an incubation of the specific repair enzyme with samples slides after cell lysis step. The enzymes induce additional ruptures at oxidized base sites and increase DNA at the comet tail (Glei et al., 2016). To analyze the result of the Comet assay in parallel with the enzyme incubation, a slide is incubated only with buffer, and the score of that control slide is subtracted from the score of the enzyme to provide enzyme-sensitive sites (Benedetti et. al., 2018; Collins et al., 2008). The same experimental framework was developed to measure the DNA repair activity induced by plant extracts in human cells and animal tissues (Moller, 2018).

According to Moller (2018) the early 1990s marked the first study of biomonitoring in healthy subjects using the Comet assay, which showed no effect of age on the average level of DNA breaks, although older individuals had increase highly damaged cells. In the mid-1990s, the first study of occupational exposure (exposure to styrene in laminating workers) and environmental studies (air pollution) using the Comet assay were reported. It was also at that time that the first study with antioxidants and phytochemicals was presented. Comet assay presents a wide range of applicability, and it is an important tool in research related to the area of human and environmental biomonitoring (Tice et al., 2000; Valverde and Rojas, 2009). Different forms of environmental and occupational exposure can be evaluated, such as exposure of workers in the plastics, rubber, shoe, cigarette and pharmaceutical industries (Valverde and Rojas, 2009). In agreement, our research group develops monitoring involving occupational and environmental factors. We have evaluated the exposure of individuals to compounds such as coal, nicotine, pesticides (mainly complex mixtures of them) in different agricultural crops, using the Comet assay as a tool to assess DNA damage (Alves et al., 2016; Benedetti et al. 2018; Kahl et al., 2018a,b; Rohr et al., 2013a). The production of different crops leads to a large number of producers being exposed to different chemical compounds, as well as to complex mixtures thereof. One such crop is the production of soybeans, which according to Benedetti et al. (2018), involves the use of different pesticides for crop protection and pest control. This exposure may lead to serious toxicological consequences, as observed in rural workers exposed to these pesticides, allowing to explain the link between exposure to pesticides and adverse health outcomes. Through Comet assay performed with whole blood collected from producers exposed to soybean crop, Benedetti et al. (2018) found significant damage index in soybean farmers exposed to complex mixture of pesticides when compared to a non-exposed group. Exposure to pesticides can induce oxidative stress, increase lipid peroxidation and reduce antioxidant defenses (Mostafalou and Abdollahi, 2013). For the enzyme-modified Comet assay (hOGG1), authors observed induction of oxidation of purine nucleobases, including 8-oxoguanine (8-oxo-dG) (Collins et al., 2008).

Like soybeans, another class of workers who are routinely exposed to agrochemicals in complex mixtures are tobacco growers. To improve crop quality and productivity, farmers apply pesticides (insecticides, herbicides, fungicides and plant growth regulators) on tobacco plants. In this culture the workers' contact with the leaves of the plant provides the absorption of organic and inorganic pesticides, as well as a high concentration of nicotine, which is a natural pesticide produced by the tobacco plant (Alves et al., 2016; Da Silva et al., 2010; Kahl et al., 2016a, 2018a,b). According Kahl et al. (2018a,b) the effects of pesticide mixtures can be more genotoxic and cause greater risks to exposed populations than individual pesticides, thereby increasing concern about their impact on human health. In the study conducted by Alves et al. (2016), whole blood samples were collected from tobacco farmers exposed to pesticides. Samples were analyzed through the Comet assay and the results demonstrated a significant (about threefold) increase in DI and DF in the exposed group compared to a non-exposed group. Another study with tobacco growers was developed by Kahl et al. (2018a). Farmers who reported being involved in spraying/handling pesticides for at least 5 years were considered occupationally exposed. The results showed that occupational exposure to pesticides and nicotine from tobacco plants was significantly associated with increased DNA damage index. Authors also observed that the years of exposure is an important factor contributing to the increase in levels of genomic damage in occupationally exposed group (Kahl et al., 2018a).

In Italy, between the provinces of Bari and Taranto, a study evaluated the exposure of agricultural workers to pesticides. In this region the relevant agricultural production is based on vegetables, grapes and olive trees. Samples collected from the exposed workers and from an unexposed group were evaluated through the Comet assay. Using lymphocyte cells, the results demonstrated increased DNA damage in the agricultural workers group (Intranuovo et al., 2018). Farmworkers of different crops (vegetables, orchards, cotton, rice and wheat) from various districts of Punjab, India, participated in a survey to assess DNA damage from spray application of pesticides (Kaur et al., 2011). Through the Comet assay, from blood samples, the results showed significant DNA damage in the producers exposed to pesticides. A second sample was collected from some workers followed up; this collection was at low or no spray time, and a significant decrease in the frequency of damaged cells was observed in comparison with the first samples of newly exposed workers. The decrease in DNA damage in matched cases could be attributed to three independent physiological processes: repair of DNA damage, elimination of cells due to the death of highly damaged cells or dilution of cells carrying DNA damage by the production of undamaged lymphocytes from stem cells. Comet assay is more efficient in detecting continuous exposure than an accumulation of exposure. No relationship between DNA damage and exposure time was observed (Kaur et al., 2011).

One study evaluated the possible genotoxic effects of occupational exposure to lead in workers in a factory, divided into two distinct parts of production, in Portugal. They used both traditional Comet assay and endonuclease-modified Comet assay (hOGG1). The results demonstrated genotoxicity of lead. They showed that the oxidative stress induced by exposure to lead causes lipid peroxidation, an increase in the activity of antioxidant enzymes, but did not observe a significant difference in the analysis for oxidative damage between exposed and control groups. However, they were able to evaluate a significant difference in oxidative damage among those exposed in the two distinct parts of the plant, suggesting that the type of activity developed is related to oxidative DNA damage (García-Lestón et al., 2014).

Our research group has also used Comet assay for occupational exposure to other agents than pesticides. Rohr et al. (2013a) investigated the potential genotoxic effect of coal in open pit workers. The results demonstrated a genotoxic and mutagenic effect of exposure to coal in miners, and the damage done to both damage index and damage frequency showed increases indicating DNA damage. The authors further suggest that DNA damage may be associated with increased inorganic elements, such as magnesium, aluminum, copper and zinc (Rohr et al., 2013a). Footwear-workers were also evaluated by our research group, as they are exposed to complex mixtures of solvents, besides glues, primers and degreasers. Comet assay could detect increase in DNA damage for workers, which was associated to a risk genotype of GSTP1 gene, from detoxification pathway (Heuser et al. 2007). The test was also sensible enough to identify higher levels of DNA damage in footwear-workers exposed to solvent-based adhesives than those to water-based adhesives (Heuser et al., 2005).

Valverde and Rojas (2009) reviewed data from 122 studies that employed the assay for human biomonitoring. The review evaluated environmental and occupational exposures and the levels of DNA damage in cells of individuals exposed to different agents as complex mixtures. This review demonstrated the high concordance of Comet assay results with cytogenetic assays conducted in parallel, the negative results obtained in the absence of genotoxins, and the ability of the Comet assay to detect low levels of DNA damage in different cell types (blood cells, nasal, buccal, tear duct epithelial cells, rectum cells), as well as the importance of the need to establish standard methodological conditions that affect DNA damage indexes. Given the available data, it is valid to say that Comet assay is recognized worldwide. The test has highly applicability in many areas of research, such as a predictive test of genotoxicity and widely used in human and environmental biomonitoring, as shown recently in an international workshop of Comet assay (Koppen et al., 2017). It is an ally for assessing genetic damage and even with more than 30 years of use, it is an innovative technique and still has much to offer as it is a method that is always being improved.

Micronucleus Test

The Micronucleus test for human biomonitoring is a cytogenetic assay developed by Fenech and Morley (1985). The test is used as a chromosomal instability biomarker, based on the identification and counting of cells with one or more micronuclei. The micronucleus is an additional nucleus separate from the cell main nucleus, consisting of chromosomal fragments or whole chromosomes that were not included in the main nucleus during mitosis. The micronucleus may originate due to a modification of the chromosomal structures or mitotic spindle faults during the telophase (Fenech et al., 2011a). Increased micronucleus frequency has been associated with several types of pathologies, such as cancer (Bonassi et al., 2007), neurodegenerative (Coppedè and Migliore, 2015) and cardiovascular diseases (Simon and Vijayakumar, 2013), diabetes (Corbi et al., 2014) and Down syndrome (Bolognesi et al., 2015). Micronuclei frequency is a predictive biomarker of cancer risk in healthy populations, as seen in a database study where medium and high frequencies of MN showed significant increase in all cancers incidence, beyond a decrease in cancer-free survival (Bonassi et al., 2007). This may be due to a characteristic feature of MN: sensitivity to identify mutagens, i.e., MN are not to be repaired anymore. With the establishment of the nuclear abnormality, genomic instability is increased, leading to higher probability of tumorigenesis (Bonassi et al., 2007).

In addition, it has been considered a simple and sensitive test, enabling the use of different cell types and tissues, such as lymphocytes, oral and nasal mucosa, bladder cells, among others (Dahl et al., 2011). The MN test in bladder cells is able to identify as many parameters as oral and lymphocytes settings and may also be useful as a diagnostic tool for detection and prognosis of bladder cancer. Although the system test has achieved an improved protocol (Nersesyan et al., 2014), it still remains less used than MN test in lymphocytes and oral cells in occupational exposures, most likely due to its difficult access and logistic as regarding sample collection. The use of nasal mucosa, on the other hand, is quite promising due to its very non-invasive approach. However, as this system is still new to the area, further standardization of experimental protocols is required (Knasmueller et al., 2011).

During cell division by mitosis, the separation of the sister chromatids occurs in the anaphase, and fragments derived from breaks or loss of entire chromosomes that are not bound to the spindle, will not peel off to the poles of the cell during migration. Thus, during karyokinesis in telophase phase, the whole chromosome or its fragments will not be included in the nuclei of the daughter cells, leading to the formation of one or more micronuclei (Fenech, 2007). Micronucleus test is widely used in toxicological genetics studies *in vitro* and *in vivo*, as it allows evaluating the genotoxicity caused by spontaneous or induced damages. The presence of a whole chromosome in MN can occur when the xenobiotic causes defects in the mitotic machinery or at the centromere. However, the formation of MN by acenteric fragments can be induced by chemicals that compromise the phosphodiester backbone of DNA, inhibit DNA repair mechanisms and/or cause DNA replication stress (Fenech et al., 2016a). The Micronucleus test itself is not able to detect if the origin of the micronucleus occurred by chromosomal breaks or whole chromosomes. Therefore, in some studies the use of centromeric (Hovhannisyan et al., 2016) and/or telomeric DNA probes (Kanagaraj et al., 2017) are useful for this distinction. Centromeric probes determine the frequency of centromere, while telomeric probes demarcate the proximal and distal ends of the chromosome (sub-telomeric and telomeric regions) possibly found in micronuclei (Kus et al., 2017).

The Micronucleus Test in peripheral blood lymphocytes, called Cytokinesis-block micronucleus Cytome assay (CBMN) is a simple and commonly used test in biomonitoring of genotoxic agents. The test can be applied both *in vitro*, for the analysis of physical and chemical substances, and *in vivo*, for population monitoring (Fenech, 2007). Lymphocytes are cells produced by the bone marrow, which have a defense activity in the body. Because they have the ability to circulate through various organs and have a long-life span, lymphocytes have been one of the preferred cells for the Micronucleus Test in humans (Bonassi et al., 2007). In order for micronucleus to form, the cells must pass through at least one mitotic division, so the CBMN has been improved with the use of cytochalasin B for a blockade of cytokinesis. Cytochalasin B acts by inhibiting the polymerization of actin, preventing the formation of the ring of microfilaments and the separation of the daughter cells after mitosis (Kazimirova et al., 2012). Thereby, the cell division is blocked after telophase, with an accumulation of binucleated cells in the G1 phase, thus guaranteeing at least one cell division (Annangi et al., 2016; Hintzsche et al., 2018). CBMN allows the evaluation of other nuclear abnormalities, beyond MN, such as nucleoplasmic bridge (NPB), nuclear bud (NBUD), apoptosis and necrosis. NPB is used as a biomarker for genomic instability and is formed by the binding of the nuclei of a binucleate cell. The emergence of NPB can occur for a number of reasons, for example, chromosomal rearrangements involving more than one centromere, chromatids migrating to opposite poles during anaphase, and final fusions of telomeres following a double strand break of DNA. The mechanisms of NBUD formation are still uncertain, but may be related to gene amplification, in which the amplified DNA is deleted from the nucleus during the S phase of the cell cycle, thus forming a budding structure attached to main nucleus (Fenech, 2007; Mesic and Nefic, 2014).

The CBMN has been used in several studies of occupational exposure, as shown by a recent special issue of Mutation Research journal (In Vivo Chemical Genotoxin Exposure and DNA Damage in Humans measured using the lymphocyte Cytokinesis-Block Micronucleus Assay Edited by Siegfried Knasmueller, Armen Nersesyan, Michael Fenech. Volume 770, Part A, Pages 1-216 [October–December 2016]). Fourteen systematic reviews from a scientific effort using the same criteria for analyzing micronuclei induction in lymphocytes as biomarker for DNA damage induced during human exposure to chemicals validated the CBMN in lymphocytes. All systematic reviews found consistent increases of MN frequencies in exposed subjects versus controls in all genotoxic compounds of chemicals groups investigated (Kirsch-Volders et al., 2018). Exposure to anesthetic gases (Vodicka et al., 2016) and cytostatic / antineoplastic drugs (Villarini et al., 2016) showed increasing in MN frequencies, although only in 62% of studies in the review of Villarini et al. (2016). Metals are recognized DNA stability disruptors. Exposure to Pb, Hg, Ar and Cr show agreement of MN increasing with other genomic instability endpoints (Annangi et al., 2016; Nersesyan et al., 2016). Although Cd is a clear tumorigenic xenobiotic, induction of chromosomal damage is still under scrutiny, as well as Ni and Va, due to lack of strong correlations (Annangi et al., 2016; Nersesyan et al., 2016). Butadiene exposure is highly associated with leukemia emergence (Bolognesi and Kirsch-Volders, 2016), while ethylene oxide is a Class I carcinogen (Ghosh and Godderis, 2016), but both chemicals have inconclusive results as regard MN frequencies (Bolognesi and Kirsch-Volders, 2016; Ghosh and Godderis, 2016). Such outcome is also true for nanomaterials, for which the tissue and cellular targets are still not clear and, therefore, their results for MN are contradictory (Gonzalez and Kirsch-Volders, 2016). On the other hand, CBMN appears to be an excellent tool for human occupational exposure to (a) formaldehyde, a Class I carcinogen as well, in which 62% of reviewed studies showed increased MN associated with formaldehyde concentration (Fenech et al., 2016b); (b) styrene, with all reviewed studies showing mutagenicity (Costa et al., 2016); (c) airborne particles, such as dusts and asbestos (Bonassi et al., 2016); (d) polycyclic aromatic hydrocarbons, for individuals working in cove oven, aluminum industry, rubber factory, road construction, and airport workers, regardless gender and smoking habit (Sram et al., 2016); (e) pesticides, for which authors found positive findings between the occupational exposure and MN increasing in 74% of reviewed studies (Bolognesi and Holland, 2016); and (f) miscellaneous chemicals (Da Silva, 2016).

Micronucleus test in buccal cells, mainly known as buccal micronucleus Cytome assay (BMCyt) is also considered a simple and less expensive technique. However, its more relevant characteristic is to be minimally invasive. The oral mucosa is formed by a stratified squamous epithelium that has high vascularization and absorption capacity. Its rate of division and cellular propensity determines its capacity of regeneration. Oral mucosa cells are in constant contact with ingested and inhaled toxic substances, making them useful as a biomarker of genotoxic events (Thomas and Fenech, 2011). To obtain the cells a scraping of the oral mucosa is done at right and left sides of inner cheeks with the aid of a brush. Subsequently, these cells are 'washed' in an inert substance for disposal of debris. Fixation and staining of slides may be done by different techniques and dyes, such as Giemsa (Antoniazzi et al., 2018) and Feulgen-Fast-Green (Li et al., 2018). Afterwards, the slides are analyzed microscopically, in duplicates. Usually, 1500 cells are analyzed in each slide, being 1000 referring to cellular damage and 500 to cell death (Bolognesi et al., 2013; Thomas et al., 2009).

The BMCyt assay allows the evaluation of proliferative potential, cytokinetic defects, DNA damage and cell death (Bolognesi et al., 2017). In order to evaluate the proliferative potential, normal basal cells are counted, allowing the study of regenerative capacity of the epithelial tissue (Thomas et al., 2009). Defects of cytokinesis are evaluated by means of binucleated cells which have two major nuclei due to a failed cytokinesis in the last nuclear division (Bolognesi et al., 2015). Thomas et al. (2009) says that the identification of cytokinetic defects helps to determine regenerative capacity and genomic instability, and such factors may be associated with early aging and Alzheimer's disease. DNA damage is assessed by MN and NBUD frequencies, similar to what is seen in CBMN. Additionally, the broken-egg cells found in BMCyt have been associated with gene amplification, although their origin is quite unclear. Cell death evaluation is achieved by the frequency of condensed chromatin, karyorrhectic, pyknotic and karyolitic cells, which are representatives of early stage of apoptosis, late stage, early maturation and epithelial death, and last stage of cell death, respectively. (Benvindo-Souza et al., 2017; Yang et al., 2017).

In human biomonitoring studies BMCyt has been used to evaluate exposure to various substances. Exposure to wood dust (Bruschweiler et al., 2014) and anesthetics drugs (Souza et al., 2016) lead mainly to increase in cytotoxicity, i.e., cell death parameters. Ladeira et al. (2013) observed increase in all cell parameters evaluated by BMCyt in workers exposed to formaldehyde, in association with some metabolism gene polymorphisms. Complex mixtures of substances used in road construction increased MN frequency in buccal cells (Çelik et al., 2013), which was similar to what Singh et al. (2013) observed in individuals exposed to lead, in addition to higher frequencies of binucleated cells as well. Open-cast coal miners showed elevated levels of basal cells, MN and binucleated cells, showing changes in cellular division, most likely due to oxidative stress generation (Rohr et al., 2013b). Also related to oxidative damage generation, soybean workers had increased frequencies of MN, NBUD and cell death due to exposure to mixtures of pesticides (Benedetti et al., 2018). Tobacco farmers showed exacerbated MN, NBUD and binucleated buccal cells with increased levels of oxidative parameters. Additionally, polymorphisms of organophosphate metabolism (PON1) and of oxidative balance (SOD2) influenced on frequencies of MN and NBUD (Kahl et al., 2018b).

However, in human biomonitoring studies, in addition to the chemical substances themselves, some variables should be taken into account when analyzing genomic instability, such as age, sex, smoking habit and time of exposure. Da Silva (2016) reports that a higher frequency of MN occurs with age, because with aging there is a decrease in cellular functions leading to an accumulation of genetic damage. Nefic and Handzic (2013) found that the frequency of MN in females is higher than in males. Pradeep et al. (2014) identified more MN in smokers when compared to nonsmokers, however, the relationship between smoking and MN frequency is still uncertain (Bonassi et al., 2003). In addition, in some studies the dose-effect relationship has been observed in relation to the time of exposure to chemical substances (reviewed by Da Silva, 2016; Mrdjanović et al., 2014).

Occupational exposure to genotoxic and/or mutagenic substances may increase the production of reactive oxygen species (ROS) and/or damage to the mitotic spindle, causing an accumulation of genetic defects that may trigger dysregulation of cellular homeostasis, leading to mutations, chromosomal changes and DNA damage. Such genetic defects can trigger the formation of a MN, so the Micronucleus test has the ability to detect a cell with a chromosomal defect, making it a good biomarker of occupational exposure (Bolognesi and Holland, 2016). An international collaboration project on CBMN and BMCyt, involving over 30 laboratories worldwide, represents the high applicability and reproducibility of the test (Fenech et al., 2011b). Therefore, the micronucleus assay, in its both applications, is a simple, reproducible, effective and highly sensitive test in detecting fixed damage. In addition, it allows the evaluation in different cell types of several parameters related to DNA damage. Those aspects justify its worldwide application as a test used in evaluation of genotoxicity and mutagenicity of substances and environmental and human biomonitoring.

TELOMERE LENGTH IN OCCUPATIONAL EXPOSURE

Human telomeres are nucleoproteins structures composed by tandem double-strand arrays of $(TTAGGG)_n$ that protect the ends of linear chromosomes (Zakian, 2012). The telomeric DNA repeat unit ends in a single-strand (ss) 3' G-rich overhand, bound by the shelterin complex, which comprises the proteins TRF1, TRF2, POT1, TIN2, TPP1 and RAP1 (de Lange, 2002). The ss-3' overhang is able to loop back on itself and hacking into proximal repeats on the same telomere, forming then telomere-loops (t-loop), a lariat-form structure (Griffith et al., 1999). T-loops and shelterin prevents DNA damage responses (DDR) pathways at telomeres by sequestering the telomere DNA ends and protects telomeres from DNA repair by non-homologous end-joining (NHEJ), homologous recombination (HR) and end resection (Lazzerini-Denchi and Sfeir, 2016). In normal human somatic cells, telomeres shorten approximately 200 base pairs (bp) in each round of cell division, due to the end-replication problem – a limitation harbored by the replication machinery to replicate the end of linear DNA molecules (Harley et al., 1990). Therefore, human population displays significant telomere length (TL) heterogeneity, but an overall decrease in TL is observed with increasing age.

Mild dysfunctions in TL are associated with risk factor to a range of diseases, such as cardiovascular diseases, diabetes mellitus, obesity, and cancer (Kong et al., 2013). These adverse health effects are directly linked to cellular proliferative deficiencies caused by early telomere shortening. When telomeres become critically short they initiate a telomere-specific DDR, resulting in a state of permanent cell cycle arrest known as senescence (Kaul et al., 2012). Overstep of senescence results in disastrous telomere shortening, i.e., telomere crisis, which culminates in widespread genomic instability. Escape from crisis requires activation of telomere maintenance mechanism (TMM), which may happen to activation of telomerase or triggering of alternative lengthening of telomeres (Lee et al., 2014), to oppose telomere shortening and thus achieve cellular immortality (Harley, 1991). Hence telomeres are widely accepted having a tumor-suppressive role by limiting the number of cell divisions a cell can undergo (Reddel, 2010).

Only recently the discussion as if TL may be a prospective biomarker for occupational exposures have arisen: the first relevant published study is dated from 2009, in which authors observed shorter TL in traffic officers exposed to traffic pollution (Hoxha et al., 2009). It is still not well defined if TL may be a biomarker for exposure or effect, as both longer and shorter telomeres are indicative of genomic instability (Aviv et al., 2017) and the dynamics involving their shortening or elongation may represent different effects of xenobiotics.

In biomonitoring studies, the use of TL as a biomarker of occupational exposure has been done mainly by quantitative polymerase chain reaction (qPCR; Zhang et al., 2013), which demands low amounts of DNA, is high throughput, but provides a relative telomere content by telomere amplification compared to a single copy gene, in oppose to absolute or specific TL. Methods such as Micronucleus assay (Eshkoor et al., 2013; Pavanello et al., 2010, 2013; Zheng et al., 2017), Comet assay (Eshkoor et al., 2013; Ko et al., 2017), global DNA or specific site methylation (Li et al., 2015; Li et al., 2016; Pavanello et al., 2010, 2013; Wang et al., 2015; Wong et al., 2014) and telomerase expression (Pawlas et al., 2016) may be used by researchers to support the evidence of exposure effect or to provide a mechanistic explanation for telomere shortening. Telomere dysfunction is usually accompanied by increased genomic instability, which is confirmed in several studies approached here through observed higher levels of micronuclei (Eshkoor et al., 2010, 2013; Kahl et al., 2018b, c; Ko et al., 2017; Pavanello et al., 2010, 2013; Zeljezic et al., 2015; Zheng et al., 2017) and comet cells (Eshkoor et al., 2010, 2013; Kahl et al., 2018a,b). Occupational exposure to polycyclic aromatic hydrocarbons (PAHs; Pavanello et al., 2010, 2013) and vinyl chloride monomer (VCM; Zheng et al., 2017) had an inversely association between micronuclei frequencies and TL. Comet cells were not significantly different between controls and welders exposed to particulate matter and had no association with TL (Ko et al., 2017), which may be explained by a DDR activation. Comet cells are a biomarker of exposure mainly because one of its characteristics is to be liable of repair (Collins, 2004). A remarkable study on occupational exposure and TL dynamics was conducted with agricultural workers exposed to 17 different pesticides, in which authors found longer TL and higher levels of nucleoplasmatic bridges (NPB) in workers, although no correlation between the two abnormalities was observed (Zeljezic et al., 2015). Interestingly, the arising of NPB is one of the cytogenetic mechanisms by which telomeres go under the breakage-fusion-bridge cycle (Fenech et al., 2011a) and the absence of relation between them may indicate that NPBs are a mechanism of only telomere shortening but no elongation.

For many years, TL was almost exclusively linked to aging (López-Otín et al., 2013). Although at this moment telomeres are recognized as a largely non-coding structure that affects many more biological process, its relationship with aging still remains. In occupational studies, this association is not strong enough: up to this moment, only two studies observed an inverse association of TL with age for individuals exposed to automotive chemicals (Eshkoor et al., 2010) and N-nitrosamines at rubber industry (Li et al., 2011). It is possible that the small number of participants may be a reason for this outcome. As the studies reviewed here used mainly qPCR, which provides an average of TL for individuals evaluated, it would be necessary bigger groups to observe such differences. However, the occupational exposure itself can change telomere dynamics *per se*, implying that what is expected to happen in normal somatic cells may not be happening in challenged biological samples of individuals occupationally exposed to xenobiotics. This hypothesis is supported by the work of Bin et al. (2011) which observed shorter TL associated with increasing age only for control individuals, while Kahl et al. (2016a) found this same correlation when both control and exposed groups were analyzed together, probably counterbalancing the genotoxic effects of pesticides on farmers' TL.

At the same time, both years of work and level of exposure seems to be a substantial factor for TL changes. A dose-response was found between shorten TL and increased levels of exposure to lead (Pb; Pawlas et al., 2016), N-nitrosamines (Li et al., 2011) and traffic pollution (Hoxha et al., 2009). In battery manufacturing industry, where workers are exposed to Pb routinely, TL was shortened only for those with abnormal Pb levels (Wu et al., 2012).

Lead is a recognized contaminant that, even in low doses, may affect public health and the environment. However, the more substantial influence on TL observed in occupational exposure studies is related to time/years of exposure. For particulate matter (PM) exposure, steel workers and welders had shortened TL in every follow-up (Dioni et al., 2011; Wong et al., 2014). This outcome was more significant to the prior months of blood collection than to distant past evaluations (Wong et al., 2014). Although PMs are cumulative in humans, this result suggest that the damage to telomeres was more consistent with short-term than long-term effects. Welders from another study also showed reduced TL in every year of work at welding fumes (Li et al., 2015), which was also observed in coke-oven workers occupationally exposed to PAH (Pavanello et al., 2010, 2013). A lifetime exposure to radiation (Andreassi et al., 2015) showed shorter TL for catheterization laboratory workers, while lifetime exposure to pesticides was associated to both longer or shorter TL, depending on the pesticide evaluated (Andreotti et al., 2015; Hou et al., 2013).

Telomeres function may be modified by epigenetic alterations, such as methylation, phosphorylation and ubiquitination (Grace et al., 2016). Both global DNA methylation and gene-specific methylation were evaluated in occupational studies along with TL (Kahl et al., 2018a,c; Li et al., 2016; Pavanello et al., 2010, 2013; Wong et al., 2014). Hairdressers showed CDKN2A gene-specific hypomethylation associated with even shorter TL when in this condition. CDKN2A is a gene highly linked to bladder cancer, which is a malignancy frequented observed in hairdressers (Li et al., 2016). The DNA methylation of LINE-1 and Alu repetitive elements showed a dose-response of positive correlation between them and TL in boilermakers occupationally exposed to metals (Wong et al., 2014). Recent research suggests that metals can influence gene expression through epigenetic mechanisms, assigning a severe complexity of metal-mediated gene expression (Cheng et al., 2012). In tobacco farmers, individuals who had p16 hypermethylated had also shorter telomeres than non-hypermethylayed p16 ones (Kahl et al., 2018a). The p16 gene is a tumor suppressor that plays an important role in cell cycle progression by decelerating the transition between G1 to S phase (Rayess et al., 2012). Similar to such results, both p53 hypomethylation and lower expression of p21 were linked to TL changes in exposures to PAH (Pavanello et al., 2010, 2013) and omeothane (Duan et al., 2017).

The main mechanism that seems to influence TL and genomic instability in occupational exposure is oxidative stress generation. Mainly, excessive reactive oxygen species (ROS) formation is a biological reaction to which telomeres are highly susceptible (Fouquerel et al., 2016). The main reason is the G rich content of telomere sequences, presumably putting them as a major target for 8-oxo-7,8-dihydro-2'-deoxyguanosine (8-oxo-dG), the most common oxidative DNA base damage (Melis et al., 2013). Exposure to Pb (Pawlas et al., 2016) and pesticides at tobacco fields (Kahl et al., 2016a, 2018a,b) were shown to increase levels of oxidative stress, while reducing TL in workers. More than that, oxidative stress was negatively associated with TL in Pb occupational exposure (Pawlas et al., 2016). Ko et al. (2017) found increasing in malondialdehyde (MDA) in steel workers occupationally exposed to PM, while in welding fume workers, also exposed to PM, there was no difference in 8-oxo-dG between workers and control group (Li et al., 2015). Interestingly, the first work observed marginally shorter TL in the exposed group (Ko et al., 2017). In the second work, although authors did not observe differences in TL between groups, every work year of exposure to PM reduced TL, even after age-adjustment (Li et al., 2015). A recent review thou show that the link between oxidative stress exacerbation and telomere shortening seems to be tissue-dependent or narrowed to some categories, such as gender or age-dependent (Reichert and Stier, 2017). The effect of PAHs on telomeres was more outstanding in men than women (Bin et al., 2011), which was also true for individuals exposed to ionizing radiation in a plutonium production facility (Scherthan et al., 2016). A systematic review and meta-analysis of 36 cohorts showed that on average females have longer telomeres than males (Gardner et al., 2014). However, most studies available in literature present controversy results in this aspect, and occupational exposure may play an additional role in potential differences between genders' telomere dynamics.

Interestingly, the studies reviewed here have evaluated TL in occupational exposure to xenobiotics that are recognized ROS disruptors.

ROS can alter chromosomal DNA, leading to genomic instability, and may work as signaling molecules that affect cell proliferation, survival, metabolism, angiogenesis and metastasis (Wu et al., 2012), leading to stimulation of immune system. Shorter TL, even after age-adjusted, were observed in individuals exposed to polychlorinated biphenyls (PCBs) in a recycling company, associated with inhibition of telomerase in a dose-dependent manner (Ziegler et al., 2017). Authors also observed changes in T cell proliferation in these workers, suggesting that telomere shortening due to exposure to PCBs may lead to limitations of cell renewal (Ziegler et al., 2017), mainly by inducing cellular senescence. This hypothesis is supported by the idea that naïve T cells diversity reaches its proliferation limit through telomere attrition in elderly individuals (Gill et al., 2018).

In general, only a few studies found longer telomeres in occupational exposures to xenobiotics, while the majority observes shortened TL in occupational stress. The most reliable explanation may be the mechanism by which the exposure agent is acting on telomeres. In this aspect, only one study stated influence of blood PCBs levels on telomerase inhibition in T cells (Ziegler et al., 2017), and the potential TMM for longer telomeres in occupational exposure was not assessed in the remaining works. Telomere biology opens a plethora of possibilities as regard its use as indicative of an individual or groups of individuals' health. There is long way to go on the occupational exposure risk field when it comes to use TL as a biomarker but is already possible to stablish TL as a reliable biomarker mainly for xenobiotics where there are more studies and more concise results, such as pesticides and PAHs exposures, for instance.

Factors of Variability in the Individual's Response

Many inter-individual variables and lifestyle habits, such as, gender, age, smoking status, alcohol consumption, hours of sleep and dietary intake, can influence in the effects of occupational exposure that result on genomic and epigenetic instability (Fenech and Bonassi, 2011). In addition to these more obvious variables, the features of genetic susceptibility involving genes of metabolism and damage repair are also shown to play a role in incorporate harmfulness (da Silva et al., 2008; Rohr et al., 2011). Therefore, human inter-individual variability is a source of uncertainty in occupational risk assessment.

Evidences shows that MN frequency tend to be greater in females relative to males. A meta-analysis confirmed the statistical significance and consistency of this observation (Bonassi et al., 2001). The increase in MN frequency in females can be accounted for by the greater tendency of the X chromosome to be lost as a MN compared to other chromosomes, and to the fact that females have two copies of the X chromosome compared to only one in males (Norppa and Falck 2003). The study of Guo et al. (2014) with workers exposed to PAH shows that women workers had higher levels of urinary monohydroxylated PAH metabolites (OH-PAHs) and plasma benzo[a]pyrene-r-7, t-8, t-9,c-10-tetrahydotetrol-albumin (BPDE-Alb) adducts then men workers. It was also demonstrated that, after adjustment for working years and passive-smoking, women workers consistently showed significantly higher levels of urinary 8OHdG and 8-iso-PGF2a, as well as higher lymphocyte MN frequencies. No significant association was found between gender and Comet assay, BMCyt assay and cholinesterase activity for soybean farmers exposed to pesticides (Benedetti et al., 2013). Interestingly, in opposition to MN, females tend to have longer telomeres than males, according to a meta-analysis carried out by Gardner et al. (2014) from 36 cohorts involving 36,230 participants.

The effects of ageing on MN in lymphocytes was recognized in the mid-1980s (Fenech and Morley, 1985). Since then, several international laboratories have consistently shown that MN frequencies increase steadily with age in both sexes (Fenech and Bonassi, 2011; Rohr et al., 2011). The increase of MN with age is likely due to a cumulative effect of acquired mutations in genes involved in DNA repair, chromosome segregation and cell cycle checkpoint, besides the combination with unhealthy lifestyle. However, Benedetti et al. (2013) found no significant results for age in terms of the different parameters of Comet assay and BMCyt assay for pesticide-exposed population. In Sinitsky et al. (2016), the correlation coefficient for age and nuclear division index and cells with different number of nucleus in coal miners was also not significant. The reduction of telomere length and the increase in % of DNA methylation were related to aging in coal workers (Souza et al., 2018). Telomeres have been shown to shorten faster due to exogenous influence. Many different research groups have approached TL biology and change in its dynamics as regard human diet (Cassidy et al., 2010; Freitas-Simões et al., 2016), lifestyle habits (Astuti et al., 2017; Dimauro et al., 2017; Latifovic et al., 2016; Puterman et al., 2010), psychological stress (Puterman et al., 2010; Shalev et al., 2013) and to environmental and occupational exposures (reviewed by Kahl and Da Silva, 2016). Over the last decade, many international research groups have been testing TL as a general prognostic marker of aging and disease (Gorenjak et al., 2018). Since telomere biology is out of question associated with ageing, Müezzinler et al. (2013) performed a systematic review of leukocyte TL and age in adults. Five longitudinal studies reviewed by them found TL to decrease with age, while for the 124 cross-sectional studies, different results were observed according to their aim and scope. In most cases, however, even when not statistically significant, there was an inverse correlation between ageing and TL (Müezzinler et al., 2013).

In a review on the genotoxicity of pesticides, Bolognesi (2003) found that different studies supported a positive association between years of work and chromosome aberration and MN frequencies. Kahl et al. (2018a) observed that DNA damage, detected by the Comet assay, increase as the years of working in tobacco fields. On the other hand, there are studies that do not show influence of the period of service in the parameters of genotoxicity analysis, such as Rohr et al. (2013b) found no association with BMCyt parameters, and Sinitsky et al. (2016) on the cytogenetic markers frequency and the index of cell proliferation, both in coal workers. Benedetti et al. (2013) also found no correlation for exposure time in terms of different parameters of Comet assay and BMCyt assay in soybean workers. Other studies support this outcome, demonstrating no relationship between years of work and DNA damage (Da Silva et al., 2010; Da Silva et al., 2012a; Paiva et al., 2011). Kahl et al. (2016a) assessed a broad range of lengths of tobacco working time, from 8 months to 60 years, and found no correlation between absolute telomere length and years of work on tobacco fields. When TL was analyzed based on years of work in individuals occupationally exposed to different xenobiotics (Eshkoor et al., 2012; Li et al., 2016; Pavanello et al., 2010), no statistical relationship was found for increasing exposure time and shorter TL.

Sleeping properly is a recognized lifestyle habit that may influence human activities, welfare and health in general (Bannai and Tamakoshi, 2014; Kumar, 2008). Huang et al. (2009) evaluated the effect of sleeping hours habit in a study conducted among 208 healthy adults (19–59 years) male Japanese hard-metal workers. Lifestyle quality was strongly negatively associated with MN frequency in cultured human lymphocytes. Nutritional imbalance, lack of regular exercise (<2 times per week), insufficient sleep (<6 h per day) and overtime working (>9 h per day) each contributed significantly to higher MN frequencies (Huang et al., 2009). Perceived stress and psychopathology had also been linked to changes in telomere length. A meta-analysis comprising over 19,000 participants showed significant results of the association between anxiety and telomere shortening (Malouff and Schuttle, 2017). Fujishiro et al. (2013) found no evidence of TL been affected by employment status, work category or job stress. On the other hand, women working long-term full-time had shorter TL in a study with 608 individuals in the Sister Study (Parks et al., 2011), while individuals with perceived severe exhaustion at work showed shorter TL than the ones with no exhaustion, even after adjustment to social statuses and lifestyle habits (Ahola et al., 2012).

The choice and the amount of foods and supplements intake have a strong influence on the cellular concentration of micronutrients required as cofactors in DNA synthesis and repair. Enzymes and proteins involved in these processes and in chromosome segregation require micronutrients either as a substrate or as a cofactor or as an integral part of the enzyme. Nutrition is a complex aspect of environmental exposure that varies between individuals and communities depending on food choices, cultural aspects or availability. Therefore, the impact of dietary patterns and multi-nutrient supplements will depend on the effect of a nutrient and its impact on the various DNA metabolism pathways. Studies in humans have shown that MN frequency in lymphocytes and telomere maintenance are significantly associated with either dietary intake levels or plasma concentration of folate, vitamin B12, riboflavin, biotin, pantothenate, beta-carotene, vitamin E, nicotinic acid retinol and calcium (reviewed by Bull and Fenech, 2008). Several studies have demonstrated that intake of fruits and vegetables can protect DNA from damage caused by xenobiotics (Franke et al., 2005; Nunes et al., 2011). In a study with 2284 females, telomere length was associated with fibers intake, while inversely associated with polyunsaturated fatty acid intake and waist circumference (Cassidy et al., 2010). Kahl et al. (2018c) observed a correlation between telomere length and intake of lipids, while inverted correlation with fibers intake in individuals occupationally exposed to pesticides at tobacco fields. Dietary antioxidants and consumption of antioxidant-rich, plants-derived foods, adherence to Mediterranean diet (Freitas-Simões et al., 2016) and the use of multivitamins (reviewed by Kahl and Da Silva, 2016) can help to maintain stable and functional telomeres.

Studies that have investigated the association of alcoholism and its genotoxic effects found that this consumption is associated with higher MN frequency (Ishikawa et al., 2007; Kim et al., 2005; Maffei et al., 2002). Occupational exposure to manganese can lead to a dose-dependent increase of liver enzyme concentrations and interact with alcohol drinking to potentially aggravate the liver damage (Deng et al., 2013). Manganese induces neurotoxicity through ROS generation and genotoxicity (Bornhorst et al., 2013). Correlation between alcohol drinking and DNA damage was not found in individuals exposed to chromium (Ambreen et al., 2012). Chromium metal and its compounds are strongly mutagenic to human cells (Beyersmann and Hartwig, 2008). Both chromium and manganese impaired DNA-repair, which may be exacerbated by poor lifestyle habits (Beyersmann and Hartwig, 2008; Bornhorst et al., 2013). Eshkoor et al. (2012) and Strandberg et al. (2012) showed that drinkers have decreased TL, while other occupational risk studies have not supported this for individuals occupationally exposed to PAH (Pavanello et al., 2010) and pesticides (Kahl et al., 2016a), for instance.

Tobacco use is the second cause of mortality worldwide (Marjani et al., 2010). Smoking is the main cause of cancer of the lungs, larynx, pharynx, nasal meatus, nasal sinuses, esophagus, ureter, kidneys, pancreas, stomach, liver, cervix, and myeloid leukemia (Al-Eisa et al., 2016). Smoking in the workplace is particularly concerning and studies already have discussed a correlation between smoking and occupational stress. Radi et al. (2007) demonstrated that risk of smoking was higher in men under high occupational stress and tension. Kouvonen et al. (2005) also pointed to the relationship of smoking with occupational stress and concluded that less occupational stress enhances smoking cessation. The effect of tobacco smoking on the frequency of MN in human lymphocytes has been the object of many population studies. A pooled re-analysis of 24 databases from the HUMN international collaborative project was performed with aiming to understand the impact of smoking habits on MN frequency (Bonassi et al., 2003). The complete database included 5710 subjects, with 3501 non-smokers, 1409 current-smokers and 800 former-smokers, among subjects in occupational and environmental surveys. The overall result of the re-analysis confirmed a small non-significant decrease of MN frequencies in current-smokers and in former-smokers, when compared to non-smokers. This analysis confirmed that smokers generally do not experience an overall increase in MN frequency, but when considering the interaction with occupational exposure, heavy smokers were the only group showing a significant increase in genotoxic damage measured by the MN assay in lymphocytes (Bonassi et al., 2003). Dobrzynska et al. (2014) shows that leukocytes DNA damage, detect by Comet assay in smokers and nonsmokers individuals exposed to ionizing radiation, was similar, and surprisingly, slightly lower for smokers. There were no significant differences between the levels of damage to DNA between control group and exposed smokers. Kahl et al., (2016a, 2018a) in their studies with tobacco farmers suggested an influence of smoking in TL in assessment of the entire population (Kahl et al., 2016a), and only in non-exposed group (Kahl et al., 2018a), suggesting that smoke itself modifies TL, independently from exposure. Eshkoor et al. (2012) also observed that smoking affects TL in both workers from mechanical workshops and control groups. A recent systematic review relates shorter TL in smokers compared to non-smokers, and among current smokers compared to never or former smokers (Astuti et al., 2017). Smoking cessation seems to be a remarkable benefit when considering molecular stability.

The DNA sequence along human chromosomes are constantly changing, and this process is involved in human evolution, adaption and disease susceptibility. Science have long been aware of genetic variation including polymorphisms (Feuk et al., 2006). The polymorphisms analysis allows to observe the variant alleles of a given gene and to seek associations of these with the individual susceptibility to the effects of the xenobiotics present in the occupational environment (Angerer et al., 2007; Bonassi and Au, 2002). Individual susceptibility to the effects of xenobiotics is modulated by three main mechanisms: the ability to metabolize, the detoxification capacity and the efficiency of the repair system (for review see Iarmarcovai et al., 2008). Studies of polymorphisms involved in the development of genotoxic/carcinogenic effects may provide useful information regarding the role of individual genetic propensity and the relationship with xenobiotic exposure. Metabolizing enzymes and detoxification reactions can be used to assess human exposure, and variations in these polymorphic genes turned out to be unfavorable, since they are associated with an increase of the activation or with the reduction of the detoxification activity of dangerous substances and can imply in increase susceptibility (Bolognesi, 2003; Manno et al., 2010).

Among the most studied polymorphisms in the response to xenobiotic exposure, it is possible to mention the polymorphisms in CYP1A1 and CYP2E1 genes from the cytochrome P450 (CYP) superfamily of enzymes. CYP1A1 was associated with higher values of DNA damage, detected by MN and NPB in lymphocytes, suggesting that CYP1A1 polymorphisms may modulate the effect of coal exposure in occupational settings (Souza et al., *in prep.*). These polymorphisms have also been shown to be associated with moderate to high risk of lung cancer in Asians (Hayashi et al., 1991), Caucasian and Hawaiian populations (Kawajiri et al., 1990; Marchand et al., 1998). On the other hand, the polymorphisms that occur in the GSTM1, GSTP1 and GSTT1 genes of the glutathione S-transferase (GST) family, the most important group of detoxifying enzymes, are important in modulating the frequency of chromosomal damage (Bolognesi, 2003; Iarmarcovai et al. 2008). Individual susceptibility also plays a critical role in the response to pesticide exposure, determining the onset or absence of clinical symptoms, as well as acute poisoning. In individuals exposed to pesticides, this sensitivity could be directly associated with polymorphisms of key metabolism enzymes such as paraoxonase 1 (PON 1) (Costa et al., 2013). A consequence of variants in this gene is the differential response regarding the incidence of DNA damage in individuals exposed to organophosphates (Morahan et al., 2007). The wild type of PON1 *Gln192Arg*, was found associated with increase in buccal micronucleus in tobacco farmers (Alves et al., 2016), as well as significantly increased frequency of cell death (Da Silva et al., 2012b). However, no significant difference was observed for the parameters of DNA damage or nuclear fragmentation detect by MN in relation to the gene PON1 in the Adad et al. (2015) conducted with individuals exposed to pesticides, including organophosphates. PON1 polymorphisms had no effect on the inflammatory markers studied by Kahl et al., (2018d) in tobacco farmers. However, farmers harboring both mutated PON1 and XRCC1 mutated polymorphisms had increased frequencies of NPBs (Kahl et al., 2018d).

The polymorphisms in the OGG1 (8-oxoguanine DNA glycosylase), XRCC1 (X-ray repair cross-complementing protein 1) and XRCC4 (X-ray repair cross-complementing protein 4) genes are responsible for repairing DNA strands breaks (Zhu et al., 2008). OGG1 and XRCC1 appear to influence repair of ruptures of individual filaments detected by the Comet assay (Aka et al., 2004), while XRCC4 genotypes are part of the double-stranded, non-homologous end joining (NHEJ) repair pathway. Kahl et al. (2018b,d) provide a body of evidence that tobacco farmers' exposure to mixture of pesticides leads to increased DNA damage and alter the immune system's response, and that XRCC1 and OGG1 polymorphisms are shown to interfere in both results. The study of Rohr et al. (2011) shows an influence of BER pathway polymorphisms on MN frequencies in individuals exposed to pesticides. Individuals with the wild-type XRCC4 genotype had lower MN frequencies compared to individuals with the presence of the mutant. The influence of XRCC4 was also observed in NBUD and NPB frequencies in the study of Souza et al. (*in prep.*) with coal mine workers. As mentioned before, NBUD formation seems to be related to elimination of amplified genetic material or DNA repair complexes (Fenech et al., 2011a). On the other hand, shorten telomeres may be recognized as double-strand breaks by the DNA repair machinery, mainly, the NHEJ mechanism (Kahl and da Silva, 2016). Therefore, it seems reasonable that variations in the XRCC4 gene have an influence on NPB frequency, since it alters the enzymatic repair activity, and the final telomere junction is one of the most relevant mechanisms for the NPB formation. The results described so far in the literature demonstrate that the inhibition of DNA repair, essentially the BER pathway, is also a common mechanism in metal induced genotoxicity (Hartwig and Schwerdtle, 2002). In addition, OGG1 encodes a glycosylase that repairs the damage by removing and catalyzing 8-hydroxyguanosine, which can result from PAHs exposure (Jarvis et al., 2014).

Individual features such as age, gender, diet and lifestyle are factors that may confound the results of biomarkers used to predict stress caused by occupational exposure. A thorough understanding and measurement of these factors is therefore essential when performing studies of suspected exposure to genotoxic agents. It is important to highlight the relevance in considering the individual susceptibility in metabolizing, detoxification and repair of incorporate DNA damage, as these processes act in a coordinated manner to determine the final response. The fact that inter-individual variables have a profound effect on the alteration of biomarkers in humans emphasizes the plausibility and importance of a disease prevention strategy by appropriate improvements in nutrition and lifestyle habits at the individual, occupational and population level.

SYSTEM BIOLOGY

System biology is an interdisciplinary tool that seeks to understand the interactions between components of a biological system (Chen, 2011) or networks of biological processes, which can be either between molecules, cells, organisms or species (Galas, 2015). The main goal is to understand how these interactions can influence a complex organism (Zhang et al., 2010), using software, databases and experimental techniques (Espindola et al., 2010).

The interdisciplinarity of this science involves the integration of different areas of knowledge, such as biology, physics, statistics, mathematics and engineering (Chen, 2011; Espindola et al., 2010). The progress of molecular biology, mainly the sequencing of the genome, has increased the application of this tool within molecular biology allows scientists to collect data on a given system behavior. System biology has been used to understand how a single gene acts on a given system in order to understand as all genes and the result of the gene products of a unit, as the cell, work together. (Galas, 2015; Potters, 2010). To this end, the development and improvement of omics science techniques (genomics, transcriptomics, proteomics, metabolomics, epigenomics, among others) has demonstrated that a biological function is not related to the action of a single molecule, but to the interactions between different molecules presents in a cell (Espindola et al., 2010; Ravasz et al., 2002). Due to this feature of integrates data from different fields and allow researchers to evaluate different biological levels, System biology tools are able to assist toxicology risk assessment (Geenen et al., 2012).

The study of cellular biological networks relates the system of molecular components and interactions, showed as graphs, formed by nodes, which represent the elements of the system connected by edges (Barabás and Oltvai, 2004; Shannon et al., 2003). In a protein interaction network, the nodes represent proteins, while the edges represent the interaction between the proteins. Several types of interaction webs or networks are formed by the sum of interactions: protein-protein, metabolic, signaling and transcription-regulation networks (Barabás and Oltvai, 2004). These networks do not act separately but form complex interactions that occur among numerous molecules found in a cell, demonstrating cellular processes (Barabási and Oltvai, 2004; Ravasz et al., 2002).

The Systems biology approach has been responsible for some of the most important developments in the field of human health when evaluating the integration of biological networks and how chemicals or other xenobiotics affect these processes. Named as system chemo-biology, a branch of Systems biology, this tool allows observing the interaction between chemical compounds and the protein-protein interaction network and what are the damage mechanisms involved. Systems biology have been used to study the interaction of multiple exposures and biological pathways involving chronic diseases, for example, particulate matter (PM) found in air pollution (DeBord et al., 2015). Several studies detected the effects of PM exposure in modulation of gene expression both *in vitro* and *in vivo*, implicated in negatives effects to human health such as the risk for cardiopulmonary disease (Heidenfelder et al., 2009; Floyd et al., 2008; Graff et al., 2007). Studies by Wang et al. (2012) that used genome-wide epigenomic and Systems biology approaches, suggests that the modulated activities of DNA methyltransferase (DNMT), histone acetylase (HAT) and histone deacetylase (HDAC) may contribute to the epigenetic modifications induced by PM or PM-related chemicals, being able to alter these epigenetic markers that may also have an important role in the development of disease (DeBord et al., 2015). Similar effects were found in studies by Zhang et al. (2010), which used toxicogenomic studies for evaluation of human benzene exposure. This study observed DNA methylation induced by benzene exposure for numerous specific genes to methylation patterns, such as ELK1, EFNB1, MYCL2, VBP1, DNASE1L1, DKC1 and CDM (Zhang et al., 2010). This information can help in the definition of biomarkers of anticipated effect in individuals occupationally exposed to chemicals, in order to predict the development of diseases (Zhang et al., 2010) and may be useful as early cancer detectors (DeBord et al., 2015).

Currently the lack of data on the action and toxicity response of chemicals used by occupationally exposed workers worldwide, whether from different activities, has made it difficult for risk assessment and risk management decisions. Usually these individuals are not exposed to a single compound, but to complex mixtures of several chemicals that may have additive, synergistic or antagonistic effects (DeBord et al., 2015). Yu et al.

(2006) identified the system-based approach as a reliable tool for interpretation of dose- and time-dependent toxicity, which may proof important for risk assessment (Yu et al., 2006).

Occupational exposure to chemicals may directly or indirectly induce alterations either in the gene expression (transcriptomics) or the protein expression (proteomics), or even in epigenetic modifications (epigenomics) (DeBord et al., 2015; Zhang et al., 2010). An example of this is a study conducted by our research group by Kahl et al. (2016b), who related through chemo-biology analysis that pesticides and nicotine exposure can cause a decrease in telomere length in tobacco farmers. Pesticides can cause inhibition of the ubiquitin proteasome system (UPS) and consequently increase proteins of the shelterin complex, avoiding the access of telomerase to the telomere; while nicotine activates UPS promoting degradation of human telomerase reverse transcriptase (hTERT), decreasing telomerase activity (Kahl et al., 2016b).

Other study using systems biology as a tool to understand the interrelationship of tobacco protein-protein, was performed by Feltes et al. (2013). In this study, authors evaluated molecular pathways associated with the effects of tobacco during embryonic development in pregnant female smokers. The results demonstrated that nicotine influences cell differentiation, affecting retinoic acid signaling, during embryonic development, inhibiting its receptors, and affecting the differentiation of osteoblasts. In addition, results showed a systemic effect of nicotine, which can trigger the effect of cellular stress at different molecular levels (Feltes et al., 2013).

Studies such as that of Kahl et al. (2016b) and Feltes et al. (2013) using System biology tools are fundamental to understanding gene-environment interactions, and these data may provide new information in order to develop new biomarkers of exposure (exposome- encompasses life-course environmental exposures from the prenatal period onwards), early effect (responsome), and susceptibility (genome) (Zhang et al., 2010). Systems biology holds great promise for the future of early biological effects on workers exposed to chemical agents (DeBord et al., 2015), and offers the possibility of simultaneous advances in the coming decades (Potters, 2010).

This tool provides faster and cheaper information than animal and human testing (DeBord et al., 2015), as long as a framework is developed in which such data can be used to predict new biomarkers in a given disease (Kitano, 2002) or biomarkers of early effect for occupational exposure to chemical agents (DeBord et al., 2015). Therefore, the standardization and validation of system chemo-biology methods need to be established before being used in routine risk assessments.

CONCLUSION

Human exposure to different xenobiotics at work places arises from unhealthy activities that can be associated to either biological, chemical or physical stressors. In such context, human biomonitoring through occupational risk evaluations is a relevant research area in order to identify and prevent work-related diseases, as cancer. However, occupational exposure assessment is a complex discipline as, in most cases, individuals are exposed to complex mixtures of different agents, which may have different effects, including long-term ones. In this context, the use of biomarkers of early effects is a major tool in approaching the occupational exposure to complex mixtures, helping to increase risk prediction. As detailed in this review, biomarkers of exposure work mainly as a screening to assess exposure by all routes and complement information obtained in workplace environment monitoring. For that reason, they also can indicate an increased risky to diseases development, as they help to comprehend by which route individuals are exposed, or what are the main risks in their work routine. They also assist in which strategy may be undertaken when moving forward in occupational risk evaluations, which improves the ability of researchers in associate more properly the relation between the exposure and any health outcome. Biomarkers of effect are usually the next step in biomonitoring and indicate the biochemical or functional alterations including a wide range of biological responses. Higher frequencies of micronucleated cells are well accepted as cancer risk indicators. Similar, telomere length dynamics is a great indicative of molecular imbalance, being related to different pathologies. As those biomarkers are recognized to have an association with several diseases, including cancer, they may help in early detection and prevention of such pathologies. Biomarkers of effect are mainly used as group indicators, being sensitive but not specific, and aiming to decrease the inter-individual differences. However, it is intrinsic to each individual how they tolerate and/or respond to exogenous agents and this is beyond the exposure itself. When the occupational exposure takes place, it exacerbates the lack of ability of susceptible workers to either detoxicate or repair any eventual damages. Biomarkers of susceptibility are, therefore, an appropriate strategy to improve the risk prediction of pathologies associated with occupational exposure. Individual susceptibility is a relevant aspect as regard the interactions between xenobiotics exposure and development of many diseases, including carcinogenesis. Additionally, as discussed in this chapter, new scientific tools such as System biology approach, are taken place as fundamental in providing new information. They relate the linkage among chemicals, biological molecules and stress response, which assist in predict both new biomarkers to be use or diseases risk. Given this, studies in occupational exposure area approached the use and the importance of such biomarkers as key strategies to help in management decisions. The studies have shown genotoxic effects of exposure to pesticides, solvents, dust, metals, organic chemicals, coal, and different complex mixtures. Some results were able to associate damage with specific genetic susceptibility for each type of exposure and, also with the non-use or inappropriate use of the personal protection equipment, age, exposure time and diet adequacy. This review show how important is continuous education for exposed workers in order to minimize effects of occupational exposure and the risk of disease associated with the occupational or environmental settings.

REFERENCES

Adad, LM; de Andrade, HH; Kvitko, K; Lehmann, M; Cavalcante, AA; Dihl, RR. Occupational exposure of workers to pesticides:

Toxicogenetics and susceptibility gene polymorphisms. *Genet. Mol. Biol.* 2015 38, 308-15.

Ahola, K; Sirén, I; Kivimäki, M; Ripatti, S; Aromaa, A; Lönngvist, J; et al. Work-related exhaustion and telomere length: a population-based study. *PLoS One* 2012 7, e40186.

Al-Eisa, E; Alghadir, AH; Gabr, SA; Iqbal, ZA. Exercise intervention as a protective modulator against metabolic disorders in cigarette smokers. *J. Phys. Ther. Sci.* 2016 28, 983-991.

Alves, JS; Da Silva, FR; Da Silva, GF; Salvador, M; Kvitko, K; Rohr, P; et al. Investigation of potential biomarkers for the early diagnosis of cellular stability after the exposure of agricultural workers to pesticides. *Ann. Braz. Acad. Sci.* 2016, 88, 349-360.

Ambreen, K; Khan, FH; Bhadauria, S; Kumar, S. Genotoxicity and oxidative stress in chromium-exposed tannery workers in North India. *Toxicol. Ind. Health* 2014 30, 405-414.

Andreassi, MG; Piccaluga, E; Gargani, L; Sabatino, L; Borghini, A; Faita, F; et al. Subclinical carotid atherosclerosis and early vascular aging from long-term low-dose ionizing radiation exposure: a genetic, telomere, and vascular ultrasound study in cardiac catheterization laboratory staff. *JACC. Card. Interv.* 2015 8, 616-627.

Andreotti, G; Hoppin, JA; Hou, L; Koutros, S; Gadalla, SM; Savage, SA; et al. Pesticide use and relative leukocyte telomere length in the Agricultural Health Study. *PLoS One* 2015 10, e0133382.

Angerer, J; Ewers, U; Wilhelm, M. Human biomonitoring: state of the art. *International J. Hyg. Environ. Health* 2007 210, 201-228.

Annangi, B; Bonassi, S; Marcos, R; Hernández, A. Biomonitoring of humans exposed to arsenic, chromium, nickel, vanadium, and complex mixtures of metals by using the micronucleus test in lymphocytes. *Mutat. Res.* 2016 770, 140-161.

Antoniazzi, RP; Lago, FB; Jardim, LC; Sagrillo, MR; Ferrazzo, KL; Feldens, CA. Impact of crack cocaine use on the occurrence of oral lesions and micronuclei. *Int. J. Oral Maxillofac. Surg.* 2018, doi: 10.1016/j.ijom.2017.12.005.

Astuti, Y; Wardhana, A; Watkins, J; Wulaningsih, W. Cigarette smoking and telomere length: a systematic review of 84 studies and meta-analysis. *Environ. Res.* 2017 158, 480-489.

Aviv, A; Anderson, JJ; Shay, JW. Mutations, cancer and the telomere length paradox. *Trends Cancer* 2017 3, 253-258.

Azqueta, A; Arbillaga, L; De Cerani, AL; Collins, AR. Enhancing the sensitivity of the comet assay as a genotoxicity test, by combining it with bacterial repair enzyme FPG. *Mutagenesis* 2013 28, 271–277.

Azqueta, A; Slyskova, J; Langie, SAS; Gaivão, IÓ; Collins AR. Comet assay to measure DNA repair: approach and applications. *Front. Genet.* 2014 5, 1-8.

Bannai, A; Tamakoshi, A. The association between long working hours and health: a systematic review of epidemiological evidence. *Scand. J. Work Environ. Health* 2014 40, 5-18.

Barabás, AL; Oltvai, ZN. Network biology: Understanding the cell's functional organization. *Nat. Rev. Genet.* 2004 5, 101-113.

Benedetti, D; Alderete, BL; De Souza, CT; Dias, JF; Niekraszewicz, L; Cappetta, M; et al. DNA damage and epigenetic alteration in soybean farmers exposed to complex mixture of pesticides. *Mutagenesis* 2018, 33, 87-95.

Benedetti, D; Nunes, E; Sarmento, M; Porto, C; dos Santos, CEI; Dias, JF; et al. Genetic damage in soybean workers exposed to pesticides: Evaluation with the comet and buccal micronucleus cytome assays. *Mutat. Res.* 2013 752, 28-33.

Benvindo-Souza, M; Assis, RA; Oliveira, EAS; Borges, RE; Santos, LRS. The micronucleus test for the oral mucosa: global trends and new questions. *Environ. Sci. Pollut. Res.* 2017 24, 27724-27730.

Beyersman, D; Hartwig, A. Carcinogenic metal compounds: recent insight into molecular and cellular mechanisms. *Arch. Toxicol.* 2008 82, 493-512.

Bin, P; Leng, SG; Cheng, J; Duan, HW; Pan, ZF; Dai, YF; et al. Association between polymorphisms of metabolic genes and telomere length in workers exposed to polycyclic aromatic hydrocarbons. *Zhonghua Lao Dong Wei Sheng Zhi* 2011 29, 401-404.

Bolognesi, C. Genotoxicity of pesticides: a review of human biomonitoring studies. *Mutat. Res.* 2003 543, 251–272.

Bolognesi, C; Bonassi, S; Knasmueller, S; Fenech, M; Bruzzone, M; Lando, C; Ceppi M. Clinical application of micronucleus test in exfoliated buccal cells: A systematic review and metanalysis. *Mutat. Res.* 2015 766, 20-31.

Bolognesi, C; Holland, N. The use of the lymphocyte cytokinesis-block micronucleus assay for monitoring pesticide-exposed populations. *Mutat. Res.* 2016 770, 183-203.

Bolognesi, C; Kirsch-Volders, M. The ex vivo L-CBMN assay detects significant human exposure to butadiene. *Mutat. Res.* 2016 770, 73-83.

Bolognesi, C; Knasmueller, S; Nersesyan, A; Roggieri, P; Ceppi, M; Bruzzone, M; et al. Inter-laboratory consistency and variability in the buccal micronucleus cytome assay depends on biomarker scored and laboratory experience: results from the HUMNxl international inter-laboratory scoring exercise. *Mutagenesis* 2017 32, 257-266.

Bolognesi, C; Knasmueller, S; Nersesyan, A; Thomas, P; Fenech, M. The HUMNxl scoring criteria for different cell types and nuclear anomalies in the buccal micronucleus cytome assay–An update and expanded photogallery. *Mutat. Res.* 2013 753,100-113.

Bonassi, S; Au, WW. Biomarkers in molecular epidemiology studies for health risk prediction. *Mutat. Res.* 2002 511, 73-86.

Bonassi, S; Fenech, M; Lando, C; Lin, YP; Ceppi, M; Chang, et al. HUman MicroNucleus project: international database comparison for results with the cytokinesis-block micronucleus assay in human lymphocytes: I. Effect of laboratory protocol, scoring criteria, and host factors on the frequency of micronuclei. *Environ. Mol. Mutagen.* 2001 37, 31-45.

Bonassi, S; Milić, M; Neri, M. Frequency of micronuclei and other biomarkers of DNA damage in populations exposed to dusts, asbestos and other fibers. A systematic review. *Mutat. Res.* 2016 770, 106-118.

Bonassi, S; Neri, M; Lando, C; Ceppi, M; Lin, YP; Chang, WP; et al. Effect of smoking habit on the frequency of micronuclei in human lymphocytes: results from the Human MicroNucleus project. *Mutat. Res.* 2003 543, 155-166.

Bonassi, S; Znaor, A; Ceppi, M; Lando, C; Chang, WP; Holland, N; et al. An increased micronucleus frequency in peripheral blood lymphocytes predicts the risk of cancer in humans. *Carcinogenesis* 2007 28, 625-631.

Bornhorst, J; Meyer, S; Weber, T; Böker, C; Marschall, T; Mangerich, A; et al. Molecular mechanisms of Mn induced neurotoxicity: RONS generation, genotoxicity, and DNA-damage response. *Mol. Nutr. Food Res.* 2013 57, 1255-1269.

Bruschweiler, ED; Hopf, NB; Wild, P; Huynh, CK; Fenech, M; Thomas, P; et al. Workers exposed to wood dust have an increased micronucleus frequency in nasal and buccal cells: results from a pilot study. *Mutagenesis* 2014 29, 201-207.

Bull, C; Fenech, M. Genome-health nutrigenomics and nutrigenetics: nutritional requirements or "nutriomes" for chromosomal stability and telomere maintenance at individual level. *Proceed. Nutr. Sci.* 2008 67, 146-156.

Cassidy, A; De Vivo, I; Liu, Y; Han, J; Prescott, J; Hunter, DJ; et al. Associations between diet, lifestyle factors, and telomere length in women. *Am. J. Clin. Nutr.* 2010 91, 1273-1280.

Çelik, A; Yildirim, S; Ekinci, SY; Taşdelen, B. Bio-monitoring for the genotoxic assessment in road construction workers as determined by the buccal micronucleus cytome assay. *Ecotoxicol. Environ. Saf.* 2013 92, 265-270.

Chen, J. Systems Biology: New Institute and Applications. *Yale J. Biol. Med.* 2011 84, 59, 61.

Cheng, TS; Choudhuri, S; Muldon-Jacobs, K. Epigenetic targets of some toxicologically relevant metals: a review of the literature. *J. App. Toxicol.* 2012 32, 643-653.

Collins, AR. The comet assay for DNA damage and repair: principles, applications and limitations. *Mol. Biotechnol.* 2004 26, 249-261.

Collins, AR. Measuring oxidative damage to DNA and its repair with the comet assay. *Biochimica et Biophysica Acta* 2014 1840, 794-800.

Collins, AR. The comet assay: a heavenly method! *Mutagenesis* 2015 30, 1-4.

Collins, AR; Oscoz AA; Brunborg, G; Gaivão, I; Giovannelli; L, Kruszewski, M; et al. The comet assay: topical issues. *Mutagenesis* 2008 23, 143–151.

Coppedè, F; Migliore, L. DNA damage in neurodegenerative diseases. *Mutat. Res.* 2015 776, 84-97.

Corbi, SC; Bastos, AS; Orrico, SR; Secolin, R; Dos Santos, RA; Takahashi, CS; et al. Elevated micronucleus frequency in patients with type 2 diabetes, dyslipidemia and periodontitis. *Mutagenesis* 2014 29, 433-439.

Costa, S; Ceppi, M; Costa, C; Silva, S; Pereira, C; Laffon, B; et al. The cytokinesis-block micronucleus (CBMN) assay in human populations exposed to styrene: A systematic review and meta-analysis. *Mutat. Res.* 2016 770, 92-105.

Costa, LG; Giordano, G; Cole, TB; Marsillach, J; Furlong, CE. Paraoxonase 1 (PON1) as a genetic determinant of susceptibility to organophosphate toxicity. *Toxicology* 2013 307, 115-122.

Da Silva, J. DNA damage induced by occupational and environmental exposure to miscellaneous chemicals. *Mutat. Res.* 2016 770, 170-182.

Da Silva, FR; Da Silva, J; Allgayer, MC; Simon, DF; Dias, JF; dos Santos, CE; et al. Genotoxic biomonitoring of tobacco farmers: biomarkers of exposure, of early biological effects and of susceptibility. *J. Hazard. Mat.* 2012a 225, 81-90.

Da Silva, FR; Da Silva, J; Nunes, E; Benedetti, D; Kahl, V; Rohr, P; et al. Application of buccal micronucleus Cytome assay and analysis of PON1Gln192Arg and CYP2A6*9 (-48T>G) polymorphisms in tobacco farmers. *Environ. Mol. Mutagen.* 2012b 53, 525-534.

Da Silva, FR; Erdtmann, B; Dalpiaz, T; Nunes, E, Da Rosa, DP; Porawski, M; et al. Effects of dermal exposure to *Nicotiana tabacum* (Jean Nicot, 1560) leaves in mouse evaluated by multiple methods and tissues. *J. Agric. Food Chem.* 2010 58, 9868–9874.

Da Silva, J; Moraes, CR; Heuser, VD; Andrade, VM; Silva, FR; Kvitko, K; et al. Evaluation of genetic damage in a Brazilian population occupationally exposed to pesticides and its correlation with polymorphisms in metabolizing genes. *Mutagenesis* 2008 23, 415-22.

Dahl, EL; Curren, R; Barnett, BC; Khambatta, Z; Reisinger, K; Ouedraogo, G; et al. The reconstructed skin micronucleus assay (RSMN) in EpiDerm™: detailed protocol and harmonized scoring atlas. *Mutat. Res.* 2011 720, 42-52.

de Lange, T. Protection of mammalian telomeres. *Oncogene* 2002 21, 532-540.

DeBord, DG; Burgoon, L; Edwards, SW; Haber, LT; Kanitz, MH; Kuempel, E; et al. Systems Biology and Biomarkers of Early Effects for Occupational Exposure Limit Setting. *J. Occup. Environ. Hyg.* 2015 12, 41-54.

Deng, Q; Liu, J; Li, Q; Chen, K; Liu, Z; Shen, Y; et al. Interaction of occupational manganese exposure and alcohol drinking aggravates the increase of liver enzyme concentrations from a cross-sectional study in China. *Environ. Health* 2013 12, 30.

Dimauro, I; Sgura, A; Pittaluga, M; Magi, F; Fantini, C; Mancinelli, R; et al. Regular exercise participation improves genomic stability in diabetic patients: an exploratory study to analyse telomere length and DNA damage. *Sci. Reports* 2017 7, 4137. doi: 10.1038/s41598-017-04448-4.

Dioni, L; Hoxha, M; Nordio, F; Bonzini, M; Tarantini, L; Albetti, B; et al. Effects of short-term exposure to inhalable particulate matter on telomere length, telomerase expression, and telomerase methylation in steel workers. *Environ. Health Perspec.* 2011 119, 622-627.

Dobrzynska, MM; Pachocki, KA; Gajowik, A; Radzikowska, J; Sackiewicz, A. The effect occupational exposure to ionizing radiation on the DNA damage in peripheral blood leukocytes of nuclear medicine personnel. *J. Occup. Health* 2014 56, 379-386.

Duan, X; Yang, Y; Wang, S; Feng, X; Wang, T; Wang, P; et al. Changes in the expression of genes involved in cell cycle regulation and the relative telomere length in the process of canceration induced by omethoate. *Tumour Biol.* 2017 93, doi: 10.1177/1010428317719782.

Dusinska, M; Collins, AR. The Comet assay in human biomonitoring: gene-environment interactions. *Mutagenesis* 2008 23, 191-205.

Eshkoor, SA; Ismail, P; Rahman, SA; Moin, S. Dos GSTP1 polymorphism contribute to genetic damage caused by ageing and occupational exposure? *Arh Hig Rada Toksikol* 2010 62, 291-298.

Eshkoor, SA; Ismail, P; Rahman, SA; Adon, MY; Devan, RV. Contribution of CYP2E1 polymorphism to aging in the mechanical workshop workers. *Toxicol. Mech. Methods* 2013 23, 217-222.

Espindola, FS; Calábria, LK; Rezende, AAA; Pereira, BB; Santana, FA; Amaral, IMR; et al. Bioinformatic resources applied on the omic sciences as genomic, transcriptomic, proteomic, interatomic and metabolomic. *J. Biosc.* 2010 26, 463-477.

Feltes, BC; Poloni JF; Notari, DL; Bonatto, D. Toxicological Effects of the Different Substances in Tobacco Smoke on Human Embryonic Development by a Systems Chemo-Biology Approach. *Plos One* 2013 8, e61743.

Fenech, M. Cytokinesis-block micronucleus cytome assay. *Nature Prot.* 2007 2, 1084-1104.

Fenech, M; Bonassi, S. The effect of age, gender, diet and lifestyle on DNA damage measured using micronucleus frequency in human peripheral blood lymphocytes. *Mutagenesis* 2011 26, 43-49.

Fenech, M; Kirsch-Volders, M; Natarajan, AT; Surralles, J; Crott, JW; Parry, J; et al. Molecular mechanisms of micronucleus, nucleoplasmic bridge and nuclear bud formation in mammalian and human cells. *Mutagenesis* 2011a 26, 125-132.

Fenech, M; Holland, N; Zeiger, E; Chang, WP; Burgaz, S; Thomas, P; et al. The HUMN and $HUMN_{xl}$ international collaboration projects on human micronucleus assays in lymphocytes and buccal cells – past, present and future. *Mutagenesis* 2011b 26, 239-245.

Fenech, M; Knasmueller, S; Bolognesi, C; Bonassi, S; Holland, N; Migliore, L; et al. Molecular mechanisms by which in vivo exposure to exogenous chemical genotoxic agents can lead to micronucleus formation in lymphocytes in vivo and ex vivo in humans. *Mutat. Res.* 2016a 770, 12-25.

Fenech, M; Nersesyan, A; Knasmueller, S. A systematic review of the association between occupational exposure to formaldehyde and effects on chromosomal DNA damage measured using the cytokinesis-block micronucleus assay in lymphocytes. *Mutat. Res.* 2016b 770, 46-57.

Fenech, M; Morley AA. Measurement of micronucleus in lymphocytes. *Mutat. Res.* 1985 147, 29-36.

Feuk, L; Carson, AR; Scherer, SW. Structural variation in the human genome. *Nat. Rev. Genet.* 2006 7, 85-97.

Floyd, HS; Chen, LC; Vallanat, B; Dreher, K. Fine ambient air particulate matter exposure induces molecular alterations associated with vascular disease progression within plaques of atherosclerotic susceptible mice. *Inhal. Toxicol.* 2009 21, 394–403.

Fouquerel, E; Lormand, J; Bose, Arindam; Lee, H-T; Kim, GS; et al. Oxidative guanine base damage regulates human telomerase activity. *Nat. Struct. Mol. Biol.* 2016 23, 1092-1100.

Franke, SIR; Prá, D; Da Silva, J; Erdtmann, B; Henriques, JAP. Possible repair action of vitamin C on DNA damage induced by methyl methasulfonate, cyclophosphamide, $FeSO_4$ and $CuSO_4$ in mouse blood cells in vivo. *Mutat. Res.* 2005 583, 75-84.

Freitas-Simões, T-M; Ros, E; Sala-Vila, A. Nutrient, foods, dietary patterns and telomere length: update of epidemiological studies and randomized trials. *Metabolism* 2016 65, 406-415.

Fujishiro, K; Diez-Roux, AV; Landsbergis, PA; Jenny, NS; Seeman, T. Current employment status, occupational category, occupational hazard exposure and job stress in relation to telomere length: the Multiethnic Study of Atherosclerosis (MESA). *Occup. Environ. Med.* 2013 70; 552-560.

Galas, D. Encyclopedia Britannica. Systems biology. 2015. Available from: (academic- eb-britannica. ez45. periodicos. capes. gov. br/ levels/ collegiate/article/ systems-biology/601866). [accessed on 27/03/2018].

García-Lestón, J; Roma-Torres, J; Vilares, M; Pinto, R; Prista, J; Teixeira, JP; et al. Genotoxic effects of occupational exposure to lead and influence of polymorphisms in genes involved in lead toxicokinetics and in DNA repair. *Environ. Int.* 2012 43, 29-36.

Gardner, M; Bann, D; Wiley, L; Cooper, R; Hardy, R; Nitsch, D; et al. Gender and telomere length: systematic review and meta-analysis. *Exp. Gerontol.* 2014 51, 15-27.

Geenen, S; Taylor, PN; Snoep, JL; Wilson, ID; Kenna, JG; Westerhoff, HV. Systems biology tools for toxicology. *Arch. Toxicol.* 2012 86, 1251-1271.

Ghosh, M; Godderis, L. Genotoxicity of ethylene oxide: A review of micronucleus assay results in human population. *Mutat. Res.* 2016 770, 84-91.

Gill, Z; Nieuwoudt, M; Ndifon, W. The Hayflick limit and age-related adaptive immune deficiency. *Gerontology* 2018 64, 135-139.

Glei, M; Schneider, T; Schlörmann, W. Comet assay: an essential tool in toxicological research. *Arch. Toxicol.* 2016 90, 2315-2336.

Gonzalez, L; Kirsch-Volders, M. Reprint of "Biomonitoring of genotoxic effects for human exposure to nanomaterials: The challenge ahead." *Mutat. Res.* 2016 770, 204-216.

Gorenjak, V; Akbar, S; Stathopoulou, MG; Visvikis-Siest, S. The future of telomere length in personalized medicine. *Front. Biosci.* 2018 23, 1628-1654.

Grace, C; Pogribny, IP; Guyton, KZ; Rusyn, I. Epigenetic alterations induced by genotoxic occupational and environmental human chemical carcinogens: a systematic literature review. *Mutat. Res.* 2016 768, 27-45.

Graff, DW; Schmitt, MT; Dailey, LA; Duvall, RM, Karoly, ED; Devlin, RB. Assessing the role of particulate matter size and composition on gene expression in pulmonary cells. *Inhal. Toxicol.* 2007 19, 23–28.

Griffith, JD; Comeau, L; Rosenfield, S; Stansel, RM; Bianchi, A; Moss, H; et al. Mammalian telomeres end in a large duplex loop. *Cell* 1999 97, 503-514.

Guo, S; Zi, X; Schulz, VP; Cheng, J; Zhong, M; Koochaki, SHJ; et al. Non-stochastic reprogramming from a privileged somatic cell state. *Cell* 2014 156, 649-662.

Harley, CB. Telomere loss: mitotic clock or genetic time bomb? *Mutat. Res.* 1991 256, 271-282.

Harley, CB; Futcher, AB; Greider, CW. Telomeres shorten during ageing of human fibroblasts. *Nature* 1990 345, 458–460.

Hartwig, A; Schwerdtle, T. Interactions by carcinogenic metal compounds with DNA repair processes: toxicological implications. *Toxicol. Lett.* 2002 127, 47-54.

Hayash, S; Watanabe, J; Nakachi, K; Kawajiri, K. Genetic linkage of lung cancer associated Mspl polymorphisms with amino acid replacement in the heme binding region of the human cytochrome P450IA1 gene. *J. Biochem.* 1991 110, 407-411.

Heidenfelder, BL; Reif, DM; Harkema, JR; Cohen Hubal, EA; Hudgens, EE; Bramble, LA; et al. Comparative microarray analysis and pulmonary changes in Brown Norway rats exposed to ovalbumin and concentrated air particulates. *Toxicol Sci.* 2009 108, 207–221.

Heuser, VD; Andrade, VM; Da Silva, J; Erdtmann, B. Comparison of genetic damage in Brazilian footwear-workers exposed to solvent-based or water-based adhesive. *Mutat. Res.* 2005 583, 85-94.

Heuser, VD; Erdtmann, B; Kvitko, K; Rohr, P; Da Silva, J. Evaluation of genetic damage in Brazilian footwear-workers: biomarkers of exposure, effect, and susceptibility. *Toxicology* 2007 232, 235-247.

Hintzsche, H; Montag, G; Stopper, H. Induction of micronuclei by four cytostatic compounds in human hematopoietic stem cells and human lymphoblastoid TK6 cells. *Sci. Rep.* 2018 8, 3371.

Hou, L; Andreotti, G; Baccarelli, AA; Savage, S; Hoppin, JA; Sandler, DP; et al. Lifetime pesticide use and telomere shortening among male pesticide applicators in the Agricultural Health Study. *Environ. Health Persp.* 2013 121, 919-924.

Hovhannisyan, G; Aroutiounian, R; Babayan, N; Harutyunyan, T; Liehr, T. Comparative analysis of individual chromosome involvement in micronuclei induced by mitomycin C and bleomycin in human leukocytes. *Mol. Cytogenet.* 2016 9, 49.

Hoxha, M; Dioni, L; Bonzini, M; Pesatori, AC; Fustinoni, S; Cavallo, D; et al. Association between leukocyte telomere shortening and exposure to traffic pollution: a cross-sectional study on traffic officers and indoor office workers. *Environ. Health* 2009 8, 41. doi: 10.1186/1476-069X-8-41.

Huang, P; Huang, B; Weng, H; Nakayama, K. and Morimoto, K. Effects of lifestyle on micronuclei frequency in human lymphocytes in Japanese hard-metal workers. *Prev. Med.* 2009 48, 383-388.

Iarmarcovai, G; Bonassi, S; Botta, A; Baan, RA; Orsiere, T. Genetic polymorphisms and micronucleus formation: A review of the literature. *Mutat. Res.* 2008 658, 215-33.

Intranuovo, G; Schiavulli, N; Cavone, D; Birtolo, F; Cocco, P; Vimercati, L; et al. Assessment of DNA damages in lymphocytes of agricultural workers exposed to pesticides by comet assay in a cross-sectional study. *Biomarkers* 2018 2, 1-12.

Ishikawa, H; Ishikawa, T; Yamamoto, H; Fukao, A; Yokoyama, K. Genotoxic effects of alcohol in human peripheral lymphocytes modulated by ADH1B and ALDH2 gene polymorphisms. *Mutat. Res.* 2007 615, 134-142.

Jarvis, IWH; Dreij, K; Mattsson, A; Jernström, B; Stenius, U. Interactions between polycyclic aromatic hydrocarbons in complex mixtures and implications for cancer risk assessment. *Toxicology* 2014 321, 27-39.

Kahl, VFS; Da Silva, J. Telomere length and its relation to human health. In: Larramendy M, Fenech M, editors. *Telomeres – A Complex End of a Chromosome*. Croatia: InTech; 2016; pg. 20-41.

Kahl, VFS; Simon, D; Salvador, M; Branco, CS; Dias, JF; Da Silva, FR; et al. Telomere measurement in individuals occupationally exposed to pesticide mixtures in tobacco fields. *Environ. Mol. Mutagen.* 2016a 57, 74-84.

Kahl, VFS; Da Silva, J; Da Silva, FR. Influence of exposure to pesticides on telomere length in tobacco farmers: a biology system approach. *Mutat. Res.* 2016b 791, 19-26.

Kahl, VFS; Dhillon, VS; Simon, D; Da Silva, FR; Salvador, M; Branco, CS; et al. Chronic occupational exposure endured by tobacco farmers from Brazil and association with DNA damage. *Mutagenesis* 2018a 33, 119-128.

Kahl, VFS; Da Silva, FR; Alves, JS; da Silva, GF; Picinini, J; Dhillon, VS; et al. Role of *PON1, SOD2, OGG1, XRCC1,* and *XRCC4* polymorphisms on modulation of DNA damage in workers occupationally exposed to pesticides. *Ecotoxicol. Environ. Saf.* 2018b 7, 164-171.

Kahl, VFS; Dhillon, VS; Fenech, M; de Souza, MR; da Silva, FN; Marroni, NAP; et al. Occupational exposure to pesticides at tobacco fields: the integrated evaluation of nutritional intake and susceptibility on genomic and epigenetic instability. *Oxid. Med. Cell. Longev.* 2018c, *in press.*

Kahl, VFS; Simon, D; de Souza, MR; Vieira, HR; Nicolau, C; Da Silva, FR; et al. Base excision repair (OGG1 and XRCC1) and metabolism (PON1) gene polymorphisms act on modulation of DNA damage and immune parameters in tobacco farmers. *Mutat. Res.* 2018, DOI: https://doi.org/10.1016/j.mrgentox.2018.04.001.

Kanagaraj, K; Raavi, V; Visweswaran, S; Selvan, TG; Dhanashekaran, S; Perumal, V. Technical note on cytokinesis-arrested binucleated cell and micronucleus assay. J. *Rad. Cancer Res.* 2017 8, DOI: 10.4103/jrcr.jrcr_40_17.

Kaul, Z; Cesare, AJ; Huschtscha, LI; Neumann, AA; Reddel, RR. Five dysfunctional telomeres predict onset of senescence in human cells. *EMBO Reports* 2012 13, 52-59.

Kaur, R; Kaur, S; Lata, M. Evaluation of DNA damage in agricultural workers exposed to pesticides using single cell gel electrophoresis (comet) assay. *Ind. J. Hum. Genet.* 2011 17, 179-187.

Kawajiri, K; Nakachi, K; Imai, K; Yoshii, A; Shinoda, N; Watanabe, J. Identification of genetically high risk individuals to lung cancer by DNA polymorphisms of the cytochrome P45 0IA1 gene. *FEBS Letters* 1990 263, 131-133.

Kazimirova, A; Magdolenova, Z; Barancokova, M; Staruchova, M; Volkovova, K; Dusinska, M. Genotoxicity testing of PLGA–PEO nanoparticles in TK6 cells by the comet assay and the cytokinesis-block micronucleus assay. *Mutat. Res.* 2012 748, 42-47.

Kim, JS; Kim, YJ; Kim, TY; Song, JY; Cho, YH; Park, YC; et al. Association of ALDH2 polymorphism with sensitivity to acetaldehyde-induced micronuclei and facial flushing after alcohol intake. *Toxicology* 2005 210, 169-174.

Kirsch-Volders, M; Fenech, M; Bolognesi, C. Validity of the Lymphocyte Cytokinesis-Block Micronucleus Assay (L-CBMN) as biomarker for human exposure to chemicals with different modes of action: a synthesis of systematic reviews. *Mutat. Res.* 2018. DOI: https:// doi.org/10.1016/ j.mrgentox.2018.05.010.

Kitano, H. Systems Biology: A Brief Overview. *Science* 2002 295, 1662-1664.

Knasmueller, S; Holland, N; Wultsch, G; Jandl, B; Burgaz, S; Misik, M; et al. Use of nasal cells in micronucleus assays and other genotoxicity studies. *Mutagenesis* 2011 26, 231-238.

Ko, JL; Cheng, YJ; Liu, GC; Hsin, IL; Chen, HL. The association of occupational metals exposure and oxidative damage, telomere shortening in fitness equipment manufacturing workers. *Ind. Health* 2017 55, 345-353.

Kong, CM; Lee, XW; Wang, X. Telomere shortening in human disease. *FEBS J.* 2013 280, 3180-3193.

Koppen, G; Azqueta, A; Pourrut, B; Brunborg, G; Collins, AR; Langie, SAS. The next three decades of the Comet assay: a report of the 11th International Comet Assay Workshop. *Mutagenesis* 2017 32, 397-408.

Kouvonen, A; Kivimäki, M; Virtanen, M; Pentti, J; Vahtera, J. Work stress, smoking status, and smoking intensity: an observational study of 46,190 employees. *J. Epidemiol. Community Health* 2005 59, 63-69.

Kumar, VM. Sleep and sleep disorders. *Indian J. Chest. Dis. Allied Sci.* 2008 50, 129-135.

Kus, A; Kwasniewska, J; Hasterok, R. Brachypodium distachyon–A Useful Model in the Qualification of Mutagen-Induced Micronuclei Using Multicolor FISH. *PloS One* 2017 12, e0170618.

Ladeira; C; Viegas, S; Carolino, E; Gomes, MC; Brito, M. The influence of genetic polymorphisms in XRCC3 and ADH5 genes on the frequency of genotoxicity biomarkers in workers exposed to formaldehyde. *Environ. Mol. Mutagen.* 2013 54, 213-221.

Latifovic, L; Peacock, SD; Massey, TE; King, WD. The influence of alcohol consumption, cigarette smoking, and physical activity on leukocyte telomere length. *Cancer Epidemiol. Biomarkers Prev.* 2016 25, 374-380.

Lazzerini-Denchi, E; Sfeir, A. Stop pulling my strings - what telomeres taught us about the DNA damage response. *Nat. Rev. Mol. Cell Biol.* 2016 epub 2016/05/12. doi: 10.1038/nrm.2016.43. PubMed PMID: 27165790.

Lee, M; Hills, M; Conomos, D; Stutz, MD; Dagg, RA; Lau, LM; et al. Telomere extension by telomerase and ALT generates variant repeats by mechanistically distinct processes. *Nucleic Acid Res.* 2014 42, 1733-1746.

Li, H; Akerman, G; Lidén, C; Alhamdow, A; Wodjacz, TK; et al. Alterations of telomere length and DNA methylation in hairdressers: a cross-sectional study. *Environ. Mol. Mutagen.* 2016 57, 159-167.

Li, H; Hedmer, M; Wodjacz, T; Hossain, MB; Lindh, CH; Tinneberg, H; et al. Oxidative stress, telomere shortening, and DNA methylation in relation to low-to-moderate occupational exposure to welding fumes. *Environ. Mol. Mutagen.* 2015 56, 684-693.

Li, H; Jonsson, BA; Lindh, CH; Albin, M; Broberg, K. N-nitrosamines are associated with shorter telomere length. *Scand. J. Work Environ. Health* 2011 37, 316-324.

Li, G; Yang, P; Hao, S; Hu, W; Liang, C; Zou, BS; et al. Buccal mucosa cell damage in individuals following dental X-ray examinations. *Scient. Rep.* 2018 8, 2509.

López-Otín, C; Blasco, MA; Partridge, L; Serrano, M; Kroemer, G. The hallmarks of aging. *Cell* 2013 153, 1194-1217.

Maffei, F; Forti, GC; Castelli, E; Stefanini, GF; Mattioli, S; Hrelia, P. Biomarkers to assess the genetic damage induced by alcohol abuse in human lymphocytes. *Mutat. Res.* 2002 514, 49-58.

Malouff, JM; Schutte, NS. A meta-analysis of the relationship between anxiety and telomere length. *Anxiety Stress Coping.* 2017 30, 264-272.

Manno, M; Viau, C; Cocker, J; Colosio, C; Lowry, L; Mutti, A; et al. Biomonitoring for occupational health risk assessment (BOHRA). *Toxicol. Lett.* 2010 192, 3-16.

Marchand, LL; Sivaraman, L; Pierce, L; Seifried, A; Lum, A; Wilkens, LR; et al. Associations of CYP1A1, GSTM1, and CYP2E1 Polymorphisms with Lung Cancer Suggest Cell Type Specificities to Tobacco Carcinogens. *Cancer Res.* 1998 58, 4858-4863.

Marjani, HA; Biramijamal, F; Hossein-Nezhad, A; Islami, F; Pourshmas, A; Semmani, S. Prevalence of esophageal cancer risk factors among Turkmen and non-Turkmen ethnic groups in a high incidence area in Iran. *Arch. Iran Med.* 2010 13, 111-115.

Melis, JP; van Steeg, H; Luijten, M. Oxidative DNA damage and nucleotide excision repair. *Antioxid. Redox Signal.* 2013 18, 2409-2419.

Mesic, A; Nefic, H. Assessment of the genotoxicity and cytotoxicity in environmentally exposed human populations to heavy metals using the cytokinesis-block micronucleus cytome assay. *Environ. Toxicol.* 2015 30, 1331-1342.

Moller, P. The Comet assay: ready for 30 more years. *Mutagenesis* 2018 33, 1–7.

Morahan, JM; Yu, B; Trent, RJ; Pamphlett, R. A geneenvironment study of paraoxonose 1 gene pesticides in amyotropic lateral sclerosis. *Neurotoxicol.* 2007 28, 532-540.

Mostafalou, S; Abdollahi, M. Pesticides and human chronic diseases: evidences, mechanisms and perspectives. *Toxicol. App. Pharmacol.* 2013 268, 157-177.

Mrdjanović, J; Šolajić, S; Dimitrijević, S; Đan, I; Nikolić, I; Jurišić, V. Assessment of micronuclei and sister chromatid exchange frequency in the petroleum industry workers in province of Vojvodina, Republic of Serbia. *Food Chem. Toxicol.* 2014 69, 63-68.

Müezzinler, A; Zaineddin, AK; Brenner, H. A systematic review of leukocyte telomere length and age in adults. *Ageing Res. Rev.* 2013 12, 509-519.

Nefic, H; Handzic, I. The effect of age, sex, and lifestyle factors on micronucleus frequency in peripheral blood lymphocytes of the Bosnian population. *Mutat. Res.* 2013 753, 1-11.

Nersesyan, A; Kundi, M; Fenech, M; Bolognesi, C; Misik, M; Wultsch, G; et al. Micronucleus assay with urine derived cells (UDC): a review of its application in human studies investigating genotoxin exposure and bladder cancer risk. *Mutat. Res.* 2014 762, 37-51.

Nersesyan, A; Kundi, M; Waldherr, M; Setayesh, T; Mišík, M; Wultsch, G; et al. Results of micronucleus assays with individuals who are occupationally and environmentally exposed to mercury, lead and cadmium. *Mutat. Res.* 2016 770, 119-139.

Norppa, H; Falck, GC. What do human micronuclei contain? *Mutagenesis* 2003 18, 221-233.

Nunes, RS; Kahl, VFS; Sarmento, MS; Richter, MF; Costa-Lotufo, LV; Rodrigues, FAR; et al. Antigenotoxicity and antioxidant activity of acerola fruit (*Malpighia glabra* L.) at two stages ripeness. *Plant Foods Hum. Nutr.* 2011 66, 129-135.

OECD. Organization for Economic Co-operation and Development. 2014. OECD guideline for the testing of chemicals. Available at https://ntp.niehs.nih.gov/iccvam/suppdocs/feddocs/oecd/oecd-tg489-2014.pdf, accessed May 13th 2018. 25 pages.

Parks, CG; DeRoo, LA; Miller, DB; McCaniles, EC; Cawthon, RM; Sandler, DP. Employment and work schedule are related to telomere length in women. *Occup. Environ. Med.* 2011 68, 582-589.

Pavanello, S; Pesatori, AC; Dioni, L; Hoxha, M; Bollati, V; Siwinska, E; et al. Shorter telomere length in peripheral blood lymphocytes of workers exposed to polycyclic aromatic hydrocarbons. *Carcinogenesis* 2010 31, 216-221.

Pavanello, S; Dioni, L; Hoxha, M; Fedeli, U; Mielzynska-Svach, D; Baccarelli, AA. Mitochondrial copy number and exposure to polycyclic aromatic hydrocarbons. *Cancer Epidemiol. Biomarkers Prev.* 2013 22, 1722-1729.

Pawlas, N; Plachetka, A; Kozlowska, A; Mikolajczyk, A; Kasperczyk, A; Dobrakowski, M; et al. Telomere length, telomerase expression, and oxidative stress in lead smelters. *Toxicol. Ind. Health* 2016 32, 1961-1970.

Potters, G. Systems Biology of the Cell. *Nature Educ.* 2010 3, 33.

Pradeep, MR; Guruprasad, Y; Jose, M; Saxena, K; Deepa, K; Prabhu, V. Comparative study of genotoxicity in different tobacco related habits using micronucleus assay in exfoliated buccal epithelial cells. *J. Clin. Diagn. Res.* 2014 8, ZC21-24.

Puterman, E; Lin, J; Blackburn, E; O'Donovan, A; Adler, N; Epel, E. The power of exercise: buffering the effect of chronic stress on telomere length. *PLoS One* 2010 5, e10837. doi: 10.1371/journal.pone.0010837.

Ravasz, E; Somera, AL; Mongru, DA; Oltvai, ZN; Barabási, AL. Hierarchical Organization of Modularity in Metabolic Networks. *Science* 2002 297, 1551-1555.

Rayess, H; Wang, MB; Srivatsan, ES. Cellular senescence and tumor suppressor gene p16. *Int. J. Cancer* 2012 130, 1715-1725.

Reddel, RR. Senescence: an antiviral defense that is tumor suppressive. *Carcinogenesis* 2010 31, 19-26.

Reichert, S; Stier, A. Does oxidative stress shorten telomeres in vivo? A review. *Biol. Lett.* 2017 13, doi: 10.1098/rsbl.2017.0463.

Rohr, P; da Silva, J; Erdtmann, B; Saffi, J; Guecheva, TN; Henriques, JAP; et al. BER gene polymorphisms (OGG1 Ser326Cys and XRCC1 Arg194Trp) and modulation of DNA damage due to pesticides exposure. *Environ. Mol. Mutagen.* 2011 52, 20-27.

Rohr, P; Kvitko, K; Da Silva, FR; Menezes, APS; Porto, K; Sarmento, M; et al. Genetic and oxidative damage of peripheral blond lymphocytes in workers with occupational exposure to coal. *Mutat. Res.* 2013a 758, 23-28.

Rohr, P; Da Silva, J; da Silva, FR; Sarmento, M; Porto, C; Debastiani, R; et al. Evaluation of genetic damage in open-cast coal mine workers using the buccal micronucleus cytome assay. *Environ. Mol. Mutagen.* 2013b 54, 65-71.

Scherthan, H; Sotnik, N; Peper, M; Schrock, G; Azizova, T; Abend, M. Telomere length in aged Mayak PA nuclear workers chronically exposed to internal alpha an external gamma radiation. *Radiat. Res.* 2016 185, 658-667.

Shalev, I; Entringer, S; Wadhwa, PD; Wolkowtiz, OM; Puterman, E, Lin, J; et al. Stress and telomere biology: a lifespan perspective. *Psychoneuroendocrinology* 2013 38, 1835-1842.

Shannon, P; Markiel, A; Ozier, O; Baliga, NS; Wang, JT; Ramage, D; et al. Cytoscape: A Software Environment for Integrated Models of Biomolecular Interaction Networks. *Genome Res.* 2003 13, 2498-2504.

Simon, AS; Vijayakumar, T. Molecular studies on coronary artery disease—a review. *Ind. J. Clin. Biochem.* 2013 28, 215-226.

Singh, NP. The Comet assay: reflections on its development, evolution and applications. *Mutat. Res.* 2016 767, 23-30.

Singh, Z; Chadha, P; Sharma, S. Evaluation of oxidative stress and genotoxicity in battery manufacturing workers occupationally exposed to lead. *Toxicol. Int.* 2013 20, 95-100.

Sinitsky, MY; Minina, VI; Gafarov, NI; Asanov, MA; Larionov, AV; Ponasenko, AV; et al. Assessment of DNA damage in underground coal miners using the cytokinesis-block micronucleus assay in peripheral blood lymphocytes. *Mutagenesis* 2016 31, 669-675.

Souza, KM; Braz, LG; Nogueira, FR; Souza, MB; Bincoleto, LF; Aun, AG; et al. Occupational exposure to anesthetics leads to genomic instability, cytotoxicity and proliferative changes. *Mutat.Res.* 2016 791, 42-48.

Souza, MR; Kahl, VFS; Rohr, P; Kvitko, K; Cappetta, M; Lopes, WM; et al. Shorter telomere length and DNA hypermethylation in peripheral blood cells of coal workers. *Mutat. Res.* 2018 doi: https:// doi.org/ 10.1016/ j.mrgentox.2018.03.009.

Souza, MR; Kahl, VFS; Rohr, P; Kvitko, K; Cappetta, M; Lopes, WM; et al. *The influence of polymorphisms of xenobiotic-metabolizing and DNA repair genes in DNA damage, telomere length and global DNA methylation evaluated in open-cast coal mining workers.* In prep.

Sram, RJ; Svecova, V; Rossnerova, A. Systematic review of the use of the lymphocyte cytokinesis-block micronucleus assay to measure DNA damage induced by exposure to polycyclic aromatic hydrocarbons. *Mutat. Res.* 2016 770, 162-169.

Strandberg, TE; Strandberg, AY; Saijonmaa, O; Tilvis, RS; Pitkälä, KH; Fyhrquist, F. Association between alcohol consumption in healthy midlife and telomere length in older men. The Helsinki Businessmen Study. *Eur. J. Epidemiol.* 2012 27, 815-822.

Thomas, P; Fenech, M. Buccal micronucleus cytome assay. In: *DNA Damage Detection In Situ, Ex Vivo, and In Vivo*. Totowa: Humana Press 2011, pg. 235-248.

Thomas, P; Holland, N; Bolognesi, C; Kirsch-Volders, M; Bonassi, S; Zeiger, E; et al. Buccal micronucleus cytome assay. *Nature Prot.* 2009 4, 825-837.

Tice, RR; Agurell, E; Anderson, D; Burlinson, B; Hartmann, A; Kobayashi, H; et al. Single Cell Gel/Comet Assay: guidelines for In Vitro and In Vivo genetic toxicology testing. *Environ. Mol. Mutagen.* 2000 35, 206-221.

Valverde, M; Rojas, E. Environmental and occupational biomonitoring using the Comet assay. *Mutat. Res.* 2009 681, 93-109.

Villarini, M; Gianfredi, V; Levorato, S; Vannini, S; Salvatori, T; Moretti, M. Occupational exposure to cytostatic/antineoplastic drugs and cytogenetic damage measured using the lymphocyte cytokinesis-block micronucleus assay: A systematic review of the literature and meta-analysis. *Mutat. Res.* 2016 770, 35-45.

Vodicka, P; Musak, L; Fiorito, G; Vymetalkova, V; Vodickova, L; Naccarati, A. DNA and chromosomal damage in medical workers exposed to anaesthetic gases assessed by the lymphocyte cytokinesis-block micronucleus (CBMN) assay. A critical review. *Mutat. Res.* 2016 770, 26-34.

Wang, Y; Duan, X; Zhang, Y; Wang, S; Yao, W; Wang, S; et al. DNA methylation and telomere damage in occupational people exposed to coal tar pitch. *Zhonghua Lao Dong Wei Sheng Zhi* 2015 33, 507-511.

Wang, T; Garcia, JGN; Zhang Wei. Epigenetic regulation in Particulate matter-mediated cardiopulmonary toxicities: A system biology perspective. *Curr. Pharmac. Personal. Med.* 2012 14, 314-321.

Wong, JYY; De Vivo, I; Lin, X; Grashow, R; Cavallari, J; Christiani, DC. The association between global DNA methylation and telomere length in a longitudinal study of boilermakers. *Genetic Epidemiol.* 2014 38, 254-264.

Wu, Y; Liu, Y; Ni, N; Bao, B; Zhang, C; Lu, L. High lead exposure is associated with telomere length shortening in Chinese battery manufacturing plant workers. *Occup. Environ. Med.* 2012 69, 557-563.

Yang, P; Hao, S; Gong, X; Li, G. Cytogenetic biomonitoring in individuals exposed to cone beam CT: comparison among exfoliated buccal mucosa cells, cells of tongue and epithelial gingival cells. *Dentomaxillofac. Radiol.* 2017 46, 20160413.

Yu, X; Griffith, WC; Hanspers, K; Dillman, JF; Ong, H; Vredevoogd, MA; et al. A system-based approach to interpret dose- and time-dependent microarray data: quantitative integration of gene ontology analysis for risk assessment. *Toxicol. Sci.* 2006 92, 560-577.

Zakian, VA. Telomeres: the beginning and ends of eukaryotic chromosomes. *Exper. Cell Res.* 2012 318, 1456-1460.

Zeljezic, D; Bjelis, M; Mladinic, M. Evaluation of the mechanism of nucleoplasmic bridge formation due to premature telomere shortening in agricultural workers exposed to mixed pesticides: indication for further studies. *Chemosphere* 2015 120, 45-51.

Zhang, X; Lin, S; Funk, WE; Hou, L. Environmental and occupational exposure to chemicals and telomere length in human studies. *Occup. Environ. Med.* 2013 70, 743-749.

Zhang, L; McHale, CM; Rothman, N; Li, G; Ji, Z; Vermeulen, R; et al. Systems biology of human benzene exposure. *Chem. Biol. Interac.* 2010 184, 86-93.

Zheng, GQ; Zhang, GH; Xu, XW; Wang, JW; Yu, LB, Zhang, YN; et al. Association of telomere length with chromosomal damage among Chinese workers exposed to vinyl chloride monomer. *Journal of Occup. Environ. Med.* 2017 59, e252-e256.

Ziegler, S; Schettgen, T; Beier, F; Wilop, S; Quinete, N; Esser, A; et al. Accelerated telomere shortening in peripheral blood lymphocytes after occupational polychlorinated biphenyls exposure. *Arch. Toxicol.* 2017 91, 289-300.

Editors' Contact Information

Nicola Mucci, MD, PhD
Junior Researcher in Occupational Medicine,
Department Experimental and Clinical Medicine,
University of Florence, Florence, Italy
Email: nicola.mucci@unifi.it

Gabriele Giorgi
Professor and Full Researcher,
Organizational Psychology (M-PSI/06),
Department of Human science,
Università Europea di Roma, Rome, Italy
Email: gabriele.giorgi@unier.it

Francesco Sderci
Research Grantholder in Occupational Medicine
University of Florence, Florence, Italy
Email: fsderci@gmail.com

Giulio Arcangeli
Professor of Occupational Medicine,
University of Florence, Florence, Italy
Email: giulio.arcangeli@unifi.it

INDEX

D

E

F

G

H

I

J

L

M

N

O

P

R

S

T

W

Y

Z